"This book is Conrad Mbewe's equivalent of Paul's pastoral letters. It is the wisdom of the Scriptures steeped in decades of personal experience. It is delivered in fresh African illustrations and applications that help even this North American pastor understand God's Word better. Having known Mbewe for a quarter of a century, having been in his church and he in mine, I could not think of a better person to write such a volume. This book well reflects the teaching of the Bible in ways that both encourage and challenge today's readers. Mbewe's writing is clear and simple, elegant and gospel-celebrating. This book is delightful. Enjoy and be edified. The last chapter is gold."

Mark Dever, Pastor, Capitol Hill Baptist Church, Washington, DC

"It's the subtitle of this book that explains its vision: Conrad Mbewe is not only laying out a biblical and practical exposition of the church but is doing so for 'African pastors and ministry leaders.' Mbewe, longtime pastor of Kabwata Baptist Church in Lusaka, Zambia, points out that he writes as 'a son of the African soil,' and therefore he has earned the right to challenge his fellow Africans in frank ways that missionaries could never deploy without being dismissed as foreigners. In twenty short but probing chapters, Mbewe writes with such clarity and prophetic faithfulness that the book deserves wide study not only in Africa but around the world.

D. A. Carson, Emeritus Professor of New Testament, Trinity Evangelical Divinity School; Cofounder, The Gospel Coalition

"I love Conrad Mbewe, and I love this boac-
tical exploration of the doctrine of the ch ble
with a Baptist point here or there, but t all
enthusiasm. Mbewe has written an excel ral
dynamics of Africa but beneficial for Chri and
accessible work finds a wide audience."

Kevin DeYoung, Senior Pastor, Christ Covenant Church, Matthews, North Carolina; Assistant Professor of Systematic Theology, Reformed Theological Seminary, Charlotte

"With biblical insight and down-to-earth illustrations, Conrad Mbewe's *God's Design for the Church* takes us on an insider's exploration of the nature, character, and challenges of the rapidly expanding church in Africa. His comprehensive but easy-to-read analysis confirms much of what is visible and does not shy away from often hidden 'hot potatoes,' such as money matters, issues of discipline, and other trends that define, enhance, or undermine the life and witness of the church. His perspective has implications for the future of the body of Christ, not only in Africa but also in other parts of the world."

Femi B. Adeleye, Director, Langham Preaching Africa, Ghana

"This is a timely book! It addresses with clarity the confused identity and practices of the church in Africa. As a grace carrier, and as a bold, honest, and effective communicator, Conrad Mbewe has vindicated the concerns of the leaders of the church on our continent by addressing the elephant in the room. He has called by name what appeared to be a no-go area and described it as unacceptable. But he has also demonstrated that there is still a remnant who have not 'bowed their knees to Baal.' Above all, Mbewe has offered practical, Bible-based solutions to the current weaknesses and problems of the church. A thoroughly readable and thought-provoking book, it has left me with renewed hope for the church in Africa. I enthusiastically recommend it to all church leaders on our continent and especially to our leadership training institutions."

Paul E. Mususu, President, Evangelical Fellowship of Zambia

"The church is the bride of Christ. It is God's plan 'A' in his work of redemption. As such, it is paramount that we know and understand God's design for the church. In this volume, Conrad Mbewe has done yeoman's work in that regard. In an age when pragmatism and innovation are held in higher esteem than doctrine and theology, this book is a breath of fresh air. With the accuracy of a theologian and the tender heart of a shepherd, Mbewe weaves a tapestry that combines timeless truths and contemporary insights into a helpful resource for Christians of every stripe. In this time of biblical and ecclesiological illiteracy, the usefulness of this book cannot be overestimated."

Voddie Baucham Jr., Dean of the School of Divinity, African Christian University

"Some books I enjoy recommending. A few I'm honored to recommend, as with this one. Conrad Mbewe has labored in faith and love for decades, studying the Scriptures and then leading his flock to follow them. This book shows the accumulated wisdom of all that study and work. It's wise, pastorally conscientious, rigorously biblical, and excellent. And I plead with pastors to read his book slowly, carefully, prayerfully, with your Bible open, and looking for ways to apply Mbewe's instruction in your own congregation."

Jonathan Leeman, Elder, Cheverly Baptist Church, Bladensburg, Maryland; Editorial Director, 9Marks

"Conrad Mbewe's ministry at Kabwata Baptist Church has been the example of faithfulness and fruitfulness that I have pursued in my own ministry for more than a decade now. His was the first preaching that I heard that was shrouded in African style, illustrations, and application, while at the same time communicating faithfully and powerfully the glorious truths of our great God. Kabwata Baptist Church and other congregations that belong to their family of churches were the first to expose me to the idea of a healthy church. The compelling witness of members of Kabwata, who loved selflessly and pursued God in the Word fervently, helped me see the beauty of God's plan for his church. In a time when the truths of God's Word are labeled as Western, and error is defended as African, Mbewe has sketched for us a biblical portrait of the church that comes accompanied with a historical witness of fruitfulness in the African context. Read this book with your Bible open. Let him convince you from the Word. Where you see a need to correct course, in prayer, patience, and humility, join in pursuing God's design for the church."

Kenneth Mbugua, Lead Pastor, Emmanuel Baptist Church, Nairobi, Kenya; Managing Director, Ekklesia Afrika

"With keen biblical insight, deep faithfulness to the Scriptures, and refreshing African illustrations, Conrad Mbewe sets his sights on the needs and concerns of the African church and hits the bull's-eye. He makes it clear that Africa needs gospel-centered, Bible-drenched churches made up of true believers, covenanted together in gospel love, who unflinchingly know, live, and proclaim the gospel of Christ. Christians around the world should offer urgent prayers that African pulpits would be filled with African men who understand and apply the truths in this book—especially as the locus of gospel vibrancy moves more and more to the Global South. Any non-African who reads this book will gain insight about Africa and Africans, but don't miss that Mbewe's clarion call is not for an African church, but rather for a biblical church. This book is not just for Africans—it is for all cultures and contexts. It's for anyone who desires to anchor themselves in the Bible's design for church."

J. Mack Stiles, Pastor, Erbil International Baptist Church, Erbil, Iraq

"What is an ideal church and how can you tell? Conrad Mbewe seeks to address God's design for the church. He writes in a vivid, concise, and penetrating way, exalting the supremacy of Jesus Christ in the church. Mbewe is a living testimony of the biblical principles contained in this down-to-earth book. While it is still today and the opportunity is ours, we need Christian leadership that is spiritually and intellectually incisive. It is this leadership that is evident in this book. Mbewe is a voice that must be listened to, and this is a book that must be reckoned with. May the Lord use it to keep his church—particularly the church in Africa—strong and true to the faith."

Joe Mundamawo, Bishop's Chaplain, Reformed Evangelical Anglican Church in Zimbabwe; Former Board Chairman, Harare Theological College

God's Design for the Church

*A Guide for African Pastors
and Ministry Leaders*

Conrad Mbewe

Foreword by Glenn Lyons

With Study Guides by The Ekklesia Afrika Ltd.

:: CROSSWAY®

WHEATON, ILLINOIS

God's Design for the Church: A Guide for African Pastors and Ministry Leaders

Copyright © 2020 by Conrad Mbewe

Published by Crossway
        1300 Crescent Street
        Wheaton, Illinois 60187

Cover design: Daniel Farrell

First printing 2020

Printed in the United States of America

Unless otherwise noted, Scripture quotations are from the ESV® Bible (The Holy Bible, English Standard Version®), copyright © 2001 by Crossway, a publishing ministry of Good News Publishers. Used by permission. All rights reserved.

The Scripture quotation marked KJV is from the King James Version of the Bible.

Trade paperback ISBN: 978-1-4335-6642-4
ePub ISBN: 978-1-4335-6645-5
PDF ISBN: 978-1-4335-6643-1
Mobipocket ISBN: 978-1-4335-6644-8

Library of Congress Cataloging-in-Publication Data

Names: Mbewe, Conrad, author.
Title: God's design for the church : a guide for African pastors and ministry leaders / Conrad Mbewe.
Description: Wheaton, Illinois : Crossway, [2020] | Includes bibliographical references.
Identifiers: LCCN 2020007244 (print) | LCCN 2020007245 (ebook) | ISBN 9781433566424 (paperback) |
    ISBN 9781433566431 (pdf) | ISBN 9781433566448 (mobi) | ISBN 9781433566455 (epub)
Subjects: LCSH: Christianity—Africa. | Church. | Church—Biblical teaching.
Classification: LCC BR1360 .M3895 2020 (print) | LCC BR1360 (ebook) | DDC 262.0096—dc23
LC record available at https://lccn.loc.gov/2020007244
LC ebook record available at https://lccn.loc.gov/2020007245

Crossway is a publishing ministry of Good News Publishers.

BP   31   30   29   28   27   26   25   24   23   22   21
14   13   12   11   10   9   8   7   6   5   4   3   2

To my fellow elders
In gratitude for our joint labors to see God's design for
the church realized at Kabwata Baptist Church

Contents

Foreword

Matrilineal succession, ancestor veneration, and *ubuntu* may not be the expected topics of discussion in most traditional church doctrine resources, but you will find all these African considerations, and even more, in this biblical instruction on God's design for the church. The chapters that follow are all driven by the need for God's people to better understand the Scriptures in order to rightly "behave in the household of God" (1 Tim. 3:14–15).

As you journey through these pages, you will also discover a pastor's heart for the body of Christ, particularly the family of believers in Africa. Here we learn from a teacher who delights to celebrate the church's strengths but also lovingly to call out her weaknesses. He will not avoid bringing God's Word to bear on the controversial issues, but without quibbling over disputable matters. Each subject is addressed and communicated in such a way that it is within the grasp of the mature as well as the new believer. Without fail, the necessary corrective is repeatedly applied: "What does the Bible say?"

We are all too aware of the need for the church to grow up into the fullness of her maturity in Christ. Across the African continent, our gathered congregations' primary need is to have God's Word faithfully taught, contextually applied, and consistently obeyed—and all this to be accomplished on our knees! The remedy is really that simple, and pastor Conrad Mbewe has, under God, given us helpful guidance in applying that remedy.

It is my privilege to commend this timely teaching to the church in Africa—and beyond. May it richly benefit all who read *and* apply it.

Build your church, Lord! Amen.

Glenn Lyons
Presiding Bishop
Reformed Evangelical Anglican Church–South Africa

Acknowledgments

The writing of this book has been a team effort. I wish to thank the pastors of sister churches in Lusaka, Zambia, who took time out of their very busy schedules across 2019 to meet with me and our pastoral interns each time I finished working on a chapter so that we could go through it together. They were the first proofreaders. They also ensured that my applications scratched where it was really itching. Without their sacrifice in terms of time, this book would not have been half as relevant as it has turned out to be. Without trying to be exhaustive, among the pastors and pastoral interns who met with me consistently throughout the writing of the book are German Banda, Curtis Chirwa, Saidi Chishimba, Million Kambuli, Uaundja Karamata (intern from Namibia), Kennedy Kawambale, Mwindula Mbewe, Emmanuel Mukisa (intern from Uganda), Jadder Mulonde, Thomson Musukwa, Joe Shoko (intern from Zimbabwe), Chipita Sibale, Oswald Sichula, Wege Sinyangwe, and Marvin Ssuuna (intern from Uganda). It was a truly international team!

The work that I do is almost impossible without the help of assistants. Let me thank my office assistant, Irene Maboshe, and my ministry assistant, Francis Kaunda, for the work they were doing behind the scenes that freed me so that I could concentrate on the primary work of an author. They know what I am talking about.

I would also like to thank the staff at the African Christian University for their enthusiasm for this book project. Their input when I presented an overview of the book to them toward the end of the writing period helped me to make the book more balanced. So, to the ACU Vice Chancellor, Dr. Celestine Musembi, and her staff, thank you very much.

I have dedicated this book to my fellow elders at Kabwata Baptist Church because of their spiritual courage. Whenever we have studied the Bible and seen that there are areas in our church belief or practice that we need to modify, they have not been afraid to do so. Sometimes it has taken a little long to do so, but their courage to obey has been inspirational. Without this, I would have been asking others to do what I have not been doing. So, Charles Bota, Chola Chakonta, John Chundu, John Kumwenda, Chipita Sibale, Alfred Sakwiya, George Sitali, and Emmanuel Matafwali (as one untimely born), this book is really for you!

Let me also thank Crossway, the Gospel Coalition, the Gospel Coalition Africa, 9Marks, and Ekklesia Afrika for the encouragement they gave me as I was writing the book. It was your gospel partnership that initially brought this book to birth. And I know that long after the manuscript has been submitted, you will continue to work behind the scenes to ensure that the book blesses the churches in Africa.

Lastly, and by no means the least, I am very grateful to my wife, Felistas, who sacrificed many hours of our marital bliss and fellowship so that I could try to beat the deadline for the project. I have no doubt that in heaven she will enjoy some of the reward that the Lord Jesus Christ will bestow on us for this labor of love.

Introduction

If you are wondering, as you pick up this book, why we should have yet another book on the church when many have already been written, I do not blame you. I was of the same mind when the idea for this writing project came up. Here is the story: I was approached to comment on the distribution across Africa of a very good book on the church. I had read it long before and would recommend it to anyone even today. However, the more I thought about this distribution project, the more I realized that the book would not meet the needs of the church at a practical level on the continent. I commented more or less as follows:

> The book flies at 10,000 feet above sea level. It gives us the general principles that ought to guide us in the life of the church. However, what the church here desperately needs is someone to take us through the African jungle by the hand, showing us trees and animals to be wary of if we are going to stay the course.

In other words, the greatest need was for a book that deals with some of the major issues that are hindering the church in Africa from being what God designed it to be.

Let me illustrate it this way. A friend recently told me the story of a man who was tired of people using a footpath along the perimeter wall around his house and urinating on a certain section of his wall. He put up a sign that said, "This is not a toilet. Please do not urinate here." This did not stop the people from urinating there. He changed the sign to read, "Anyone found urinating here will be prosecuted." Alas, the vice continued unabated. Finally, he put up a sign that read, "Please urinate here. We need human urine for some rituals." He said that the vice not only stopped but the footpath was completely abandoned!

I am sure that, for many Western minds, the appeal to simple common sense ("This is not a toilet") or the appeal to the law ("You will be prosecuted") would have sufficed to arrest this vice. If it did not, certainly the appeal to superstition (such as witchcraft) would have also failed. Yet, to the African mind, there is something more powerful than common sense and the state—it is witchcraft. This belief is what did the trick in the story I have narrated. It is important for an author to recognize this when writing for an African audience. The world of the spirits is so real and near that it needs to be addressed in order to produce authentic Christian practice.

While I do not agree that Christianity in Africa must be different from Christianity in the East or West, I recognize the need for the application of Christian truth to vices that are peculiarly African. To my mind, these two approaches are different. The first tries to create a divide that the Bible knows nothing about and would not even want to encourage. For instance, it wants us to deliberately and intentionally worship differently from our brethren in the West, many of whom live among us in our cosmopolitan cities. This self-conscious effort is foreign to New Testament Christianity, which tries to bring all of us into one body—". . . Greek and Jew, circumcised and uncircumcised, barbarian, Scythian, slave, free; but Christ is all, and in all" (Col. 3:11). The second, which this book is about, tries to apply biblical principles to what is obtaining in Africa so that we are drawn back to belief and practice that follows God's design for the church. I am not trying to make the Bible more African; I am trying to get the church in Africa to be more biblical.

Having said all that, there is a lot that is happening in the African church that is very positive and should be encouraged. There is a lot of good that the church on other continents will do well to imitate. Here are a few of these areas.

The church in Africa is growing by leaps and bounds. This is certainly a matter to thank God for, especially when one compares this to what is happening in the church in the West. It is disheartening to any Christian who goes from Africa to, say, Europe, and finds church buildings that have been turned into libraries, museums, restaurants, and bars. It is equally sad to see so many churches with mainly elderly people tottering to their graves and almost all the pews empty. Where are the people? Where are the young people? How can such churches survive? It is so refreshing to return to Africa and find churches meeting in every conceivable place as new churches sprout up almost every week. It is said that the number of Christians in Africa at the beginning of the twentieth century was about 9 million and that by the end of the twentieth century it was about 380 million. Church structures cannot cope with this kind of growth. So, churches are simply meeting in classrooms, in grass-thatched makeshift structures, and under trees—and yet they are still growing! It is also refreshing to see in attendance young parents with their toddlers, teenagers and young adults, all the way to octogenarians. It speaks well for the future of the church in Africa.

The church in Africa is full of zeal, though sometimes this zeal lacks knowledge (Rom. 10:2). This zeal is seen in evangelistic fervor. Anyone with eyes to see cannot miss this, and it is the explanation behind the quantum leap in growth. African society generally is very open to the Christian message, though openness to listening is not the same thing as openness to responding to the message. If they know that you are a pastor who has come to visit their home, most parents will call everyone in the home to come and listen to you. The door of opportunity is still wide open. Individuals whose knowledge of the Bible is still at kindergarten level will soon be found leading a church in a village. Some of them do not even have a full Bible. Yet they are preaching wherever they find ears that are willing to listen. You will find lay preachers in streets and on buses and trains. Personal witnessing takes place in schools, colleges, and universities. There is a desperate need for more training in order to reduce the wildfires being produced by this zeal where knowledge is lacking. The normal "Bible College" structures used in the Western world to train future leaders and pastors cannot cope with this zeal and growth. Other forms need to be brought in that would function more like the combine harvester does on huge commercial farms. All such "problems" aside, however, the church in Africa is refreshingly zealous.

The church in Africa is communal and has respect for authority. This is something that comes largely from African culture, and it is commendable. Later in the book I speak about the *ubuntu* phenomenon, which captures something of the tendency by the African people to prize human relations more than anything else. This is the fountain out of which relationships in the church tend to run deep and which also means that the elderly and those in positions of leadership are respected. Pastors living within certain distances of each other will have pastor "fraternals," where they not only meet to listen to each other teach but also share their common lives as pastors and meet each other's needs. They develop deep relationships in those groupings, and many of these are beyond immediate denominational circles. The "one another" imperatives of Scripture are already in practice in the culture before they are augmented with biblical teaching. People have a greater sense of belonging to churches than they normally do in the West. If there were to be a fault, perhaps it would be that people do not question the actions of their leaders as much as they ought to because of their respect for authority. Some biblical balance may be necessary.

The church in Africa is respected by the community and the state because it often provides for the basic needs of society. In my own country of Zambia, the church provides 60 percent of the health facilities of the entire nation. The church also runs the best schools in the country, in terms of both the physical structures and the holistic development of the students. Even when there has been need for disaster relief, the church has tended to be the vehicle chosen by donors to deliver help at the grassroots level. This has helped the nations of Africa that are on the brink of abject poverty to appreciate the church and to still have hope for the younger generation. The love shown by the church has won the ears of community and state leaders. Therefore, when church leaders express concern about an important matter in society, local and national leaders tend to listen. This means that the church is able to speak into the moral issues of the day and gain a hearing. This is one reason why the leaders of African nations have been able to withstand the pressure from the West to redefine human sexuality and marriage to suit those with a homosexual agenda. This is despite the fact that some Western countries are tying their aid to an acceptance of this agenda. Although some church leaders have abused the listening ear of state leaders for their own personal gain, this relationship still augurs well for the ambience that enables the church to do its evangelistic work. What was true in the Western world some two hundred years ago is currently still true on the African continent.

So, there is a lot to be said for the health and prosperity of the church in Africa. As the reader begins to make progress in reading this book and finds some areas of grave concern being addressed, these positive characteristics of African Christianity should not be forgotten. You would have to be of a very pessimistic spirit to feel discouraged about what God is doing on the continent.

This book is written to give the biblical foundations of what the church is meant to be. Many people who make up the church in Africa—including church pastors and ministry leaders—simply inherited the church. They have adopted what they have found in the church without really knowing why they do what they do. Without being anchored in the Bible's teaching about the church, they have been at the mercy of the winds that are blowing and the waves that are beating against the church, and consequently, they sometimes take the church in directions that hurt its spiritual life. This is because they are simply flowing with the tide. This zeal that lacks knowledge sometimes results in the church finding itself in seriously unbiblical practices. There is a desperate need for a book that explains God's design for the church so that those who lead the church can do so in accordance with God's mind. This is the positive goal of this book.

Another reason why this book has been written is to address the obvious wrong practices that are in vogue in the African church today. My approach will be to lay out what the Bible teaches concerning various areas of church life and then to take that torch and shine it upon the current practices. I have tried to use questions as headings for the various chapters so that those who want to use it as a guide can go straight to the chapter that asks the question that they are asking. They will not only get the biblical answers but will also see what areas need to change in the light of what the Bible says. Where the Bible is not very clear on a matter, I have honestly said so. In such situations, denominations that equally respect the authority of the Bible have different applications, and I have avoided being too dogmatic. However, where the Bible's teaching is well-defined, I have sought to be faithful to the Scriptures so that the readers are left in no doubt about God's design for the church. It is my prayer that the reader will have the humility to admit where the practices of a particular church are in opposition to the teaching of the Bible and will make the changes necessary to receive the approbation of God. Church leadership is a stewardship and not an ownership. The church belongs to God, and our job is to look after it on his behalf.

This book goes out with the prayer that its fragrance will spread across the landscape of Africa and will result in a therapeutic effect on the church. The church on this continent currently has the greatest potential to bless the global church if only it can be healed of the vices that are crippling its effectiveness. This transformation can take place by the power of the Holy Spirit once the word of God is known. God has designed his church to function in a particular way and has revealed that design in the Bible. May this be known and applied to the health of the church in Africa and to the glory of God alone. Amen!

STUDY GUIDE FOR THE INTRODUCTION
God's Design for the Church

Summary

Biblical Christianity is the same everywhere. It speaks into the different manners and customs that people have and speaks to them in ways they can understand, but the message of the Bible is still the same everywhere. By and large, churches in Africa are growing. They enjoy certain advantages that our brothers in the West do not have, e.g., respect in the society and the presence of a young, future generation. There is, however, a deep need to recover a biblical understanding of God's design for a church, and to forsake practices that are false to God's word.

Study Questions

1. The author identifies a number of blessings that churches in Africa still have which many in the West no longer enjoy. Can you identify them? Which of these blessings are true in your setting?

2. What do you think are the differences between a church that follows God's design for the church and a church that does not?

3. The author also says that the church is "a stewardship and not an ownership." What do you think is the difference between these two ways of viewing the church? In what ways have you seen pastors in your country practicing the one or the other?

4. Some have said that it is a waste of time to explore God's design for the local church in Africa, since Africa's greater need is to hear the gospel, not to reform its churches. Do you agree?

   How do churches that follow God's design promote evangelization of the community?

5. Are there any ways you think your current church has missed the Bible's design for what a church should be? What ways are these?

   Consider beginning to pray for your church in these areas as you work through this book. At the end of the book, you can come back to this list and compare it with what you have learned.

1

What Is the Church?

Like many individuals in Africa, I grew up going to church. From the earliest memories of my childhood, I recall being helped to dress up in my best clothes on Sunday and being shepherded into the family car before going with my parents and siblings to church. I remember the Sunday school years, with their riveting stories of Samson and Delilah, David and Goliath, Daniel in the lions' den, Moses and Pharaoh, and so on. I recall the stories about Jesus that endeared him to my heart even as a young, unconverted boy.

I also remember the eloquence of the pastor. Standing out in my childhood memories was the way in which about halfway through the sermon on Sundays, at some high point, women in the church would suddenly burst forth in a chorus and the pastor would pause to sip some water. I always waited for that refreshing midpoint in the sermon. Church was the climax of my week, and the mid-sermon singing was the great crescendo of that climax.

This background defined what church was for me. It was a place. It was a building. It was where you went in your best clothes to meet people in their best clothes and to hear wonderful Bible stories. Most often those stories ended with some moral application about how we should live in ways that pleased God. They also helped us to become more loving neighbors.

It was not until many years later that I began to understand that a church was in fact not a building. It was not even a place. It was a gathered people who come together for the purpose of worship and fulfilling the mission given to them by Jesus Christ. In that sense, it was different from a bank or a shop. This change of understanding happened when I became a true Christian through regeneration and conversion. The more I studied the Bible, the more I began to understand that the church was not the building you went to on Sundays. It was the people engaged in the activities that took place in that building. It was the people who met there. I can go further and say that the church was not even *everyone* who met there. It was the people who had experienced conversion in Christ and had covenanted together to live as a family according to the law of Christ. These were the church. That was a new concept for me.

Ekklesia and the Body of Christ

In the forty years of my Christian life I have come to realize that my wrong concept of the church was in fact the most common understanding all around me. The first picture used in the Bible for "church" is best captured in the Greek word *ekklesia*, which means, "the called-out ones." Perhaps the closest phrase in English would be the word "assembly," which refers to people who are called out from wherever they are and are gathered into one place. Sometimes this word was used to refer to other assemblies who were not the church. We see this in Acts 19:32, 39, 41:

> Now some cried out one thing, some another, for the assembly was in confusion, and most of them did not know why they had come together. . . .
>
> [The town clerk said] 'But if you seek anything further, it shall be settled in the regular assembly.' . . . And when he had said these things, he dismissed the assembly.

The New Testament church chose to use this Greek word for assembly to refer to its own gatherings.

In the Gospels, this Greek word is used only three times. It is used when Jesus said, "And I tell you, you are Peter, and on this rock I will build my church, and the gates of hell shall not prevail against it" (Matt. 16:18). It is used twice when Jesus said, "If he refuses to listen to them, tell it to the church. And if he refuses to listen even to the church, let him be to you as a Gentile and a tax collector" (Matt. 18:17). In both cases, these were the words of Jesus. In the rest of the New Testament *ekklesia* is used more than 110 times. The usage of the word emphasizes that the church is not a building but people. It also emphasizes that these people are separated, through salvation, from other people. They are "called out" from other people. In this case, believers are called out to live separate lives from what the Bible calls "the world." Finally, this word emphasizes that the people of God are called out in order to be together. They are an assembly. The sense of togetherness cannot be missed when one reads the following description of the church in its very earliest days:

> And all who believed were together and had all things in common. And they were selling their possessions and belongings and distributing the proceeds to all, as any had need. And day by day, attending the temple together and breaking bread in their homes, they received their food with glad and generous hearts, praising God and having favor with all the people. And the Lord added to their number day by day those who were being saved. (Acts 2:44–47)

A second picture that the Bible uses for the church is that of "the body of Christ." We see this especially in the writings of the apostle Paul. To the Romans Paul says, "For as in one body we have many members, and the members do not all have the same function, so we, though many, are one body in Christ, and individually members one of another. Having gifts that differ according to the grace given to us, let us use them" (Rom. 12:4–6). To the Ephesians Paul writes, "And he gave the apostles, the prophets, the evangelists, the shepherds and teachers, to equip the saints for the work of ministry, for building up the body of Christ" (Eph. 4:11–12). This refers to the church's relationship with Jesus Christ. Jesus is the head of the body (Eph. 5:23; Col. 1:18). We are joined to him when the Holy Spirit regenerates us and baptizes us into his body (1 Cor. 12:12–13). Just as the human head controls what the body does, so also Jesus by his Spirit and his word determines what the church does. This concept of the body of Christ also emphasizes the variety of gifts that we have as

Christians, as we noted in both the Romans and Ephesians passages quoted earlier. We are like the eyes, ears, mouth, nose, arms, and legs of the human body. Each of us fulfills a distinct function in the body. Finally, this body concept illustrates the way in which Christians are to care for one another in the church. As Christians, we are members of the body of Christ in the same way that the human body has various parts. Each part functions for the good of the rest of the body. "If one member suffers, all suffer together; if one member is honored, all rejoice together" (1 Cor. 12:26).

The Church Universal and Local

According to the Bible, the church is both universal and local. The universal church comprises all those who from the beginning of human history up to the end of history have been (or will be) purchased by the blood of Jesus and are already assembled and enrolled in heaven (Heb. 12:23). We will one day be gathered around the throne of God from every tribe, language, people, and nation (Rev. 5:9). For God, who sees the end from the beginning (Isa. 46:10), this church is ever present before his eyes. The author of the letter to the Hebrews seems to suggest this when he tells the Hebrew Christians that they have come ". . . to the assembly of the firstborn who are enrolled in heaven" (Heb. 12:23). The apostle Paul seems also to have alluded to this ever-present reality when he says,

> Christ loved the church and gave himself up for her, that he might sanctify her, having cleansed her by the washing of water with the word, so that he might present the church to himself in splendor, without spot or wrinkle or any such thing, that she might be holy and without blemish. (Eph. 5:25–27)

That makes sense only if it refers to all the believers right across history. At any one time, part of that number is here on earth awaiting glorification and the other part has already arrived in heaven. In Christian literature, the former is called "the church militant" while the latter is called "the church triumphant." Wonderful terms, I think!

The church militant, being the sum total of Christians on earth, has been growing over time. The numbers sometimes reduce in some parts of the world due to persecution or worldliness. Sometimes it is evident that a growing hardness to the gospel sweeps over an entire geographical area. As older Christians die and very few people are converted, the number of Christians in that area reduces and the church militant gets smaller. However, generally speaking, the church militant has continued to grow around the world over the years. This has been primarily because of its evangelistic and missions work. In the most dangerous places for Christians to live, and especially where tyrannical regimes have been in power, sometimes the church militant has largely disappeared. In fact, believers have simply gone "underground" (see 1 Kings 19:18). They are still there, but for fear of their lives they no longer meet publicly. However, once the situation changes and freedom of religion is guaranteed, the church militant has popped up again and the world has been amazed to discover that it has grown substantially while in hiding.

Belonging to the Local Church

The local church ought to comprise those who have repented of their sins, put their faith in the Lord Jesus Christ, and undergone public baptism. (Some church denominations include the children of believers, but that issue is beyond the scope of this book.) Jesus, the head of the church, wants all those who claim to belong to him to be baptized and become part of such visible and localized bodies so that they can be taught the implications of belonging to him. We read this in the statement that we call "the Great Commission." Jesus said,

> All authority in heaven and on earth has been given to me. Go therefore and make disciples of all nations, baptizing them in the name of the Father and of the Son and of the Holy Spirit, teaching them to observe all that I have commanded you. And behold, I am with you always, to the end of the age. (Matt. 28:18–20)

As shown in this passage, baptism signifies the public confession by which a person becomes a member of the local church and comes under the instruction of church leaders.

All Christians should belong to a local church. This is not optional. It is in the local church that they will be instructed, as we have already observed. It is also in the local church that they will primarily experience the richness of Christian fellowship with other believers. Everything we have learned about *ekklesia* and the body of Christ will be experienced at a very practical level in the context of the local church. Christians will learn to live with other believers in the local church even though they may have serious personal disagreements and disputes from time to time. It is in the local church that they will learn to serve one another and to serve together in extending the kingdom of God according to the gifts that God has given them. Every Christian should become an active member of a local church. I repeat, this is not optional.

Distinguishing Characteristics of a True Church

Not every institution that calls itself a church is really a true church. In the Bible, some such institutions are called "synagogues of Satan" (Rev. 2:9; 3:9). So, how can we tell if a church is really a church? When the New Testament church began in Acts 2, it was described this way: "So those who received his word were baptized, and there were added that day about three thousand souls. And they devoted themselves to the apostles' teaching and the fellowship, to the breaking of bread and the prayers" (Acts 2:41–42). There was the preaching of God's word, the sharing of the common life, the ordinances, and prayer. From this list, I want to draw out two distinguishing characteristics of true churches and then add another one that became part of church life later. A true church can be *distinguished* by three primary characteristics:

1. The preaching of the word of God. That this is an essential characteristic of a true church is evident from what Jesus said in Matt. 28:20: ". . . teaching them to observe all that I have commanded you." The preaching of the word of God must be central to the very definition of the church. This is why one of the very first achievements of pioneer missionaries who came to Africa was to translate the Bible into the language of the people. They knew how important the preaching of the Bible was to the health of Christians and of churches. Sadly, in too many of our churches in Africa, preaching does not occupy a central position anymore. Rather, we have many choirs that take turns on the same day—children's choir, men's choir, women's choir, the main choir, and so on. By the time all these choirs have finished singing, everyone is ready to go home. Drama has also begun to feature quite prominently in some churches. This must change. With regard to preaching, Louis Berkhof says, "This is the most important mark of the Church. . . . It does not mean that the preaching must be perfect and absolutely pure, but that it must be true to the fundamentals of the Christian religion and must have a controlling influence on faith and practice."[1]

Closely connected with the preaching of the word of God should be the proclamation of the true gospel. This is the heart of the word of God. The church should be one place where men and women are constantly reminded of the way in which God reconciles sinners to himself. The person and work of Christ should be taught in all its fullness. Where salvation is being taught as achieved through works of righteousness—whether in part or in whole—you will not have the church of Christ there, even if the place is called a church. The true gospel must be an essential component of the definition of the church.

2. The provision of the ordinances. This refers to the administration of baptism and the Lord's Supper (see Acts 2:41–42, referred to earlier). The latter is sometimes called Communion. Whereas churches may differ on the right recipients and mode of baptism, this religious rite should be part of the activities of local churches as a means by which individuals enter into the church. While inside the church, they should participate in the Lord's Supper, which typifies the death of the Lord Jesus for his people. Again, there will be differences in the frequency and the precise way in which this meal is celebrated, but it must be part of the church's life.

3. The practice of discipline. The church is meant to be a place where godliness and truth are upheld. Where either of these is missing in the life of a person, they should be warned and urged to repent so that they are restored to a healthy spiritual life. However, where they stubbornly continue living a life of sin or holding on to and teaching heresy, they should be disciplined through public rebuke or excommunication (Matt. 18:15–20; 1 Cor. 5:1–13). In the book of

---

1. Louis Berkhof, *Summary of Christian Doctrine* (Grand Rapids, MI: Eerdmans, 1938), 153.

Revelation, Jesus warned those churches where stubborn sinners are not disciplined that he was going to do it himself (e.g., Rev. 2:16). Where that happens, often entire churches end up being closed down. We must all take this matter seriously. Discipline is part of the very definition of the church.

The only people who should remain in the church are those who show genuine faith and obedience to the Lord Jesus Christ, the great head of the church. This is seen when individuals are doing everything possible to flee from sin and pursue a righteous life. This is also seen in their love for fellow believers and for the God whom Christians worship. Where you have individuals like this filling up the membership of a local church, you can safely say that you have a true church on earth.

Some Implications of All This

All these issues are dealt with in more detail later in this book. For now, I wanted us to simply answer the question, "What is the church?" I trust that the explanation above has answered that question from the Bible. A few implications come out of this brief survey.

First, attending a church regularly does not automatically make you a member of a church. There is a difference between the local church and the Sunday congregation. You must go beyond simply attending and should become a responsible member who fulfills all the responsibilities that Christ expects you to fulfill.

Second, we must not look down on churches that do not meet in exquisite church buildings, as if they are any less churches of Christ. The rate at which Christianity is growing in Africa means that we will continue to have churches meeting in school classrooms and under trees. These are as much churches of Jesus Christ as those who meet in magnificent cathedrals. What matters is not the kind of building Christians are meeting in but whether the people meeting there are real Christians and whether they are listening to the preaching of the word of God, receiving the sacraments, and ensuring purity among themselves through the exercise of church discipline.

Third, it must be evident from this that we should rejoice in the international and global nature of the church. We must not think of the church primarily in terms of our own local church or denomination.

We belong to the body of Christ that encompasses the whole planet. The church is in Africa, in America, in Europe, in Asia, and so on. It is everywhere. Your local church is only a local manifestation of this big, international body. There is sometimes such an emphasis on being an "African church" that we can easily lose sight of the fact that we are one body—one church—right across the globe. Our local church should be in partnership with other churches in fulfilling the task that Jesus has given to his worldwide church. Our local church should also be actively helping weaker churches around us to become stronger.

Fourth, since membership in the church is open to all who are converted in Christ, we must never limit our church's membership to one tribe or one ethnic group. The language that we use in our church should simply represent the language of the people we meet in our community. That way, anyone who lives in our vicinity will feel free to belong to our church as long as they are truly believers in Christ. One of the sad realities of Africa is that you can have five churches on the same street and they all use different languages because each church "belongs" to a different tribe. Yet those who go to those churches go to the same schools and work in the same offices, where they interact or learn and work in the same language. This totally misrepresents the nature of the Christian church. If there is to be any division, let it be because of doctrinal differences. Beyond that, each local church must be open to anyone who is a Christian, and we must go out of our way to make everyone in that category feel at home.

STUDY GUIDE FOR CHAPTER 1
What Is the Church?

Summary

God's word, not our varied experiences, should teach us what a church is. A church is a gathering of those who have been called out of the sinful world through salvation and who have made a covenant with each other to care for each other and to assemble regularly to worship God. These assemblies of believers must be marked by three things: the preaching of the word, the practice of baptism and the Lord's Supper, and the practice of church discipline. The church is the body of Christ, which is both universal and local. As the head, Christ has authority over the church, and as a body we need the variety that each body part contributes.

Study Questions

1. This chapter identifies three distinctive marks of a true church. What are they? Which of them is your local church strongest at? Which one do you think you are weakest at?

2. On page 24, the author describes the church as "people who had experienced conversion in Christ and had covenanted together to live as a family according to the law of Christ." Based on this definition of a church, would you call a weekly Bible study or a home group fellowship a church? Why or why not?

3. Are there local churches in your area that have died and closed down? How would you reconcile a church closing down with Jesus's promise in Matthew 16 to build his church?

4. A pastor in rural Burundi believes that even though everyone is welcome to attend church on Sunday, the Bible teaches that only those who have been "called out" through faith and repentance can rightly become members. However, he fears to teach this because he will upset the unconverted elderly, rich, long-time attendees whose money supports the church budget. What should he do?

5. From this chapter, what would you say to believers who don't think they have to be part of a local church?

2

Who Is the Church's Founder and Head?

You have only to be around churches in Africa for a short time before you come across individuals claiming to be the "founders" of the churches that they planted. This is especially the case when more churches have been established out of that individual's church. They all start going by the name of that first church. That person ensures that he is referred to as the founder of the church.

Companies have founders. These are the individuals who first see the need to start such companies and take the risk of investing funds to get them off the ground. Think of Shoprite, for instance. It is now Africa's largest food retailer, operating in at least fourteen countries across the continent and with more than 147,000 workers. Prior to November 1979, this company did not exist except, perhaps, in the mind of its founder. Then, that year, Christo Wiese decided to lead his family business to buy a small, struggling chain of retail outlets in South Africa. That was the birth of what we know today as the multinational retail company called Shoprite, which is among the top one hundred retail chain stores in the world. That is what founders do.

Companies also have heads. The head of an organization is the person who directs all that is going on in it. He is responsible for ensuring that it achieves the purpose of its existence. It is the responsibility of everyone else in the organization to submit to his leadership.

Today, the popular phrase for such a person is CEO—chief executive officer. I guess the phrase "head" may have its origin in the way the physical head of a human being is where the brain is, and from the brain, through the nervous system, comes all the instructions that cause us to do what we do. We speak of big enterprises as having a "headquarters," schools as having a "headmaster" or "headteacher," and so on. In each case, we are talking about the place or person where authoritative instructions come from to ensure that what needs to be done is done. The responsibility of all who are in that organization or school is to submit to and cooperate with the instructions coming from there.

In this chapter, we are asking and seeking the answer to the question, "Who is the founder and head of the church?" In the last chapter, we saw what the church is. We noted that, in the New Testament, it comprised the called-out ones and was referred to as the body of Christ. We saw that it had two major segments—those who were still on earth and those who had gone to heaven. Finally, we saw that the church had localized expressions, which we refer to as local churches. These local churches are spread right across the world. Who is behind all this development over the years? Who is the founder? Who is the head?

Jesus Christ Is the Founder of the Church

If we go to the "founding documents" of the church—the Holy Scriptures—it is tempting to identify the apostles who were appointed by Jesus as the founders of the church. We read such words as, "So then you are no longer strangers and aliens, but you are fellow citizens with the saints and members of the household of God, *built on the foundation of the apostles* and prophets, Christ Jesus himself being the cornerstone" (Eph. 2:19–20, emphasis mine). We notice in the book of Acts how the first church came into existence through the preaching of the apostle Peter on the day of Pentecost. Three thousand individuals were baptized that day and formed the membership of the first local church on earth, in Jerusalem.

We see from the Scriptures how these same apostles deliberately and purposefully went all over Asia and Europe spreading the teaching about Jesus Christ and founding local churches. Later, when difficulties arose in these churches, these apostles wrote authoritative letters to those churches defining what they should believe and how they should live and conduct their affairs. Some of those letters have survived up to this day, and we refer to them as Epistles in the New Testament of the Bible. Even today, we seek to settle any matters of dispute with respect to the running of the church by referring to those letters. Therefore, could the apostles of Jesus Christ be the founders of the church?

When you consider the sum total of the teaching of the Bible, the one who comes out at the top as the true founder and head of the church is the Son of God, the Lord Jesus Christ. Even in the passage we read earlier that spoke of the foundation of the church being the apostles and prophets, the apostle Paul ended by saying, "Christ Jesus himself being the cornerstone" (Eph. 2:20). He is the most important and unique part of the entire foundation. That only makes sense, because he is the one who chose each one of the apostles and sent them out with the express instructions,

> All authority in heaven and on earth has been given to me. Go therefore and make disciples of all nations, baptizing them in the name of the Father and of the Son and of the Holy Spirit, teaching them to observe all that I have commanded you. And behold, I am with you always, to the end of the age. (Matt. 28:18–20)

The apostles were simply obeying Jesus's instructions. The word "apostle" means "a sent-out one," a little bit like missionaries today who are sent out by a church to go and establish Christ's kingdom elsewhere, usually by planting new churches. So, the apostles were not the ultimate founders of the church. It was Jesus Christ. They were simply carrying out his instructions.

Jesus Christ Is the Head of the Church

Jesus is not only the ultimate founder of the church; he is also the church's head. Two passages in the Bible make this abundantly clear. In Colossians 1:18 Paul says, "And [Jesus Christ] is the head of the body, the church. He is the beginning, the firstborn from the dead, that in everything he might be preeminent." In Ephesians 5:22–24, Paul says, "Wives, submit to your own husbands, as to the Lord. For the husband is the head of the wife even as Christ is the head of the church, his body, and is himself its Savior. Now as the church submits to Christ, so also wives should submit in everything to their husbands." We not only see here the role of Christ as the head of the church; we also see what the role of the church is. It is to submit to his leadership.

Ultimately, it is through the work of the Holy Spirit and through the word of God that Jesus founds and leads the church. It was on the Day of Pentecost, when the Spirit of God was poured down from heaven in a most unusual manner, that the New Testament church was born. We trace its birthday to that date. It has been under the direction of the Holy Spirit that apostles and missionaries have been sent out into all the nations of the world to establish the reign of Jesus Christ in the hearts of people from every tribe and language. Thus, we read in Acts 13:1–3,

> Now there were in the church at Antioch prophets and teach-ers, Barnabas, Simeon who was called Niger, Lucius of Cyrene, Manaen a lifelong friend of Herod the tetrarch, and Saul. While they were worshiping the Lord and fasting, the Holy Spirit said, "Set apart for me Barnabas and Saul for the work to which I have called them." Then after fasting and praying they laid their hands on them and sent them off.

The church in Antioch was obeying the instructions of the Lord Jesus Christ, and the one who ensured they got the message was the Holy Spirit. He must have spoken to them through one of the prophets who was with them.

The role of the Spirit in communicating the Lord's will to his church is particularly evident as you read the messages in the book of Revela-tion that Jesus sent to each of the seven churches of Asia. In each case we read, "He who has an ear, let him hear what the Spirit says to the churches" (2:7, 11, 17, 29, 3:6, 13, 22). Jesus was making the point that he was communicating to the churches through his Spirit, and he wanted the churches to take heed to his messages because he is the head of the church. He threatened with punishment any church that did not take heed to his messages. The responsibility that the church had in those days is the same responsibility we have today. Remember, that is the role of those who are under a head. They must submit to his leadership so that he is able to accomplish the purpose for which the institution exists.

In New Testament days, the churches were at the mercy of prophets discerning the mind of the Holy Spirit and making that known to them. Today,

> we have the prophetic word more fully confirmed, to which you will do well to pay attention as to a lamp shining in a dark place, until the day dawns and the morning star rises in your hearts, knowing this first of all, that no prophecy of Scripture comes from someone's own interpretation. For no prophecy was ever produced by the will of man, but men spoke from God as they were carried along by the Holy Spirit. (2 Pet. 1:19–21)

God in his goodness has ensured that what we need to know about what to believe and how to live in order to please the great head of the church has been written in the Bible. All we need to do is read it and obey it.

What Makes Jesus the Founder and Head of the Church?

We have seen that Jesus Christ is both the founder and head of the church. Let us broadly consider other relationships that Jesus has with the church. All the pictures that we will see simply augment why it only makes sense that Jesus should be not only the founder but also the head of the church.

1. He received them. The elect, who make up the true church, were given to Jesus Christ by God the Father. In what we call the high priestly prayer of the Lord Jesus Christ, he said,

> I have manifested your name to the people whom you gave me out of the world. Yours they were, and you gave them to me, and they have kept your word. . . . I am praying for them. I am not praying for the world but for those whom you have given me, for they are

yours. All mine are yours, and yours are mine, and I am glorified in them. (John 17:6, 9–10)

Earlier in this prayer, Jesus had said to the Father that he had been given authority over all flesh so that he might give eternal life to all whom the Father had given him (John 17:2). Surely, if the people who make up the church are Christ's, then it makes sense that he has the right to rule then as he sees fit.

2. He purchased them. When Jesus died on the cross, he paid the price for the redemption of his people who make up the church. To the question "Whom did Jesus die for?" we often answer without thinking twice, "Jesus died for the world." That is true. He is "the Lamb of God, who takes away the sin of the world" (John 1:29). We find similar words in the most famous verse in the Bible, John 3:16. However, the Bible often uses the word "world" to emphasize that the gospel was not for the Jews only but also for the Gentiles. The term "world" does not always mean each and every person who has ever been born since creation. More specifically, the Bible teaches that Jesus died for his elect people, those whom the Father had given him before the foundation of the world. Jesus speaks of having died exclusively for his sheep. He says, "I am the good shepherd. The good shepherd lays down his life for the sheep. . . . I know my own and my own know me, just as the Father knows me and I know the Father; and I lay down my life for the sheep" (John 10:11, 14–15). Perhaps the passage in the Bible that shows most clearly that Jesus died for his church is Ephesians 5:25–27:

> Husbands, love your wives, as Christ loved the church and gave himself up for her, that he might sanctify her, having cleansed her by the washing of water with the word, so that he might present the church to himself in splendor, without spot or wrinkle or any such thing, that she might be holy and without blemish.

Preaching to the Ephesian elders in his farewell address, Paul said, "Pay careful attention to yourselves and to all the flock, in which the Holy Spirit has made you overseers, to care for the church of God, which he obtained with his own blood" (Acts 20:28). Jesus redeemed a people for himself who now make up the true church in heaven and on earth. So, he must have the right to do with them as he sees fit. He bought them with his own blood!

3. He betrothed them. The church is referred to as the bride of Christ. At the end of history, there will be the marriage feast of the Lamb (Rev. 19:7). The bride, referred to here as the new Jerusalem, will appear beautifully adorned to meet her bridegroom, the Lord Jesus Christ (Rev. 21:2). Hence, the church is referred to as "the wife of the Lamb" (Rev. 21:9). There will be the final wedding day of Christ and the church, whose bride price he paid when he died on the cross. This relationship of Christ to his church as husband and wife is the great argument the apostle Paul uses to define how a wife and a husband should relate to each other. Paul says,

> Wives, submit to your own husbands, as to the Lord. For the husband is the head of the wife even as Christ is the head of the church, his body, and is himself its Savior. Now as the church submits to Christ, so also wives should submit in everything to their husbands. Husbands, love your wives, as Christ loved the church and gave himself up for her. (Eph. 5:22–25)

The point is well made: The church must submit to Christ the bridegroom.

4. He shepherds them. One more important New Testament picture of Jesus as head of the church is that of his being the great shepherd of the sheep. A shepherd not only protects sheep; he also directs them where to feed. Usually, when a shepherd has many sheep, he divides them among other shepherds who then work under his immediate supervision. These are called undershepherds. That is what church leaders are. They are undershepherds under Jesus Christ, the great shepherd of the sheep. The apostle Peter used this imagery to encourage elders to do their work faithfully. He wrote,

> So I exhort the elders among you, as a fellow elder . . . shepherd the flock of God that is among you, exercising oversight, not under compulsion, but willingly, as God would have you. . . . And when the chief Shepherd appears, you will receive the unfading crown of glory. (1 Pet. 5:1–2, 4)

This emphasizes that church leaders are not the ultimate authority in the church. It is Jesus Christ. They should be carrying out their work in the way in which Jesus wants them to. When he returns, he will reward them accordingly.

Some Implications of All This

Those who have been used by God to plant churches should not see themselves as founders of the church. They are not. They are merely instruments in the hands of the great head of the church—the Lord Jesus Christ—whom he used in order to plant that church or those churches, as he did with the apostles in the Bible. Jesus alone is the founder of the church. As stated at the beginning of this chapter, we have too many church leaders in Africa today claiming to be founders of the churches that they planted. This is especially the case when more churches have been established out of the first church and all of them are now going by the name of that first church. That person ensures that the church's website and his business cards read that he is the founder of the church. Even where such a person was the church planter, it is wise to avoid such abused terms and realize we are only instruments in God's hands. As Paul would say,

> What then is Apollos? What is Paul? Servants through whom you believed, as the Lord assigned to each. I planted, Apollos watered, but God gave the growth. So neither he who plants nor he who waters is anything, but only God who gives the growth. . . . For we are God's fellow workers. You are God's field, God's building. (1 Cor. 3:5–7, 9)

Sadly, it reaches levels where, even when such a leader has fallen into grievous, scandalous sin, he insists that he can neither be removed from office nor be disciplined in any way. He demands that those who are calling for his resignation should be the ones to leave because he is the founder of the church. It is as if he has an inalienable right to be the primary leader of the church, no matter what his spiritual state might be. There is need to reverse this trend and ensure that Jesus has no competition. He alone is the founder of the church. No human being paid the price to purchase the church. Only Christ did, and he demands holiness especially from church leaders. They will give an account to him when he returns. Those who have usurped Christ's position and abused his church will pay dearly for it on that day.

Church leaders must not do with the church whatever they please. They should always ask the question "What does the Bible say?" The Holy Spirit has ensured that we have the mind of the head of the church in the Holy Scriptures. Those of us who are church leaders should go there frequently to hear what he says. When Paul sent Timothy to pastor the church in Ephesus, he was anxious that Timothy should not end up leading the church according to his own pragmatic reasoning. "It is a good idea" is not a good idea if the Bible does not sanction it. Thus, Paul sent Timothy the letter that we refer to as 1 Timothy. Paul wrote, "I hope to come to you soon, but I am writing these things to you so that, if I delay, you may know how one ought to behave in the household of God, which is the church of the living God, a pillar and buttress of the truth" (1 Tim. 3:14–15). Paul did not want to take chances. His letter to Timothy is full of instructions on things such as male and female roles in the church, who qualifies to be elders and deacons in the church, how the church should look after the vulnerable among them and also their pastors, and so on.

Today, we have churches being made to do what Jesus never said in his word that they should be doing. Church leaders sometimes want to use the power of numbers to sway political elections or even to monitor such elections. Is that what the head of the church said the church should be doing? In the next chapter we will see the purpose of the church. Suffice it now to say, I doubt that Jesus included the swaying or monitoring of elections as one of the purposes of the church.

Let us always remember that the ultimate leader of the church is the Lord Jesus Christ. He is its founder and head. He may have died, but he is not dead. He is alive and well, and he is walking among the lampstands (Rev. 2:1), trimming their wicks.

STUDY GUIDE FOR CHAPTER 2
Who Is the Church's Founder and Head?

Summary

Jesus Christ alone is the founder and head of his church. The church belongs to him because he received the church as his possession from the Father; he purchased her with his blood; he betrothed her to himself to be his bride; and he lives now to shepherd his church. The church is alive because of his Spirit, and it lives by his word. Church leaders should see themselves as servants whose work is to do Jesus's will for his church, not as executives free to do whatever they like or whatever they find wise.

Study Questions

1. The author identifies three reasons why Jesus is the head of the church. What are they? Which of these was the least obvious to you?

2. Looking around in your context, identify common ways in which church leaders or pastors compromise the authority and headship of Christ in the way they lead.

3. In 2014, a South African pastor told his congregants to eat grass to bring themselves closer to God. Many of his congregants did so. How would you advise Christians to evaluate such instructions from their pastors?

4. How can a pastor demonstrate the authority of Christ through his preaching?

How can he likewise demonstrate Christ's authority in how he leads the church?

5. What structures do you think churches can put in place to ensure that their leaders are accountable? Where would you go in the Bible for support for such structures?

3

What Is the Church's Task in the World?

They say that necessity is the mother of invention. When you lack something that you badly need, your mind goes into overdrive and comes up with solutions that you may not have thought about, had you not been under pressure. I recall once visiting a friend in the United Kingdom and needing to use a two-pin plug in a three-hole socket. He told me that it was not possible because he did not have an appropriate adapter and it was too late at night for him to buy one. I asked him for a ball-point pen, got the plastic pen cover, and pushed it into the top hole of the three-hole socket. That opened the bottom two holes in the socket and I squeezed in my two-pin plug. He exclaimed, "Wow, I never knew you could do that! Where did you learn that from?" Well, in Africa, we do that all the time. We have learned such tricks due to our lack of appropriate gadgets.

Sadly, the church has fallen into the same fate. We have ended up using the church for all kinds of human needs and, in the end, it has become a Jack of all trades and a master of none. The church is being used for running schools and health facilities, conducting weddings and funerals, taking care of nonmember widows and orphans, mediating between political parties, monitoring elections, and so on. Sometimes, it even becomes a form of livelihood for so-called "men of God" who fail to find employment elsewhere. It is important that we search the Scriptures to find out what the primary purpose of the church is. Thankfully, we do not have to look very far. Before Jesus ascended to heaven, he stated unequivocally what the marching orders of the church were. This is recorded for us in all the Gospels, but perhaps the most comprehensive statement is found in Matthew. We read,

> And Jesus came and said to them, "All authority in heaven and on earth has been given to me. Go therefore and make disciples of all nations, baptizing them in the name of the Father and of the Son and of the Holy Spirit, teaching them to observe all that I have commanded you. And behold, I am with you always, to the end of the age." (Matt. 28:18–20)

Notice how Jesus began giving these instructions by first stating the power and authority that had been given to him. It was "all authority in heaven and on earth." Only God has such power and authority. This refers, therefore, to Christ's mediatorial kingship that was about to be conferred upon him when he ascended to heaven. He could speak as though it was already his because he had earned it through his atoning work on the cross of Calvary. God took on human nature at the virgin birth. Now, upon his ascension into heaven, the human nature of Christ was going to experience the glory that Jesus had from before the foundations of the earth. He was going to be given the reins of history to rule the universe for the purpose of bringing in his elect people for whom he died. Only when the last of the elect have been brought in is Jesus going to return to earth to wind up history. Then he will hand back the reins of history to the Father, so that God "may be all in all" (1 Cor. 15:28). Until then, all authority in heaven and on earth has been given to him. He is ruler of both the church and the world!

No doubt, you must wonder how Jesus rules a world that is in rebellion against him. The answer is that he rules the world as its ultimate judge and also providentially. In other words, nothing happens in this world without his allowing it to happen. Remember how, in Job 1 and 2, Satan had to obtain permission from God in order to destroy Job's property, family, and health? Remember how, in Acts 4:23–31, the disciples stated unequivocally in prayer that even the death of Jesus Christ took place because God permitted it to happen?

All that power is now vested in Jesus Christ, as the great God-man. He controls even the evil deeds of men and women and thus sets their boundaries—otherwise this world would be much worse than it is. He controls all human activity primarily in order to bring about the salvation of his people. When Jesus returns, the other aspect of his rule will also be visible, when he summons the whole of creation in order to punish or reward.

It is with this background that the Lord Jesus Christ now gives three instructions to his disciples. These three remain the work of his church throughout the whole of history until he returns. They spell out the purpose of the church up to this very day. Jesus is the head of the church, as we saw in the last chapter. He has every right to give the church its responsibilities. What are those responsibilities?

Making Disciples of All Nations

As we have seen, the first responsibility that Jesus gave to the church is that of making disciples of all the nations (Matt. 28:18–20). In the other Gospels, Jesus gives the church the responsibility to ensure that the gospel of salvation is preached to all nations. In the Gospel of Mark, Jesus says, "Go into all the world and proclaim the gospel to the whole creation" (Mark 16:15). In the Gospel of Luke, Jesus says, "Thus it is written, that the Christ should suffer and on the third day rise from the dead, and that repentance for the forgiveness of sins should be proclaimed in his name to all nations, beginning from Jerusalem" (Luke 24:46–47). And, finally, in the Gospel of John, we read, "Peace be with you. As the Father has sent me, even so I am sending you" (John 20:21). In this last passage, Jesus was referring to his work as an itinerant preacher of the gospel. He was now sending his disciples to do the same work.

If we were to summarize what is being communicated by Jesus in these four passages, it is that his disciples were under instruction to go to all nations of the world to tell them the good news that God was now offering them forgiveness of sin through the atoning work of Christ on the cross, and that they needed to repent and trust in this Jesus in order to obtain that forgiveness. By so doing, they would become his disciples.

When you read the Acts of the Apostles, the disciples to whom Jesus spoke these words understood them to mean precisely what we have summarized. They went from Jerusalem to Judea and then to Samaria and they just kept going. As they went, they preached the gospel wherever they could (Acts 2:14ff.; 3:12ff.; 4:8ff.; 5:27ff.; 6:7; 8:1–8; etc.). Even when they were commanded to stop preaching about the death and resurrection of Jesus Christ, they refused and went on preaching. They basically said they were willing to die rather than to stop preaching this message (Acts 4:18–20). That is the first responsibility that we have as a church. It is to ensure that the gospel is proclaimed to all nations so that individuals come to Jesus Christ in repentance and faith.

Baptizing the Disciples

The next area of responsibility that Jesus gave his disciples was that of baptizing those who became his disciples in the name of the Father and the Son and the Holy Spirit (Matt. 28:19). Of the other Gospel writers, the only one who also captured this second responsibility was Mark. He wrote, "Go into all the world and proclaim the gospel to the whole creation. Whoever believes and is baptized will be saved, but whoever does not believe will be condemned" (Mark 16:15–16).

What was the significance of baptism? It was the way in which those who repented from sin and trusted in Jesus Christ for their salvation proceeded to publicly express their faith in Jesus Christ and consequently formally join others in the local communities of Jesus's disciples. It was also the way in which the person baptizing affirmed the faith of the new convert, which was an important part of the person's sense of assurance. More will be said later about what baptism signifies and its relevance to local churches. For now, it is important to take note that this was a responsibility of the church. Jesus instructed his disciples to make this part of their work until he returns from heaven.

When you read the book of Acts, you see that the apostles took the words of Jesus seriously. They did not see baptism as a by-the-way instruction that they could do away with. Wherever they went, they not only preached the gospel but they also baptized those who responded positively to their gospel message. In this way, churches were being established in the various towns and villages where they preached. Let us see a few of these historical accounts by way of example.

On the day of Pentecost, when Peter preached the gospel, the Bible records, "So those who received his word were baptized, and there were added that day about three thousand souls" (Acts 2:41). Notice the order. There was the receiving of the word that was preached, which means that they repented and believed the gospel. This was followed by baptism. Everyone who believed the gospel was baptized. This was then followed by those who were baptized being added to the other disciples, so that the church grew by three thousand people.

The necessity of baptism is also seen in the preaching of Philip the evangelist. When he shared the gospel with the Ethiopian eunuch, the Bible records, "Then Philip opened his mouth, and beginning with this Scripture he told him the good news about Jesus. And as they were going along the road they came to some water, and the eunuch said, 'See, here is water! What prevents me from being baptized?' And he commanded the chariot to stop, and they both went down into the water, Philip and the eunuch, and he baptized him" (Acts 8:35–38).

What is interesting in this account is that we are not told that Philip taught the Ethiopian eunuch about baptism. However, from the eunuch's reaction when he saw water, it is evident that Philip had mentioned it to him. So, although baptism was not essential to salvation, it must have been mentioned as something that the eunuch needed to do as an expression of his faith in the Lord Jesus Christ. He wanted to do so as soon as he saw the water. In this story, the baptism did not lead to the eunuch joining a local church, because he was still on his way home to Africa. That was an exceptional situation.

There are many other examples of baptism following the proclamation of the gospel. Allow me to end with one more. In Acts 16 we are told about the establishing of the church in Philippi. Paul and his team were preaching outside the city. We read,

> One who heard us was a woman named Lydia, from the city of Thyatira, a seller of purple goods, who was a worshiper of God. The Lord opened her heart to pay attention to what was said by

Paul. And after she was baptized, and her household as well, she urged us, saying, "If you have judged me to be faithful to the Lord, come to my house and stay." And she prevailed upon us. (Acts 16:14–15)

Later in the chapter we are told of the conversion of the Philippian jailer. Paul and Silas were in prison and witnessed the jailer wanting to kill himself because, when he found their prison doors ajar, he thought the prisoners had escaped. Paul and Silas stopped the jailer before he could harm himself. We read,

Then he brought them out and said, "Sirs, what must I do to be saved?" And they said, "Believe in the Lord Jesus, and you will be saved, you and your household." And they spoke the word of the Lord to him and to all who were in his house. And he took them the same hour of the night and washed their wounds; and he was baptized at once, he and all his family. (Acts 16:30–33)

This was how the church began in Philippi. The families who heard the gospel and were converted to Christ were baptized and thus took up membership in this new church. Of course, many others in due season joined them. This responsibility of gathering new believers into local assemblies of God's people through baptism wherever the gospel is preached remains the responsibility of the church to this very day.

Instructing the Disciples

The third and final responsibility that Jesus gave his church was that of teaching the disciples to observe everything that he had commanded them (Matt. 28:20). Whereas conversion and baptism were one-off events, this teaching was to take place in an ongoing way for the rest of the lives of the disciples. This was for the purpose of securing the spiritual growth of believers. Jesus prayed to the Father while he was still here on earth, "Sanctify them in the truth; your word is truth" (John 17:17). The apostle Paul also pictured the work of Christ in his church in this way:

Husbands, love your wives, as Christ loved the church and gave himself up for her, that he might sanctify her, having cleansed her by the washing of water with the word, so that he might present the church to himself in splendor, without spot or wrinkle or any such thing, that she might be holy and without blemish. (Eph. 5:25–27)

The word of God is the instrument by which Jesus sanctifies his church and thus makes his people holy.

The people of God are to be taught Christian doctrine. They need to know about who God is, how he created the world, and how the world became the ruin that it has become. They need to be taught in more detail and depth how God came down in the person of Jesus Christ in order to save the world from sin and destruction. They need to learn how they are to live as God's new humanity in the home and in society, especially in light of the fact that the world still is essentially opposed to the Christian faith. They will need to be encouraged to remain firm in their faith as they await the Savior from heaven, the Lord Jesus Christ. All this cannot be done in a single day. The church is to be an educational center, where all Christians are present for regular instruction in and through Bible exposition.

This emphasis is unmistakable when you read the book of Acts. Let us go back to the sermon preached on the day of Pentecost. We read, "So those who received his word were baptized, and there were added that day about three thousand souls. And they devoted themselves to the apostles' teaching and the fellowship, to the breaking of bread and the prayers" (Acts 2:41–42). Notice how the very first item that these disciples devoted themselves to was the apostles' teaching. This was in line with what Jesus had commanded.

Later, when the church in Jerusalem experienced persecution, the believers scattered. Some went to Antioch and shared the gospel there. Many people believed. This resulted in a new church being born. Barnabas was sent there from Jerusalem to help the new church. The Bible says,

When he came and saw the grace of God, he was glad, and he exhorted them all to remain faithful to the Lord with steadfast purpose, for he was a good man, full of the Holy Spirit and of faith. And a great many people were added to the Lord. So Barnabas

went to Tarsus to look for Saul, and when he had found him, he
brought him to Antioch. For a whole year they met with the church
and taught a great many people. And in Antioch the disciples were
first called Christians. (Acts 11:23–26)

Notice how the preaching of the gospel resulted in the "adding" of
people, which was later followed by the teaching of the people. Barnabas found this to be so important that he even went to look for Saul
(later known as Paul the apostle) to come and help. This teaching is
an all-important part of the work of the church.

A third example from the book of Acts is found in the words of
Paul when he was bidding farewell to the elders of the church in Ephesus. He said,

And now, behold, I know that none of you among whom I have
gone about proclaiming the kingdom will see my face again. Therefore I testify to you this day that I am innocent of the blood of all,
for I did not shrink from declaring to you the whole counsel of
God. (Acts 20:25–27).

The phrase "the whole counsel of God" must be referring to the
whole menu of God's revelation. Paul had spent time in Ephesus instructing believers in the ways of God so that they could live their lives
as God wanted them to live. This duty did not end with the death of
the last apostle. It remains our responsibility today in the Christian
church.

The need to instruct the people of God to obey everything that
Jesus had instructed is what gave birth to the apostolic epistles. These
begin with the book of Romans and go all the way to the book of
Revelation. These were letters written to churches and individual
church leaders about what Christians were to believe and how they
were to live. These letters were often necessitated by circumstances in
the lives of churches and individual Christians that were detrimental
to their well-being. The apostles knew that it was their God-given
responsibility to instruct the church so that erroneous teaching and
erroneous living did not take root. The churches of Christ needed to
reflect the mind of Christ in the world. They could do so only if indi-

vidual church members lived as Jesus wanted them to live. Since the apostles could not be in all of those churches at the same time, they wrote letters to the churches, which they expected them to read so that everyone could know what to believe and how to live.

The instruction of believers should not end with belief or with moral living. It should include the agenda of the Great Commission itself, issuing into the formation of other churches in farther regions of the world. This work of evangelism and missions is part of obeying everything Christ commanded (see Matt. 28:20; also Matt. 5:13–16; Eph. 3:10; 1 Pet. 2:9–12).

Glorifying God

Why should the church be so engrossed in the evangelization of sinners and the sanctification of God's people through the preaching of the gospel and the proclamation of the whole counsel of God? It is in order to glorify God. The constitution of Kabwata Baptist Church states, "The church has been tasked to glorify God by promoting his joyful worship through the evangelization of sinners, the planting of local churches, and by ministering spiritually and materially to the saints." Notice the emphasis on glorifying God. That is why the church should pursue the activities that have been outlined thus far in this chapter.

The apostle Paul put it this way to the Ephesians:

> To me, though I am the very least of all the saints, this grace was given, to preach to the Gentiles the unsearchable riches of Christ, and to bring to light for everyone what is the plan of the mystery hidden for ages in God, who created all things, so that *through the church* the manifold wisdom of God might now be made known to the rulers and authorities in the heavenly places. (Eph. 3:8–10, emphasis mine)

Paul captures the same thought in a doxology. He says, "Now to him who is able to do far more abundantly than all that we ask or think, according to the power at work within us, *to him be glory in the church* and in Christ Jesus throughout all generations, forever and ever. Amen" (Eph. 3:20–21, emphasis mine). That is the grand purpose of the church. It is to bring glory to God through the realization of the redemption that Christ bought on the cross of Calvary.

Sadly, this is not what we see in many churches today. Rather, we find that many Christians do not see it as their responsibility to safeguard the Lord's Day so that they can meet with other believers for fellowship and to learn from God's word. Church leaders sometimes use the church to further their own personal agendas and goals. Or, a church may be simply seeking to meet the social needs of the marginalized and the poor in society. In some cases, the church has become an opposition party in the politics of the country. In a growing number of instances, the church has become a means of financial enrichment for its leaders—especially the so-called "man of God." There is a great need to revert to the purpose of the church that Jesus Christ its head instituted it for. We must get back to fulfilling the Great Commission.

STUDY GUIDE FOR CHAPTER 3
What Is the Church's Task in the World?

Summary

We saw in chapter 2 that the church is founded and headed by Jesus Christ. Therefore, the church's purpose and task in the world is determined by him. Jesus's special assignment to the church is to make disciples by evangelizing, baptizing, and teaching people his commands. Through this the church will be built and she will achieve her ultimate and grand purpose—to bring glory to God by displaying his work and power as the Redeemer.

Study Questions

1. The author observes that "the Lord Jesus Christ began giving these instructions by first stating the power and authority that had been given to him," which he calls Jesus's "mediatorial kingship." Why do you think it was important for Jesus to underline his authority before giving the Great Commission?

2. In your own words, why does God establish local churches?

3. List some tasks that the church has been commissioned to fulfill which cannot be fulfilled by any other institution. What do you think makes these tasks so unique?

What is the difference between the duties of individual Christians scattered in the world and the task of the church as an institution?

4. There are people who have said that Africa's most urgent needs are problems like poverty, famine, political unrest, etc., and so churches need to first focus on these things before they can focus on preaching the gospel. How should pastors respond to this, based on what you have learned about the church's task in the world?

5. What challenges does your local church face in evangelism, baptism, and its teaching ministry? How does the promise in Matthew 28:20 encourage you?

4

Why Is the Gospel So Important to the Church?

Churches that have lost the gospel but continue in existence remind me of one of my most memorable childhood pastimes, which was making wire cars with my friends and imagining that they were the real thing. We often ransacked wire fences for raw materials, which we brought to the backyard at home, and turned the place into some sort of car manufacturing plant. Once a wire car came off the assembly plant, it was often an object of admiration, though sometimes it suffered disapproval. We made car noises with our voices and even skidded so that we could see how the car could perform. We did our best to imitate the shapes of real cars and even named them as such—Ford, Toyota, Mercedes Benz, and so on. This was exciting childhood stuff. As soon as we came home from school, we would quickly go to the backyard, get our cars, and drive them to a friend's home so that we could go driving together. We even had car racing days. The boys who were already very good runners always won the races. Every so often our friends would want to catch a ride with us. In order for them to do so, they formed a queue behind the driver by each person holding the shirt or dress of the person in front. Thus, you could see a wire car being pushed in the streets with a queue of neighborhood children behind it, all having the time of their lives. The cars were very cheap to run. They did not need gasoline or grease. They did not need any coolant or oil. Once they came off the assembly line, the only thing they needed was strong young legs!

Many churches today remind me of this favorite childhood pastime. They are called churches, but they are a faint imitation of the church we read about in the Bible. There is no spiritual life in them. They have to keep being pushed in order for them to do anything. The people in the church are blissfully ignorant of the fact that they are merely playing church. It is not the real thing. Every Sunday, they put on their best clothes and either walk or drive to church. They meet with friends, sing together, give a little bit of money—usually the smallest change in their pockets—and listen to some inspirational message by the pastor. Neighbors can hear their voices, especially when they are singing or encouraging the preacher with their "Amens" and "Preach it, brother" punctuating the sermons. Every so often the pastor's humor sends the packed auditorium into loud laughter. They sing the final song and close in prayer. Church is over. They have done church until the following Sunday.

Why is this the case? As I hope to show you in this chapter, the first reason is that many churches have lost the gospel. Having lost the gospel, the church members are still spiritually dead. They do not know God, nor do they love him. They have no real hunger for the teaching of God's word and they do not desire corporate prayer. They do not know what it means to fight the good fight of faith through evangelistic enterprises. Sending out missionaries is the furthest thought from their minds. The book of Acts sounds like an account of life on another planet. Church is merely a social club for people in the neighborhood or village. We need to recover the gospel if we are going to recover real New Testament church life. Let us look at this matter in a little more detail.

The Gospel Is Important for the Growth of God's Kingdom

The gospel is important to the life of the church because the church gets its members *through* the gospel. The first task of the church is the evangelizing of sinners. We saw this in the previous chapter, but let me briefly repeat what we saw. Before Jesus went to heaven, he commanded his disciples, saying, "All authority in heaven and on earth has been given to me. Go therefore and make disciples of all nations, baptizing them in the name of the Father and of the Son and of the Holy Spirit" (Matt. 28:18–19). We noted from the Gospels of Mark and Luke that this was to be done through preaching the gospel: "Go into all the world and proclaim the gospel to the whole creation. Whoever believes and is baptized will be saved, but whoever does not believe will be condemned" (Mark 16:15–16); "Thus it is written, that the Christ should suffer and on the third day rise from the dead, and that repentance for the forgiveness of sins should be proclaimed in his name to all nations, beginning from Jerusalem" (Luke 24:46–47).

It is only as men and women, boys and girls, hear the gospel and respond to it through repentance and faith in the Lord Jesus Christ that they are to be added to the church through baptism. The word "gospel" simply means "good news." It is the good news of how God sent his Son, Jesus Christ, to live and die here on earth in order to save us from our sins. He was the only one who was ever born sinless, and he lived a perfectly righteous life. Therefore, death had no claim on him. However, he died in our place as our substitute. God punished him for sins he never committed so that his righteousness could become ours if we trust in him. As Paul said, "For our sake he made him to be sin who knew no sin, so that in him we might become the righteousness of God" (2 Cor. 5:21). Jesus rose again from the dead as evidence that God was satisfied with the payment he made on our behalf. Death, which is the wages of sin (Rom. 6:23), had been fully paid for and was thus totally defeated. Jesus then ascended to heaven, from where he, together with God the Father, has sent the Holy Spirit to convict and convert sinners as they listen to the gospel. Jesus will return at the end of history to take his believing people home.

As part of the Holy Spirit's saving work, he gives new life to dead souls. He transforms our hearts and makes us new creatures in Christ. We hate the sins that we loved before, and we love the holiness that we despised before. As transformed individuals, we are now ready to be members of the church of the Lord Jesus Christ. I will say a lot more on this in the next chapter. Suffice it to say here that, without the gospel, you lack the spiritual factory in which God makes real Christians who can then become true church members. The gospel is vital to the life of the church.

The apostle James wrote, "Of his own will he brought us forth by the word of truth, that we should be a kind of firstfruits of his creatures" (James 1:18). The apostle Peter wrote, "You have been born again, not of perishable seed but of imperishable, through the living and abiding word of God" (1 Pet. 1:23). So, the Holy Spirit uses the word of God to bring us to salvation and into the kingdom of God. The heartbeat of the gospel message is Christ's life, death, burial, and resurrection on our behalf. Once we lose this message, we have lost the means by which God will add to his church on earth real citizens of his kingdom.

The Gospel Is Important for Spiritual Growth

The gospel is also important to the life of the church because of its key role in helping Christians to grow in their most holy faith. We start our spiritual lives as believers by hearing and believing the gospel. We gain a strong assurance of our salvation the more we understand the implications of what Jesus did in order to save us from sin. We grow our spiritual lives as believers also by hearing and believing the gospel. Christians must never move on from the gospel. If they do, they end up wanting to please God by their own efforts instead of through resting in the finished work of Christ on their behalf.

Paul said to the Colossians,

> Therefore, as you received Christ Jesus the Lord, so walk in him, rooted and built up in him and established in the faith, just as you were taught, abounding in thanksgiving. See to it that no one takes you captive by philosophy and empty deceit, according to human tradition, according to the elemental spirits of the world, and not according to Christ. (Col. 2:6–8)

Paul was anxious that the believers in Colossae should not move beyond their faith in Christ, through whom they had come to salvation. He told them that they should continue to walk in him and be rooted and built up in him. The truths that brought them to salvation are the same truths upon which they must build their lives. It seems as if Paul had heard about teachings doing their rounds in Colossae that were based on human traditions and not based on Christ. Later in Colossians 2, it becomes evident that some of these teachings were mere legalism. Paul warned the believers to see to it that no one fell prey to such philosophies and empty deceit. He knew that these teachings were powerless to aid people in achieving real lasting holiness. He wrote, "These have indeed an appearance of wisdom in promoting self-made religion and asceticism and severity to the body, but they are of no value in stopping the indulgence of the flesh" (Col. 2:23). Only the work of the Holy Spirit can truly sanctify God's people. The raw material that the Holy Spirit uses in order to do this is the gospel of the Lord Jesus Christ. That is why we must never graduate from the gospel. We need it to grow in holiness. Anything else will simply turn us into self-righteous hypocrites, like the Pharisees in the days of the Lord Jesus Christ. Jesus described the Pharisees as whitewashed tombs—beautiful on the outside but full of dead men's bones on the inside! (Matt. 23:27–28). That is what we become without the gospel.

We see another example of the importance of the gospel in a Christian's spiritual growth in the book of Romans. At the start of chapter 12, Paul wrote, "I appeal to you therefore, brothers, by the mercies of God, to present your bodies as a living sacrifice, holy and acceptable to God, which is your spiritual worship" (Rom. 12:1). The New Living Translation of the Bible captures this thought very well: "And so, dear brothers and sisters, I plead with you to give your bodies to God because of all he has done for you." Our commitment to the Lord must be a response of gratitude for all that he has done for us. In the earlier chapters of Romans, Paul dealt with how we are all under the wrath of God because of our ungodliness and unrighteousness. He then showed how we are saved by grace through the redemption that came through Jesus Christ. Paul explained our standing as believers before God as objects of his grace, based on the finished work of Christ. He spoke eloquently, saying, "There is therefore now no condemnation for those who are in Christ Jesus" (Rom. 8:1). In that chapter, he also spoke of how "we know that for those who love God all things work together for good, for those who are called according to his purpose" (Rom. 8:28). He then ended on a note that is hard to equal. Having spoken about the painful sufferings that Christians have to go through in this life, he wrote,

> No, in all these things we are more than conquerors through him who loved us. For I am sure that neither death nor life, nor angels nor rulers, nor things present nor things to come, nor powers, nor height nor depth, nor anything else in all creation, will be able to separate us from the love of God in Christ Jesus our Lord. (Rom. 8:37–39)

What a crescendo that is! It is all "in Christ Jesus our Lord." If the Christian life is to be lived properly, it must be a response to these glorious benefits that have been procured for us through the death, burial, and resurrection of God's own Son. That again illustrates why a proper understanding of the gospel results in a greater commitment to Christ and his church.

We find another illustration of the vital place of the gospel in Christian growth in the epistle of Paul to the Ephesians. Paul wrote about "the unsearchable riches of Christ" (Eph. 3:8), which he preached to the Gentiles. By this he meant the inexhaustible riches of Christ for the benefit of his people. Paul always prayed that all Christians would "comprehend with all the saints what is the breadth and length and height and depth, and . . . know the love of Christ that surpasses knowledge, that [they] may be filled with all the fullness of God" (Eph. 3:18–19). It was in the light of this that Paul urged Christians to live lives worthy of the calling that they had received (Eph. 4:1). This was the engine full of gasoline that would propel the car to go forward without being pushed. It is also a fresh view of this love of Christ that anchors our souls against backsliding when temptations and trials come. We are willing to suffer anything rather than leave the God who has loved us this much. The hymn writer put it so well when he prayed to God, saying,

> Oh, to grace how great a debtor daily I'm constrained to be,
> Let Thy goodness, like a fetter, bind my wondering heart to Thee;

Prone to wander, Lord, I feel it, prone to leave the God I love;
Here's my heart, O, take a seal it; Seal it for Thy courts above.[1]

An understanding of the riches of grace in Christ was also the secret of Paul's own personal Christian life. He wrote to the Galatians,

For through the law I died to the law, so that I might live to God. I have been crucified with Christ. It is no longer I who live, but Christ who lives in me. And the life I now live in the flesh I live by faith in the Son of God, who loved me and gave himself for me. I do not nullify the grace of God, for if righteousness were through the law, then Christ died for no purpose. (Gal. 2:19–21)

Paul had tasted the life of a Pharisee and found that he could not attain to the levels of holiness he was trying to achieve. He had a choice: to either remain a hypocrite or to abandon that pursuit altogether. He opted for the latter when the Lord Jesus Christ revealed himself to him on the road to Damascus. He was no longer propelled by human effort in trying to keep the law. Rather, he was propelled by a love for God. How? It was when he saw himself crucified with Christ so that it was no longer him trying to live out an impossible life. It was Christ by his Spirit who was now living in him and propelling him in true holiness. The life he was now living was one in which he concentrated his gaze on Christ, who, to borrow Paul's own words, "loved me and gave himself for me." In this way, the Christian life is a life built on the grace of God—grace that has come to us through the redemptive work of Christ, and grace that is mediated to us by the Spirit of Christ. It is the only way to live a life that pleases God. If this could be attained by human effort, then there was no need for Jesus to pay such a high price as dying for us on the cross. That was Paul's logic in the passage we have quoted from Galatians. This is why it is important for the gospel to be the main diet of the Christian pulpit.

The Gospel Is Important for Inspiring True Worship

The gospel is also important in the life of the church because it is when Christians reflect on the way in which God has saved them from sin that

---

1. Robert Robinson, "Come, Thou Fount of Every Blessing."

true worship is inspired in their hearts. In many ways, this is where the growing commitment referred to in the last section finally lands the true Christian. We already saw how the apostle Paul captured this when he wrote, "I appeal to you therefore, brothers, by the mercies of God, to present your bodies as a living sacrifice, holy and acceptable to God, which is your spiritual worship" (Rom. 12:1). Some Bible versions use the word "service" instead of "worship" in this verse. Both words lead to the same conclusion. It is as you appreciate the mercies of God that your worship is no longer about you and what you can get from God. It is about God and what service you can render to him as an act of worship.

Again, think about this. You were a sinner under God's wrath and were utterly unable to save yourself. God sent his Son to bear the consequences of your sin, and through his grace alone you have been brought from death to life. Your destination has changed from hell to heaven. God sought you by his Holy Spirit from among your friends and relatives, despite your stubbornness and rebellion. He finally apprehended you as you heard the gospel, and added you to his church. God is driving the engine of providence across history in order to build his church, and he has included you in his great plan. All this was because of his immense love for you. Surely, this must leave you in ecstasy and worship, just as it left Paul when he exclaimed,

> Oh, the depth of the riches and wisdom and knowledge of God!
> How unsearchable are his judgments and how inscrutable his ways!
>
> > "For who has known the mind of the Lord,
> >   or who has been his counselor?"
> > "Or who has given a gift to him
> >   that he might be repaid?"
>
> For from him and through him and to him are all things. To him be glory forever. Amen. (Rom. 11:33–36)

Yes, such meditations inevitably leave you "lost in wonder, love, and praise!"[2]

Without the gospel, the church soon loses true worship and can keep its numbers only by turning to entertainment. This has become

---

2. From the hymn "Love Divine, All Loves Excelling," by Charles Wesley.

common fare in many churches. You notice it in the singing. There is very little doctrinal depth simply because there is very little of it in the regular preaching. The songs are now all about some vague "blessings" that our God bestows upon us. What matters are the danceable tunes, as the congregation sings about God taking us "from there to here." It is so common today to find people in church gyrating for almost an hour to a fleshly, stimulating tune while simply saying over and over again, "Let me dance to the Lord. You don't know what he has done for me." When an attempt is made to state what those blessings are, they are inevitably about physical things—health, education, marriage, children, a home, a job, an expensive car, and so on. Even when the blood of Jesus is referred to, it is in the form of a charm to protect one's family and property. It is still physical things. Salvation from sin and hell, through the work of redemption, is conspicuous by its absence. These are wire cars. They cannot take you anywhere. They are not the real thing. They do not lead to true worship but to self-indulgence.

Once the gospel becomes the regular diet in the church, the opposite becomes true. Believers will want to sing about "every spiritual blessing in the heavenly places" (Eph. 1:3). The mind will want to feast on these blessings as the hymns being sung recount them: eternal election, the grace of God, regeneration, faith and repentance, justification by faith only, the grace of God, adoption, the indwelling work of the Holy Spirit, positional and progressive sanctification, spiritual adoption, fellowship with God and with his people, prayer, the final perseverance of the saints, heaven, and so on. All these themes are sweet to the soul of a child of God and make up the rich content of Christian worship songs. We need to return to this, and we can do so only as we make the gospel the chief content of the pulpit.

The Gospel Has Been Lost

Sadly, very few church pastors today are preaching the gospel to nonbelievers and believers. If you were to pull an average Christian aside today and ask him or her to tell you what the gospel is, you would be shocked at the level of ignorance. Words like atonement, redemption, propitiation, and substitution do not mean much to such people.

To them, grace is merely another word for mercy and love. How are such people expected to offer their bodies as living sacrifices to God as their reasonable act of worship, when they are so unaware of the unsearchable riches of Christ?

The popular sermons today are motivational speeches. They are based on worldly principles that promise people earthly benefits if they say the right words or do the right things. These draw the crowds, but the people are not interested in growth in holiness. They want entertainment and earthly treasures. There is also a very high turnover of congregants. Many become disillusioned because the principles they are being taught are not working for them and so they leave quietly. Many more come in and take their place, hoping that the magic formulas will work for them. Like the wire car passengers, they hold onto the shirt of the person in front of them, but it is all human effort. This is not the Christianity of the Bible. It is not church as God intended it to be.

It is not uncommon today to be invited to preach at a church and to discover that the topic you are given is "commitment." Usually, the thinking of those inviting you is this: "If this man can come as an outsider to tackle the subject of commitment and rebuke the lukewarm and *laissez faire* attitude that is common in this church, perhaps there will be a higher level of commitment from our church members as a result." One reason you may have received such an invitation is because the leaders of that church may have observed a higher-than-usual level of commitment from members of *your* church. They want you, in a sermon or two, to replicate what you have achieved in your own church. What they fail to realize is that sermons that simply directly address the subject of commitment will have only short-term results. They are the equivalent of pushing a wire car. As soon as you stop pushing, the car stops. This is because only the gospel provides spiritual gasoline to keep believers fired up from the inside. In order to achieve biblical commitment, believers must feed on Christ. They must regularly feast on the unsearchable riches of Christ.

STUDY GUIDE FOR CHAPTER 4
Why Is the Gospel So Important to the Church?

Summary
It is only through the gospel—the good news announcing Jesus's atoning life, death, and resurrection—that the church is built and sustained. People come to faith only when the gospel is preached; and they remain and grow in this great faith when that same gospel is expounded to them. Churches that seek growth in their numbers and commitment from their members in any way other than through the regular preaching of the gospel end up with artificial results.

Study Questions

1. What, in your own words, is the gospel? Ask this question of a trusted Christian friend, compare your answers, and discuss the differences in your answers.

2. The author emphasizes that "Christians must never move on from the gospel," and that "We must never graduate from the gospel" (pp. 62, 63). How does he show this to be true?

3. In what two main ways does the church depend on the gospel?

4. Can you think of two common songs in your context which speak only vaguely about what God can do, or has done?

   Now think of two songs that speak *specifically* about God and what he has done in the gospel.

5. What is the outcome when a church does not preach the gospel but instead preaches only positive messages and emphasizes entertainment?

5

Who Should Be in the Church's Membership?

The African matrilineal system of inheritance is quite interesting. When a clan leader or chief dies, the successor is not the man's son but his sister's son. The logic is that this is the only way you can ensure that leadership of the clan or tribe remains in the bloodline of the family. A clan leader or chief's wife could have been unfaithful to him and could have had a child with a man outside the clan or tribe. In this way, the inheritance of the clan or tribe could unknowingly pass on to the wrong people. However, a clan leader or chief's sister comes from the same womb as himself. It is very difficult to make a mistake about that. Therefore, any son from her womb is guaranteed to be a direct relative of her brother. Passing on the mantle to her son ensures that it is being passed on in the same bloodline. That was Africa's way of ensuring that clan or tribal heritage remained in the family long before DNA testing was ever invented. It was vital in an age prior to the state system, when clans and tribes were often at war with each other. It was important to secure allegiance at the leadership level. Failure to do so could result in a betrayal that could cost the permanent loss of tribal lives and property.

If it was so important for a clan or tribe to ensure that only those who qualify to be inheritors should be considered for the inheritance, it is even more important for the church. This is because the church is "the household of God" (1 Tim. 3:15). It is wrong to have in its membership individuals who are not children of God. This is even more important because anyone who is not a child of God is a child of the devil, the archenemy of God. It is worse than having a clan leader or a chief who is not really from your family line. It is like having one who is from the family that wants your clan or tribe exterminated!

Every church should have a membership application process. The fact that someone attends church regularly does not mean they have automatically become members. Partly, this is because every shepherd should know who his sheep are, even when they mingle with sheep that belong to another shepherd. Church leaders must know who their members are because they will have to give an account for them before God on judgment day. That is the assumption in the words found in Hebrews 13:17: "Obey your leaders and submit to them, for they are keeping watch over your souls, as those who will have to give an account." Who are those who attend your church who should obey and submit to your leadership, over whose souls you are keeping watch, and for whom you will give an account? It is not everyone who attends your church. It is those who are members of your church. Very well, then, who qualifies to become members?

Nonbelievers Cannot Be Church Members

Those listed as members of a local church should be only those who are regenerate and consequently have personally turned from sin and put their trust in the Lord Jesus Christ as their Savior. In order to appreciate this, let us look at the state of nonbelievers for a moment. The apostle Paul described that state in this way:

> And you were dead in the trespasses and sins in which you once walked, following the course of this world, following the prince of the power of the air, the spirit that is now at work in the sons of disobedience—among whom we all once lived in the passions of our flesh, carrying out the desires of the body and the mind, and were by nature children of wrath, like the rest of mankind. (Eph. 2:1–3)

We see at least five truths from this passage that disqualify nonbelievers from being members of the church:

1. They are spiritually dead.
2. They are enslaved by the world.
3. They are enslaved by the devil.
4. They are enslaved by their sinful nature.
5. They are under the wrath of God.

Only Believers Should Be Church Members

Church leaders should jealously guard the door into membership in the local church. Only those who repent of their sins and believe in the Lord Jesus Christ should be allowed to come into the church's membership, because repentance from sin and faith in Christ are the evidence that a person has been born of the Spirit of God. We see this in the book of Acts. When Peter was drawing toward the end of preaching the gospel on the day of Pentecost, the people cried out, "What shall we do?" He told them to repent and be baptized. The Bible records, "So those who received his word were baptized, and there were added that day about three thousand souls" (Acts 2:37–41). Notice that it is only those who received the gospel and were baptized who were "added" to the church. Toward the end of this chapter we read, "And the Lord added to their number day by day those who were being saved" (Acts 2:47). Notice, again, that it is only those who were being saved from sin that God was adding to the church. This is the pattern that we see throughout Acts.

How do we know those who are saved? There are at least two basic tests.

1. They should understand and respond to the gospel message. No one becomes a Christian who still thinks that God accepts them on the basis of their own moral or religious efforts. As a fruit of regeneration, the Holy Spirit opens the minds of sinners so that they can understand spiritual truths. They begin to understand that the Bible teaches that all have sinned and have fallen short of the glory of God (Rom. 3:23), and that there is only one response that we should expect from God in the light of the way we have lived: condemnation to hell. All our efforts at our own moral or religious change amount to nothing. Our righteousness is like "filthy rags" in the eyes of God (Isa. 64:6 KJV). This is the bad news that is the backdrop of the gospel. The gospel comes in and says that God, out of his great love and grace, sent his only Son, the Lord Jesus Christ, to live the life we totally failed to live and then to die in our place for all our sins. He did this as our substitute. After three days, he rose again from the dead because he had fully satisfied the demands of God's law. This is the gospel—the good news from heaven. Anyone who does not know and understand this good news is not a Christian. We are called to turn away from everything we know to be sinful and to trust in Jesus and his finished work for us. This is the only right response that we can make once we know this gospel. It is the response that the gospel itself demands—repentance toward God and faith in the Lord Jesus Christ (Acts 2:38; 16:31; 20:21). When we do so, God forgives all our sins. In theological circles this is referred to as "justification by faith alone." Anyone who thinks that God forgives him or her on the basis of their own efforts to please him should be taught this biblical gospel instead of being welcomed into the church's membership. As Jesus said, those who repent and believe this gospel should be baptized publicly and welcomed into the church's membership. Those to be welcomed into church membership are only those who can say,

> I need no other argument,
> I need no other plea;
> It is enough that Jesus died,
> And that he died for me.[1]

2. They should testify of a morally changed life. In other words, they should be repentant. This is the second test. When individuals are converted, God morally and spiritually changes their hearts. This is a fruit of the new birth, and it is instantaneous. The apostle Paul, writing to the Corinthians who had allowed immorality and other forms of evil in the church, said,

> Do you not know that the unrighteous will not inherit the kingdom of God? Do not be deceived: neither the sexually immoral, nor idolaters, nor adulterers, nor men who practice homosexuality, nor thieves, nor the greedy, nor drunkards, nor revilers, nor swindlers

---

1. From the hymn "My Faith Has Found a Resting Place," by Lidie H. Edmunds.

will inherit the kingdom of God. And such were some of you. But you were washed, you were sanctified, you were justified in the name of the Lord Jesus Christ and by the Spirit of our God. (1 Cor. 6:9–11).

Paul assumed that those who were legitimate members of the church in Corinth were repentant of their previous sinful lifestyle. They had been washed and sanctified by the Spirit of God. Likewise, the apostle John said, "No one born of God makes a practice of sinning, for God's seed abides in him; and he cannot keep on sinning, because he has been born of God" (1 John 3:9). We must never compromise on this. Only such individuals are God's "workmanship, created in Christ Jesus for good works" (Eph. 2:10). There are a lot of people who have a mental knowledge of the gospel because they have heard it over and over again but who have never experienced a moral transformation. They know the truth intellectually, but they betray what they know by the wicked lives they live. Such individuals are not yet converted and should be challenged to turn to Christ for salvation instead of being welcomed into the church in the hope that they will one day change. Very few of them actually do. Most of them conclude that the sermons calling sinners to repent are for those who are visiting church and not for those who are already church members. They continue to live in sin, and the church gets more and more corrupted and scandalized.

Church leaders should not simply conclude that because someone has been coming to church consistently for a few months, they have automatically become members. They should not accept people into membership simply because they belong to the tribe whose language is the primary medium of communication in that church. There should be a membership application process that includes the leaders of the church interviewing individuals who want to be identified as members. The church leaders should ask the kind of questions that enable them to discern the applicants' understanding of the gospel message and whether there has been any moral and spiritual change in their lives. Where individuals fail to answer the questions correctly, they should not be welcomed into the church's membership but instead should be advised to do some serious heart-searching to see if they are truly Christians. It is vital to lovingly implore them to seek salvation in Christ. Here are a few questions that can be asked:

1. How did you become a Christian?
2. What makes you think that you are a Christian?
3. Have you or anyone close to you observed any changes in your life since the day you said you became a Christian? If so, what are some of those changes?
4. Have you been baptized since you turned from sin and trusted in Christ for salvation?
5. Briefly, what is the gospel?
6. Suppose I was not a Christian and wanted to become one; what would you tell me to do?
7. If you were about to enter heaven and an angel asked you why he should allow you in, what answer would you give him?

In the nineteenth century there was a very well-known soul-winner in America named Dwight L. Moody. He was converted in May 1855 and then sought baptism and membership in the Mount Vernon Church in Boston, Massachusetts, where he had been converted. His first few attempts at satisfying the elders of that church that he was converted proved a failure. To the question "What has Christ done for you, and for us all, that especially entitles him to our love and obedience?" he answered, "I think he has done a great deal for us all, but I don't know of anything he has done in particular." Based on that answer, Moody was not admitted into membership but was given to some older Christians to be discipled for a while. The following year, in March 1856, he again came before the church eldership to be examined. This time he was successful and thus became a member of the church. He went on to become the foremost American evangelist of the nineteenth century. We learn from this that when someone fails to satisfy us when we ask questions related to his or her conversion, we are not rejecting them. We simply want to ensure that we are truly convinced of their salvation. We can ask other people to help them understand the way of salvation better. There should be no hurry to quickly bring them back for a membership interview, because the eternal welfare of a soul is at stake. If they are truly saved, they will still come back because they really want to belong to the people of God, as was the case with Moody.

The process of becoming a member of a local church should also include baptism. I have handled this matter in more detail in chapter 8, on baptism and the Lord's Supper. However, it is worth mentioning it here because of its relevance to the subject of church membership.

Members Should Know about the Church

Church membership is also about taking up responsibilities. Remember, we noticed that the apostle Paul called the church "the household of God" (1 Tim. 3:15). A household has values, and it also has activities. It is the smallest economic entity, where every member of the household who is old enough to participate in household chores gets to do something. We will handle what church members ought to be doing in the church in the next chapter. For now, we simply want to deal with two preliminary matters that should be dealt with when a person is becoming a member of the church, so that it will be easier for that person to participate actively in the life of that church.

1. **The church's doctrinal position.** In order for a person to participate meaningfully in the life of a church, he should wholeheartedly embrace the church's doctrinal position. The church is not a social club. It is meant to be a lampstand to shed light so that people in the world can see the truth of God. The light to be shed is what the Bible teaches. However, even where we are agreed on the content of the gospel, churches tend to see things differently on other major teachings of the Bible. One such area, for instance, will be the work of the Holy Spirit in the lives of believers. If you are not in agreement with the church's position on such teachings, you will find yourself constantly butting heads, figuratively speaking, with other church members and especially with the church's leadership. This will only result in a difficult time for you and for the church. Therefore, every church should have a written doctrinal statement that spells out in clear terms what its position is with respect to the most important doctrinal issues. New members should carefully read this document so that they can see whether it represents their own convictions as well. In some cases,

the church's position may not totally represent the position of the prospective member but that individual is willing to learn from the leadership of the church. Such an individual may still be welcomed, bearing that in mind. So, to the question, "Who should be in the church's membership?" we must add that it should be individuals who believe what the church claims to believe.

There is a story told of an individual who was asked what he believed and he answered by saying that he believed what his church believed. Upon being asked what his church believed, he cleverly answered that his church believed what *he* believed. Not to be outwitted, the person asked him what he and his church believed. But he was ready even for this question; he answered, "My church and I believe the same thing!" Such answers may cleverly get you out of a tight spot, but they cannot hide the fact that such a church member will not help his church to spread the truth that the church claims to believe.

2. The church's polity. Another area that you must agree with if you are to participate meaningfully in a church's life is that of its "polity." This refers to the way in which a church is governed. It has to do with its organizational structure and includes things like the constitution, which determines the way decisions are made. This applies to countries, organizations, and even churches. Some churches have an Episcopal system of government, others have a Presbyterian form, while others are more Congregational. Under each of these general categories there will be shades of differences as well.

It is important that those who are becoming members of a church know how it is governed and agree to function under that structure. For instance, some churches choose their own pastors, while others simply receive pastors who are sent to them from the head office. Some churches operate from a more centralized structure, while others operate from a more decentralized structure, including how the funds are spent. Individuals joining a church should be clear about such matters so that they do not needlessly come into conflict with the church's leadership on matters of organizational procedure. Every church should have a document that spells out how it is to be governed. This is normally required by the law of the country in which the church is located. Individuals wanting to join the church should be availed of this document so that they can make up their minds as to whether they are willing to be in a church with this kind of governing structure. The importance of this will become evident in the next chapter. So, to the question, "Who should be in the church's membership?" we must add that it should be individuals who accept the structures by which the church is organized.

After reading all this, you might feel discouraged from joining a church or from getting involved in processing new church members for your church. It may simply seem like too much trouble. The truth is that we do not have much of a choice. Just as there are no human beings who do not belong to families, so also there must be no Christians who do not belong to a local church. Jesus wants his sheep to be looked after by shepherds. It is also part of the way in which Christians grow. They must belong to local groups in which they experience life together and in which they are accountable to other Christians. These groups are called local churches, which should be under the leadership of qualified elders.

At the beginning of this chapter, we noted how our forefathers ensured that tribal inheritance went only to those who were truly their blood relatives. A wrong clan leader or chief could result in a most costly betrayal. We have seen how only truly converted people are able to care for the church and its purpose on earth because they alone are alive spiritually. We must never compromise on this for the sake of numbers. If we do, we will be opening a door for sin to take the church captive and thus render it ineffective. Let us take great care in ensuring that only the right people come into the membership of the church.

Sadly today, we tend to bring into the sheep pen any four-footed creatures without ensuring that they are truly sheep. Our fear of offending individuals is often what causes us to do this. "It will not look nice" is the philosophy that rules the day. Also, the view of many is that if you stop anyone from becoming a member of your church, you are the one who is consigning their souls to hell. Church is viewed like Noah's Ark. It is the safe place to be. So, when you refuse someone entrance into this safe haven, you are expressing real hatred toward them. You may be seen as a very heartless church leader and may even lose your leadership position in the church.

If the person applying for membership is, say, the child of the person who started the church, or the village headman or chief, we may find it hard to evaluate their qualification for membership. We fear the consequences if we conclude that the person is not yet converted and therefore cannot join the church. Therefore, such people are often automatically brought into the membership of the church, much to the detriment of its spiritual life. Another category of individuals that we often do not genuinely examine are those who are wealthy. We want their money and so we bring them into the church, even when we know that their testimony of salvation is suspect and their moral lives are scandalous. We even quickly give them leadership positions. That rings the death knell on the spirituality of the church.

Let us be encouraged to do what we can to ensure that only those who qualify are welcomed into the life of the church. It will save us from a lot of future difficulties, and we will be taking the first step in securing the blessing of God upon the church.

STUDY GUIDE FOR CHAPTER 5
Who Should Be in the Church's Membership?

Summary

The household of God can only be for the children of God and not the children of the enemy. Nonbelievers cannot truly belong to the church. They are still spiritually dead, enslaved to the world, the devil, and their sinful nature, and are under the wrath of God. All are welcome to the Sunday gathering, but only those who give a credible confession of faith and repentance can belong to the church. Elders should have a membership process where they try to determine this before recognizing people as members. Those who would be members should affirm the church's doctrines and submit to its leadership structures.

Study Questions

1. What three things should a church look at before they formally accept someone as a member?

2. What harm do you think is done to nonbelievers when they are recognized and affirmed as church members before actually coming to faith in Christ?

3. In the previous chapter we saw that the task of the church is the Great Commission. How does a biblical practice of church membership help in fulfilling the Great Commission?

4. Have you interacted with people who believe they are Christians but don't have a biblical understanding of the way of salvation? How have you ministered to them or observed other people minister to them?

5. As Africans, most of us are welcoming and loyal to our own people. How would you advise a pastor who finds the biblical practice of church membership difficult because it excludes some people and so feels "un-African"?

6

What Is the Role of Church Members?

My mother died when I was only nine years old. After about a year, my mother's sister came and took my two sisters and me to go and live with her and her family. We lived with them for the next six years. It was quite a change for my sisters and me. The first major change was the number of children. We came from a home with very few children. It was I, my two sisters, and a foster brother whom my parents had raised from birth so that I would have a male companion. Now we moved in with a family with eight children, twice the size of our family. We were now eleven children swarming the house! The second major change was that we went from living in a suburban context in Zambia's capital city to living out on a farm in the outskirts of a copper mining town. In our parents' home, we hardly did anything beyond keeping our bedrooms tidy because our parents employed domestic servants who did almost all the work. On the farm, all the children participated in home and farm chores. We fed and provided fresh water to the farm animals, regularly collected the eggs, and fed firewood into the boiler that heated water for the farmhouse. When it was planting, weeding, or harvesting time there was need for extra hands and we—the children in the home—were the extra hands at those critical times. When we ran out of milk in the home, we were sent with a big container to a neighboring farm that had cows. We bought the milk and walked the entire distance home carrying the heavy weight. The family kept a vegetable garden behind the farmhouse where we collected fresh vegetables every day. There were many workers on different areas of the farm. They were more professional in their work and got paid for the work they did. We worked with them and learned a lot from them. All this was initially difficult for my two sisters and me, but seeing our cousins joyfully participating in all this made us realize that this was farm life, and we soon "got into the groove" and saw it as fun. Waking up early to do one's chores before getting ready for school was the most difficult part, especially during winter when it was cold and dark at that hour of the morning. Yet not once did we think that this was child abuse. We simply went from finding the work hard to enjoying it. In the evenings, as we interacted around the family dinner table, we talked about experiences we had as we played our roles on the farm.

Church life should be more like the life we found on the farm rather than the life we lived in our home before my mother died. It should involve everyone who is a member. That picture is not common today. Many people think of church membership primarily in terms of a sense of belonging. They also want to be members simply because of what they can get out of the church rather than what they can put into it. Or, they see it merely as a place where you ensure that your name is recorded for the purpose of being allowed to marry or have your funeral in that church. They see it as a place where they will get help whenever they are in need.

As we saw in the last chapter, the church is "the household of God" (1 Tim. 3:15). At the time the New Testament was being written, households were comprised of parents, children, and servants. If the family was very wealthy and large, it would have a lot of servants. This is what Paul had in mind when he referred to the church as the household of God. He meant that God fulfills the role of parents in the home. Church leaders fulfill the role of servants in the home, ensuring that each child knows "how one ought to behave in the household of God" (v. 15). The rest of us are the equivalent of children who are being raised up in that home. We ought to participate actively in the household chores.

There are a number of references in the Bible that suggest that children in the home participated in household chores fairly actively, depending on their ages. This was especially the case with looking after domestic animals, which were often the measure of family wealth. For instance, in the Old Testament, when Samuel went to anoint a future king of Israel from the house of Jesse, the Bible says, "And Jesse made seven of his sons pass before Samuel. And Samuel said to Jesse, 'The Lord has not chosen these.' Then Samuel said to Jesse, 'Are all your sons here?' And he said, 'There remains yet the youngest, but behold, he is keeping the sheep'" (1 Sam. 16:10–11). This meant more than simply following hired shepherds around. He was given sheep to look after. On the day David killed Goliath, he explained this to King Saul:

> Your servant used to keep sheep for his father. And when there came a lion, or a bear, and took a lamb from the flock, I went after him and struck him and delivered it out of his mouth. And if he arose against me, I caught him by his beard and struck him and killed him. Your servant has struck down both lions and bears . . . (1 Sam. 17:34–36)

The life of this young shepherd was real work. It was hard work. It was dangerous work.

In case you think that this was only in Old Testament days, we find a similar example of this in the famous parable of the prodigal son in the New Testament. When the younger son returned from the far country, the Bible says, "Now his older son was in the field . . ." (Luke 15:25). If you are wondering what he was doing there, his words of anger tell us that he was working. He said, "Look, these many years I have served you, and I never disobeyed your command . . ." (Luke 15:29). He had been faithfully participating in the work on the farm. That was family life in those days. That was part of what would have been in the mind of the apostle Paul as he wrote to Timothy about the household of God. There was order, but there were also areas of responsibility for the servants and for the children according to the level of maturity they had reached. Let us now look at what the roles of church members in the local church should be, by studying relevant passages in the New Testament.

Attending the Church's Meetings

The very first role of church members in the life of the church is that of attending the church's meetings. It is amazing how many churches speak of great numbers of church members but, when you go to their church services, you find only a fraction of that number in attendance. Where are the people who make up those bloated membership lists? Many of them considered being baptized and then being registered in the membership of the church as enough to secure what they wanted. Church attendance is not seen as an obligation now that they are members.

We have seen previously that when people became Christians on the day of Pentecost, they were described thus:

> They devoted themselves to the apostles' teaching and the fellowship, to the breaking of bread and the prayers. . . . And all who believed were together and had all things in common. . . . And day by day, attending the temple together and breaking bread in their homes, they received their food with glad and generous hearts. (Acts 2:42, 44, 46)

You cannot miss the fact that the New Testament believers committed themselves to the church's meetings during the week. They certainly did not register their names on a church membership list and then disappear.

It was in attending such meetings that they learned Christian doctrine at the feet of the apostles. It was in attending these meetings that they had fellowship together, broke bread together, and prayed together. Granted, there were no Christian books then and there was no internet from which they could download sermons. However, church life is more than simply listening to sermons. You encourage other believers when you deliberately take time away from other demands of life to meet with them and to worship together with them. The writer of the letter to the Hebrews wrote, "Let us consider how to stir up one another to love and good works, not neglecting to meet together, as is the habit of some, but encouraging one another, and all the more as you see the Day drawing near" (Heb. 10:24–25). The believers were able to stir up one another to love and good works only when they faithfully met together. The first role of a church member is commitment to attending the church's meetings. Absence will happen sometimes, but it must be due to unavoidable circumstances.

Fulfilling the "One Another" Commands

The New Testament is full of "one another" commands. They are divine and apostolic appeals to Christians which point to the fact that Christians are responsible to act in specific ways toward other believers. Here are some of them:[1] "love one another" (John 13:34), "edify one another" (Col. 3:16), "honor one another" (Rom. 12:10), "live in harmony with one another" (Rom. 12:16), "do not judge one another" (Rom. 14:13), "accept one another" (Rom. 15:7), "agree with one another" (1 Cor. 1:10), "serve one another in love" (Gal. 5:13), "carry one another's burdens" (Gal. 6:2), "bear with one another in love" (Eph. 4:2), "be kind and compassionate to one another" (Eph. 4:32a), "forgive one another" (Eph. 4:32b), "speak to one another with psalms, hymns, and spiritual songs" (Eph. 5:19), "submit to one another" (Eph. 5:21), "encourage one another" (1 Thess. 4:18), "do not slander one another" (James 4:11), "do not grumble against one another" (James 5:9), "confess your sins to one another" (James 5:16), "pray for one another" (James 5:16), and so on.

It is such activities that make up the juice of fellowship in the life of the church. They show that Christians care for one another and will not allow anything to hinder their relationships. The "one another" commands should not be hindered by tribalism in the church. The only dividing line is whether those individuals are Christians. Most of these activities happen outside the context of church meetings and show that the bond of Christian unity purchased by the blood of Christ and realized by the work of the Holy Spirit is very real at a personal level. Christians serve one another by using their individual gifts, but that must wait until the next section of this chapter. Suffice it to say for now that Christians should see it as their role in the church to fulfill these "one another" commands.

The Use of Gifts in the Church

Another role of church members is that of using their individual gifts to serve the Lord Jesus Christ through his church. Paul's favorite picture

---

1. Quoted or paraphrased from various Bible translations.

of the roles church members should play in the life of the church was not that of the family but of the body—the human body. To the church in Corinth he said, "Now you are the body of Christ and individually members of it" (1 Cor. 12:27). Earlier in that chapter, he had spoken about the responsibilities of church members toward one another using the example of the way in which feet and hands play different roles in the human body. He also spoke about the different roles of ears and eyes. In the midst of explaining these different roles, he brought in the nose as well, without mentioning it, when he asked, "If the whole body were an ear, where would be the sense of smell?" (1 Cor. 12:17). His point was that believers had different God-given gifts that they should use in the church so that it could grow as God intended.

Granted, almost all the examples Paul used would be very foreign to the church today, but the principles are still applicable. He wrote,

> Now there are varieties of gifts, but the same Spirit; and there are varieties of service, but the same Lord; and there are varieties of activities, but it is the same God who empowers them all in everyone. To each is given the manifestation of the Spirit for the common good. For to one is given through the Spirit the utterance of wisdom, and to another the utterance of knowledge according to the same Spirit, to another faith by the same Spirit, to another gifts of healing by the one Spirit, to another the working of miracles, to another prophecy, to another the ability to distinguish between spirits, to another various kinds of tongues, to another the interpretation of tongues. All these are empowered by one and the same Spirit, who apportions to each one individually as he wills. (1 Cor. 12:4–11)

With the advent of the Pentecostal and Charismatic movements in the last century, there are claims that the church is supposed to function with all these gifts even today. It is beyond the scope of this book to show that these were largely gifts that were necessary in the infant phase of the New Testament church. However, it is still true that the Holy Spirit apportions gifts to individual believers in the church so that they can all participate in the church's quantitative and qualitative growth. Each church should have varieties of gifts, varieties of service, and varieties of activities, empowered by "the same God who empowers them all in everyone" (1 Cor. 12:6). These gifts are all given by the Lord "for the common good" (1 Cor. 12:7).

Paul was very emphatic that believers should use their gifts and not simply go to church in the way in which people go to movies. He wrote to the church in Rome, saying,

> For as in one body we have many members, and the members do not all have the same function, so we, though many, are one body in Christ, and individually members one of another. Having gifts that differ according to the grace given to us, *let us use them:* if prophecy, in proportion to our faith; if service, in our serving; the one who teaches, in his teaching; the one who exhorts, in his exhortation; the one who contributes, in generosity; the one who leads, with zeal; the one who does acts of mercy, with cheerfulness. (Rom. 12:4–8, emphasis mine)

Gifts are simply abilities. God wants believers to use them in the church so that the church looks after itself and also ministers in the world as directed by Jesus.

Sadly, that is not the way most churches function today. The popular image is not that of a body but of a bus. Instead of having everyone participating in church life, everything is left to a few individuals while the rest simply enjoy the ride. Most of the time they are half asleep as they wait to arrive at their destination. The only time most of the people actively participate is when the bus hits a pothole and they are suddenly awakened from their slumber. With the sudden rush of adrenaline, they hurl insults at the driver for his poor driving skills. However, the humming sound of the engine soon lulls them back to sleep for the rest of the journey.

Someone said that in most churches a third of the members do all the work, another third watch the work that is being done, and the last third haven't a clue what is going on. From my personal experience, I think that person was right—that is, if you can get that first one third to begin with! In a lot of cases, getting a third of the church to serve is like answered prayer. Too many Christians do nothing more than simply go to church. That is a far cry from what New Testament church life was meant to be.

Gifts Vary in Prominence and Use

Some gifts in the church are more central to its mission than others. Since the church's role in the world is primarily that of proclaiming the truth of God, those who have the gifts and calling related more directly to proclamation will tend to be more prominent than those who do not have such gifts. They will have a prominent pulpit to operate from in front of the church building. They will also have a higher cut in the church budget than everyone else. That is not because they are filled with a sense of self-importance or greed but because of the role they play in the edification and growth of the church. Paul instructed his protégé Timothy, saying, "Let the elders who rule well be considered worthy of double honor, especially those who labor in preaching and teaching. For the Scripture says, 'You shall not muzzle an ox when it treads out the grain,' and, 'The laborer deserves his wages'" (1 Tim. 5:17–18). In today's language, Paul is simply saying that pastors should be paid . . . and they should be paid well.

That does not mean that pastors should work alone. The rest of the church members should work with them in fulfilling the Great Commission. Let me use the example of the Sunday worship service, by which I mean the times when the whole church gathers together to pray, sing the praises of God, and hear the preaching of God's word. The pastor and his family should not be the only ones coming early to church to prepare the place for worship—turning on the lights, opening the windows to air out the room, sweeping the place, arranging the chairs and tables, putting up the decorating flowers and other paraphernalia, distributing the hymn books, and so on. Where is everyone else? They should know that, long before this day, the pastor was busy working on his sermon. They should also know that, depending on how many issues will be raised in members' lives by the sermon, he probably will also have his work cut out for the rest of the week by the number of people asking him for counsel. Surely, others should share in preparing for the worship service and closing down afterwards. They should also be involved in inviting friends, relatives, neighbors, schoolmates, and workmates to church. Many people have become Christians because a believer persisted in inviting them to church. Members of the church should also be involved in other parts of the worship service such as reading the Bible, praying, and even leading the worship service. They should also take care of visitors and follow them up later. Others could be involved in recording the sermons and, in today's internet world, ensuring that the sermons are uploaded on the World Wide Web so that others all over the world can hear the messages.

The Use of Gifts beyond Sundays

So far, I have touched only on the various roles that church members can play in relation to the worship services on Sunday. But church life does not take place only on the Lord's Day. It goes into the rest of the week. In the early days of the church, Luke wrote,

> And day by day, attending the temple together and breaking bread in their homes, they received their food with glad and generous hearts, praising God and having favor with all the people. And the Lord added to their number day by day those who were being saved. (Acts 2:46–47)

Evidently, church life spread out across the whole week as believers served one another and served together in the world "day by day." They used their homes as extensions of the church's life. This was for smaller church meetings but also for purposes of hospitality.

It is when church members realize that we have the world to win to Christ that it dawns on them that the church needs the involvement of all its members. There is no room for some to be sleeping in the back. In fulfilling the Great Commission, church members should be organized to reach the children, the youth, and the men and women in the community with the gospel of the Lord Jesus Christ. The poor and the professionals must also be reached. Seminars, conferences, and camps will need to be organized. This will need many hands in terms of publicity and preparations. During such events there will be a need for many people to work behind the scenes while those who are preaching and teaching are busy doing so. Then there is the work of follow-up, which many church members can get involved in. Often, it is during the ongoing watering of the seed that was sown during the outreach meetings that souls finally yield to the claims of Christ. Never underestimate the place of follow-up that is often done by faithful foot

soldiers of the cross of Christ. They are the ones who lay the prover-
bial final straw that breaks the camel's back.

Faithful and Generous Financial Giving

Another important area of involvement in church life in which ordinary Christians play a role is that of financial giving. While the
church is in the world, it will need finances. The giving of tithes and
offerings is, therefore, an important part of the stewardship of church
members. Whereas some Christians question whether we, as New
Testament believers, are required to bring tithes to the church to support its work, no one doubts that the work of the church is primarily
underwritten by the financial giving of its members. As early as Acts 2
we read, "And they were selling their possessions and belongings and
distributing the proceeds to all, as any had need" (Acts 2:45). Two
chapters later we read, "There was not a needy person among them,
for as many as were owners of lands or houses sold them and brought
the proceeds of what was sold and laid it at the apostles' feet, and it
was distributed to each as any had need" (Acts 4:34–35). Later, Paul
urged Timothy, a young church pastor, to ensure that elderly widows
in the church who had no relatives to look after them would be taken
care of by the church (1 Tim. 5:3–16). Those believers in the church
whom God has blessed with financial means should see it as their
God-given responsibility to contribute generously toward the care of
their brothers and sisters who are going through economically difficult
times. This should be over and above their regular giving to the church
to sustain its normal ongoing operations, such as paying its pastors
and others who serve the church in a full-time capacity. We already
saw that Paul urged Timothy in 1 Timothy 5:17 to ensure that pastors
are paid well. This can be done only when Christians are faithfully
giving financially to the church.

Sadly, in Africa, this is one area in which we are very weak as a
Christian church. Partly, this is a carryover from the pioneer missionary era when those who came to plant the church in Africa were fully
supported from the countries they were coming from. We did not
know exactly who was supporting these foreign missionaries or how
much support they were receiving. Whether believers gave financial

support to the church or not, the preachers were not affected. As a result, we got away with giving as little as possible—or even giving nothing at all. To turn this culture around has proved to be one Herculean task. Often the claim is that we do not have money. However, the people who are saying so end up with very expensive smartphones in their hands and pricey television sets in their homes. They are willing to pay that much for themselves but will say they have no money when it comes to the Lord's work and the Lord's church. There is need for a dramatic cultural shift.

In some churches, finances have been abused by church leaders. Pastors are lining their pockets by swindling the flock. I will deal with this issue under the heading of church leadership.

Praying for the Well-Being of the Church

Closely related to financial giving is the subject of prayer. In fact, prayer is even much more important and vital. Those Christians who feel pain in their pockets because of giving to God's work are usually the ones who bruise their knees in prayer as well for the same work. Jesus said, "Where your treasure is, there your heart will be also" (Matt. 6:21). The two go together. Where our giving ends, there our praying begins. We know that we can go only so far, but God can go much, much farther if he comes into our desperately needy situation. So, we give and pray. A lot of this praying will be done by individual believers on their own. Yet, when one reads the Bible, there is evidence that believers also met together to pray. It was not only an individual, private matter. The church held prayer meetings.

The New Testament church was a praying church. Luke adds prayer to the description of the church soon after it was born. He records, "And they devoted themselves to the apostles' teaching and the fellowship, to the breaking of bread and the prayers" (Acts 2:42). This was partly because the church was born in adversity. It was under persecution from the very beginning, and so it relied very much on the sustaining hand of its sovereign head. God's people knew that they needed God's intervention to survive the hostility of both the Jewish and the Roman authorities. When James was killed and Peter was arrested, they all expected Peter to suffer the same fate as James. However, an angel of God was sent to miraculously rescue him. Peter thought he was dreaming until he was safely outside the well-guarded prison walls. The Bible says, "When he realized this, he went to the house of Mary, the mother of John whose other name was Mark, where many were gathered together and were praying" (Acts 12:12). Yes, the New Testament church was truly a praying church. This is the responsibility of all church members. We must never lose sight of this, even if our church is not going through a period of trials and persecution. The Great Commission can be achieved only with God's help. Souls can be saved from sin only through the direct operations of the Holy Spirit. We must, therefore, plead with God to bless our labors for him as we go about our evangelistic work. The church prayer meetings should be at a time and place that is most convenient for church members.

One area of prayer that is specifically mentioned, which we must never neglect, is that of praying for our nation and its leadership. Paul wrote to Timothy, the young pastor of the church in Ephesus,

> First of all, then, I urge that supplications, prayers, intercessions, and thanksgivings be made for all people, for kings and all who are in high positions, that we may lead a peaceful and quiet life, godly and dignified in every way. This is good, and it is pleasing in the sight of God our Savior, who desires all people to be saved and to come to the knowledge of the truth. (1 Tim. 2:1–4)

This command was not dependent on whether you loved the ruler or president who was over your land. And the main reason was not so that your country could become prosperous, but that there might be peace, which would enable you to live out your Christian profession unhindered. The further reason is that, in such a peaceful context, the evangelistic mandate of the church can be carried on. The church should pray for the extension of God's kingdom in their society. Church members should include this in their prayers as part of their church responsibility.

Other Areas of Church Involvement

There are other areas of church life that Christians should be involved in, but the ones I have covered here are the most prominent ones.

Church government, for instance, is yet another area that all members should be involved in. Some of them will be elders and deacons. Others will be involved in leading church meetings and ministries or departments. Others will also be involved in ensuring that finances are well budgeted for and spent with transparency and integrity. Those who are not in these positions should learn to submit to and cooperate with their leaders. Depending on your church's form of government, ordinary members of the church can have other roles. For instance, in some churches almost every major decision has to be voted on. In such cases, it is important that church members make informed decisions by being well-read concerning the matters that will be voted on. In churches where they vote on all leadership levels, it is vital that church members acquaint themselves with the candidates for leadership long before voting day comes. Members must see themselves as stewards of the church of the living God.

Ensuring Personal Spiritual Growth

The personal spiritual growth of church members is not normally seen as a role of church membership, and yet it is important to include it as a way of concluding this chapter. A lot of what has been mentioned in this chapter will not be realized in a Christian's life unless he is growing spiritually. It is only a growing Christian who will want to make use of the various church meetings in order to grow even more in his Christian life. It is only a growing Christian who will be concerned about other Christians enough to carry out each of the "one another" commands that we saw earlier in the chapter. It is only a growing Christian who will want to use his gifts and finances to serve the Lord Jesus Christ in and through the church. It is only a growing Christian who will deliberately carve out time for corporate prayer in the church. Therefore, church members should be urged to make their own spiritual growth a priority in their lives. It will result in greater involvement in church life and fruitfulness.

The apostle Peter puts it this way:

> For this very reason, make every effort to supplement your faith with virtue, and virtue with knowledge, and knowledge with

self-control, and self-control with steadfastness, and steadfastness with godliness, and godliness with brotherly affection, and
brotherly affection with love. For if these qualities are yours and
are increasing, they keep you from being ineffective or unfruitful
in the knowledge of our Lord Jesus Christ. (2 Pet. 1:5–8)

Notice that Peter is urging believers to make every effort to grow
spiritually, and he ends by stating that one result of their growth is
that they will be more effective and fruitful in their knowledge of our
Lord Jesus Christ. These are the kind of Christians every church leader
longs for—believers who are growing and consequently playing their
role in the life of the church without always being pushed.

STUDY GUIDE FOR CHAPTER 6
What Is the Role of Church Members?

Summary

Like any other household, members of the household of God have work to do. Church members should faithfully attend the regular meetings of the church, where they can be taught Christian doctrine, have fellowship, break bread, and pray together. All members are also called to lovingly fulfill the "one another" commands, to use their gifts and abilities for the church's quantitative and qualitative growth, and to pray and give toward the success of the church's work. All this requires that we keep growing in our Christian maturity and our capacity to do our work of ministry.

Study Questions

1. What connection does the author make between your personal growth in Christ and your fruitfulness as a member of the church? How have you experienced this?

2. "It is when church members realize that we have the world to win to Christ that it dawns on them that the church needs the involvement of all its members" (p. 91). How do the tasks of members, as described in this chapter, contribute to the Great Commission?

3. What abilities, advantages, and opportunities do you currently have that someone in your local church can benefit from?

4. While faithful and generous financial giving is an important part of church membership, the author laments that many African Christians don't think of this as their duty, and he calls for a "cultural shift" on this issue (p. 93). Do you agree with this observation? How do you think this change could be effected while guarding against the financial exploitation rampant in many churches?

5. Prayer is one of the responsibilities of church membership. Does your church have prayer meetings? What purpose should these meetings serve? How can your church encourage members to pray outside of church prayer meetings?

7

Who Should Lead the Church?

Although many of us no longer live in villages, the view that a leader—even a church leader—is like a tribal chief still lingers in our psyche. To begin with, a chief is not primarily chosen by the people. It is hereditary. The position comes to him because "the gods" placed him in the right family tree, at the right position in that family, and at the very right time. Once he is inaugurated, it is as if the spirit of the gods comes to dwell with him. A chief, especially a paramount chief, is the highest position in the tribe. He may have many elders and advisors to help him, but his decisions are final. He is the final custodian of the vast, vast land that belongs to the entire tribe. He has an aura about him that fills the people with fear when they are in his presence. He has a special seat, which is his throne. He has many assistants around him. In a bygone era, even the lives of individuals in his tribe were at his mercy. If he demanded that you die, you would die with nowhere to appeal the decision. That was the absolute power that chiefs wielded.

When you understand this psyche, you begin to see why pastors and other church leaders in Africa tend to be treated with the dignity that leaves political leaders in the West green with envy. They end up being accountable to no one and easily abuse the money, property, and females in the church—and get away with it. We need to get back to the Bible and see what God says about who should be church leaders and how they should carry out their work.

Churches Are to Be Led by Elders

In the Bible, churches were led by elders. This concept was nothing new because, right across the Old Testament, the people of Israel were led by elders. The very word suggested that they were elderly individuals. Elders were leaders in their families, clans, and tribes, and then they came together to provide leadership to the whole nation. Thus, when Moses and Aaron were planning the great exodus of the people of Israel out of Egypt, they first met with the elders to convince them of this move (Ex. 4:29). Later, seventy elders were chosen to assist Moses in handling judicial matters in the nation (Num. 11:16, 24). These elders sat at the city gate to handle all kinds of disputes among the people and to pass judgments that resulted in people being either punished or acquitted (Deut. 21:19; 22:15).

This tradition of elders continued all the way into the New Testament, both in Jerusalem and wherever Israelites were dispersed. In the dispersion, the elders ruled in the synagogues, where they formed governing bodies. This is the way in which the religious life of the Jews was well supervised even when they were so far away from the temple in Jerusalem. The elders not only handled judicial matters; they also handled the synagogue properties, the care of the sick, and the gathering of contributions.

This concept was carried over into the life of the church from its very beginning (see Acts 11:30; 20:17; 21:18; James 5:14). Even when the apostles were still alive and overseeing the church in Jerusalem, they worked with elders (Acts 15:6, 22). In the minds of the apostles, the elders of the churches were appointed by God himself. We see this in Paul's farewell address to the elders in Ephesus: "Pay careful attention to yourselves and to all the flock, in which the Holy Spirit has made you overseers" (Acts 20:28). Paul was not referring to a supernatural prophetic utterance. Rather, he believed that, when God's people pray and providential happenings match up with biblical qualifications in a person being considered for eldership, it can rightly be said that God himself is behind that person's appointment.

The apostles considered themselves to be church elders, rather than being a group of men who were in a class of their own above the elders. The apostle Peter could write, "So I exhort the elders among you, *as a fellow elder* and a witness of the sufferings of Christ, as well as a partaker in the glory that is going to be revealed: shepherd the flock of God that is among you, exercising oversight" (1 Pet. 5:1–2, emphasis mine). Elders were the primary leaders of the church. When churches were being established, it was the responsibility of the pioneering missionaries to ensure that men in that church were mentored until they were mature enough to be appointed as elders. The work of planting churches was not finished until suitably qualified elders were installed. We read that Paul and Barnabas did so among the churches they were planting in Galatia: "And when they had appointed elders for them in every church, with prayer and fasting they committed them to the Lord in whom they had believed" (Acts 14:23). That is when they considered their work to be finished.

The work of elders is essentially that of providing oversight. This is well captured in the instructions Peter gave, part of which is quoted above. Here is the rest of the quotation: "Shepherd the flock of God that is among you, exercising oversight, not under compulsion, but willingly, as God would have you; not for shameful gain, but eagerly; not domineering over those in your charge, but being examples to the flock. And when the chief Shepherd appears, you will receive the unfading crown of glory" (1 Pet. 5:2–4). In using the word "shepherd," Peter is likening the work of elders to that of ordinary shepherds who look after sheep. This was a common scenario. David used it about God when he wrote, "The LORD is my shepherd" (Ps. 23:1). Often in the Old Testament, God used the term to refer to his people as sheep and to the elders of Israel as shepherds (e.g., Ezekiel 34). It is crucial that those who function as elders see their work in this light. The best shepherds fed the sheep on good pasture, gave them water to drink, protected them from wild animals, accounted for them individually, nursed them back to health when they were sick, and ensured they were safely in their sheep pen at the end of the day. They went after straying sheep and worked hard to find them and bring them back to safety. All those responsibilities are the work of elders in a spiritual sense. Elders are Christ's undershepherds. They lead the work with an eye on what Christ, the head of the church, wants them to do. What he wants them to do is written clearly in the Scriptures. In the quote above, Peter emphasized that elders are to do their work willingly and not because of some earthly payment. Jesus himself, the chief shepherd, will reward them when he returns to earth.

This work must be carried out in the form of servant leadership. Even in the Old Testament, the elders were to implement the mind of God among the people of God for their spiritual good in a spiritually hostile world. They did not possess absolute power to do whatever they wanted to do. Where the latter was the case, God expressed displeasure with what he was seeing. For example, we read in Jeremiah 23:1–4,

> "Woe to the shepherds who destroy and scatter the sheep of my pasture!" declares the LORD. Therefore, thus says the LORD, the God of Israel, concerning the shepherds who care for my people: "You have scattered my flock and have driven them away, and you have not attended to them. Behold, I will attend to you for your evil deeds, declares the LORD. Then I will gather the remnant of my flock out of all the countries where I have driven them, and I will bring them back to their fold, and they shall be fruitful and multiply. I will set shepherds over them who will care for them, and they shall fear no more, nor be dismayed, neither shall any be missing, declares the LORD."

The elders in Israel were not caring for God's people, and God was planning to replace them with those who would care for them.

It is the same in the New Testament church. Elders are leaders with God-given authority, but they are to use this authority with meekness and in a spirit of tender loving care for the flock—"not domineering over those in your charge, but being examples to the flock" (1 Pet. 5:3). Their persuasiveness as elders should largely come from the spiritual magnetism of their godly character, domestic management, and teaching competence.

Among the elders will be those whose work is preaching and teaching. Paul referred to such when he wrote to Timothy saying, "Let the elders who rule well be considered worthy of double honor, especially those who labor in preaching and teaching" (1 Tim. 5:17). In some churches, these are called "pastors," while in others they go by different titles. Paul's appeal here is that such individuals should be paid by the church and they should be paid well. It is beyond the pale of this book to go into details about this except to emphasize two things.

First, it is important to have someone within the church's leadership who preaches God's word regularly. Such a person should have a sense of calling to this work and should clearly be gifted as a preacher. He will fulfill the kind of role that Timothy and Titus fulfilled in the New Testament. Paul wrote to Timothy saying,

> All Scripture is breathed out by God and profitable for teaching, for reproof, for correction, and for training in righteousness, that the man of God may be complete, equipped for every good work.
>
> I charge you in the presence of God and of Christ Jesus, who is to judge the living and the dead, and by his appearing and his kingdom: preach the word; be ready in season and out of season; reprove, rebuke, and exhort, with complete patience and teaching. (2 Tim. 3:16–4:2)

A church that lacks such a person is lacking an essential gift of God to his church. The health and growth of the church will inevitably be stunted.

Second, it is equally important that such a person work within the church's leadership and not on top of it. Peter, an apostle, called himself "a fellow elder" (1 Pet. 5:1). Also, in Acts 15, when the issue of circumcision was being settled by the leaders of the church in Jerusalem, the apostles and elders did this together (Acts 15:2, 4, 6, 22). Elders do not report to a pastor. He is one of them. They work together as a team. Due to the centrality of preaching the word in the life of the church, the person designated "pastor" will provide leadership to the rest of the team of elders in the church. However, he does not do so as one to whom the rest are accountable. There should be mutual accountability between the pastor and the rest of the elders. It bears repeating: the pastor is one of the elders and not above them.

Elders Must Be Biblically Qualified

The Bible insists that churches should be led by godly pastors and elders. This is what Paul told Timothy in 1 Timothy 3:1–7. He gave similar instructions to Titus in Titus 1:5–9. Notice from these qualifications that there are three areas in which a person must qualify in order to be an elder in the church.

Personal godliness. In both of the lists of qualifications given to Timothy and Titus, Paul emphasized that the person being considered for the office of elder must be truly godly. To Timothy he said, "An overseer must be above reproach, the husband of one wife, sober-minded, self-controlled, respectable, hospitable, able to teach, not a drunkard, not violent but gentle, not quarrelsome, not a lover of money" (1 Tim. 3:2–3). To Titus he wrote, "An overseer, as God's steward, must be above reproach. He must not be arrogant or quick-tempered or a drunkard or violent or greedy for gain, but hospitable, a lover of good, self-controlled, upright, holy, and disciplined" (Titus 1:7–8). The sanctifying work of the Holy Spirit should be evident in a person's morally transformed character before he should be considered for the position of elder. His godliness should be evident to all, because an elder must not only lead by what he says; he should also be an example to the church about how a Christian should live in obedience to God.

Domestic management. In both lists of qualifications for the office of elder, Paul also mentioned the need for a person to prove himself through the way in which he manages his own family. To Timothy he wrote, "He must manage his own household well, with all dignity keeping his children submissive, for if someone does not know how to manage his own household, how will he care for God's church?" (1 Tim. 3:4–5). To Titus he wrote, "If anyone is above reproach, the husband of one wife, and his children are believers and not open to the charge of debauchery or insubordination"[1] (Titus 1:6). The reason this is vital is seen in the question that Paul asks Timothy: If someone fails the test in managing his own household, how do you honestly expect him to pass the test in taking care of God's church? He will fail again. So, do not appoint him to that position in the first place. The principles involved in leading a church are basically the same as those involved in leading a family. The need for regular instruction is the

---

1. The phrase "his children are believers" can also be rightly rendered, "his children are faithful" (see ESV footnote). The Greek word translated "believers" can also be rightly translated "faithful." The context determines which English word is appropriate to use in translation. The author prefers the word faithful here because that is a product of child training in the home. Only God can make people believers, including the children of churchgoing parents.

same. The balance between love and discipline is the same. The issue of being a good example to those being led is also the same.

Teaching competence. This quality should be seen especially in the way in which the person handles the word of God and in matters of doctrine. In Paul's list of qualifications given to Timothy, you can almost miss it because it is a very short phrase. Among the personal qualifications, the apostle wrote that an elder must be "able to teach" (1 Tim. 3:2). But to Titus he elaborated this point: "He must hold firm to the trustworthy word as taught, so that he may be able to give instruction in sound doctrine and also to rebuke those who contradict it" (Titus 1:9). This is vital to the life of the church, as elders lead God's people using the word of God. An elder should not be a maverick who keeps changing what he believes or who teaches his own beliefs that are not scripturally based. Notice, however, that this is not suggesting that every elder should be a gifted preacher of the word of God. Preaching is a specialized form of teaching. It is a public and authoritative proclamation of the word of God. Not every elder needs to be gifted in this way. However, every elder should be able to open the Bible and instruct an individual, a small group of believers, or even a larger group, depending on his level of giftedness. In this way, he will be leading God's people through sound doctrine and restoring to a sound faith those who are going astray. This is real eldership work.

It is worth mentioning here that elders in the Bible were always males. There is not even a hint of a female elder in the church in the New Testament—or even in Old Testament Israel. The fact that he will be instructing the whole church in the word of God puts this office outside the sphere of women because of what Paul stated earlier in 1 Timothy 2: "Let a woman learn quietly with all submissiveness. I do not permit a woman to teach or to exercise authority over a man; rather, she is to remain quiet" (1 Tim. 2:11–12). This is worth emphasizing today because the atmosphere of egalitarianism seems to demand a reversal of this biblical norm.

Elders Should Be Assisted by Deacons

The Lord blessed the early church with thousands of new converts. Soon it had grown so large that the elders were drowning under their workload. It became impossible for them to cope. They met together and decided that they should recommend a new office, which later came to be called the diaconate. The story of how this came about is found in Acts 6. We read,

> Now in these days when the disciples were increasing in number, a complaint by the Hellenists arose against the Hebrews because their widows were being neglected in the daily distribution. And the twelve summoned the full number of the disciples and said, "It is not right that we should give up preaching the word of God to serve tables. Therefore, brothers, pick out from among you seven men of good repute, full of the Spirit and of wisdom, whom we will appoint to this duty. But we will devote ourselves to prayer and to the ministry of the word." (Acts 6:1–4)

These men were later given the name deacons, as we shall see when we come to consider the qualifications for that office.

We learn from this passage that, as a church grows larger, they should not necessarily increase the number of elders; rather, they should consider appointing deacons as well. We also notice from this passage that the responsibilities that elders passed on to the deacons were those to do with mundane matters, such as caring for the financially needy. This today can include handling the church's finances, caring for the orphans and widows (and any other needy individuals) in the church, taking care of the church's properties, and so on. However, the teaching and preaching of the word of God should remain in the hands of the elders.

Deacons Must Be Biblically Qualified

When you read about the choosing of the first deacons in Acts 6, you discover that the apostles were concerned that those who were chosen were appropriately qualified. We read the apostles saying, "Therefore, brothers, pick out from among you seven men of good repute, full of the Spirit and of wisdom, whom we will appoint to this duty" (Acts 6:3). They were looking for truly spiritual and wise men to do this work.

When Paul gave qualifications for deacons to Timothy, there were hardly any differences from the qualifications he gave for elders. He wrote,

> Deacons likewise must be dignified, not double-tongued, not addicted to much wine, not greedy for dishonest gain. They must hold the mystery of the faith with a clear conscience. And let them also be tested first; then let them serve as deacons if they prove themselves blameless. Their wives likewise must be dignified, not slanderers, but sober-minded, faithful in all things. Let deacons each be the husband of one wife, managing their children and their own households well. (1 Tim. 3:8–12)

The one noteworthy difference was that deacons did not need to have the ability to teach, which was a requirement for elders. If a deacon ended up getting involved in preaching, like Philip in Acts 8:26–40, it was because he was already gifted as such. It is certainly not a requirement for the office of deacon in the church. Deacons were, however, to "hold the mystery of the faith with a clear conscience" (1 Tim. 3:9). That means they were to be grounded in Christian doctrine. In terms of personal godliness and being good leaders in their homes, there is no real difference between the qualifications of elders, and deacons.

Since we tackled the question of female elders it is worth saying something about female deacons. It is harder to reach a definite conclusion on this subject. Biblically, the office of deacon does not carry any authority. The very name "deacon" is simply the word "servant" in Greek. In that sense, there would be no need to preclude women from this office. Also, we have the example of Phoebe, who in Romans 16:1–2 is referred to as a "servant" ("deacon" in Greek) of the church in Cenchreae. Others argue that the word there is used in a generic sense and is not referring to an office. Then there are the women who are included in the list of qualifications for deacons in 1 Timothy 3. Who were they? Were they female deacons or simply women assisting the deacons, or were they the wives of deacons? That remains an open question. Those who think only males can be deacons sometimes cite the stipulation that deacons should be "the husband of one wife" (1 Tim. 3:12), which, they say, excludes women from this office. They may also point out that there is no example in the New Testament of a woman being ordained to any office of the church. Thus, the matter of whether women can be deacons is not as easily settled as that of female elders.

Eldership Work Must Not Be Usurped

We are seeing less servant leadership being exhibited by church leaders. Instead, we are seeing the African chief mentality that I mentioned at the start of this chapter. This is what is being reproduced in the church. The pastors are the ones who are most guilty of this. The fight for titles is one symptom of this. At one time, in the Protestant church, it was enough for pastors to be called "pastor" or "reverend" or "bishop," depending on the denominational etiquette. Today, we have many people going under the titles of "apostle" and "prophet." Sometimes, I wish we could all in the church simply be called "brother" or "sister."

Yet, the issue is not so much that of changing or banishing titles but of arresting the tendency to see church leadership in the way in which we see village or tribal chiefs. In some churches, especially those in rural areas, the top leadership is under the control of and occupied only by the most powerful family in the area. They decide who will lead the church, and it is often someone in their own family. Usually, it is a descendant of the pioneer of that church. Where such a person is related to the chief's family, this is even worse. Due to the fact that, in rural Africa, churches easily become the social center of an entire village, the village headman ends up becoming part of the church's leadership purely out of respect for his position in the community. Sometimes, people are brought into church leadership because of their wealth. That is one way they are kept from leaving the church. It is also a way in which they are rewarded for their financial contributions. In all these cases, whether the person is spiritually fit or not is not even considered. That is totally wrong. It kills the spirituality of the church.

There is also the phenomenon of self-appointed elders, which is foreign to the New Testament. How is this happening? Individuals who become disaffected with what is taking place in their church simply decide to start a new church. They start meeting in a home or a school classroom. Once they have got a small crowd, the leading men appoint themselves as elders of that church. There is no such practice in the New Testament. Individuals who would start a new church like this should first place themselves under an already established church until the elders in that established church lay hands on them to appoint them as elders. You cannot simply declare yourself to be an elder.

Sometimes the pastor appoints his own wife to become the assistant pastor. Again, there is no biblical precedent for this. It is a phenomenon that is foreign to the Scriptures, and yet it has become very common in churches across Africa. As already asserted, biblical church leadership is male. Quite apart from that, there were many church leaders in the Bible who were married—such as the apostle Peter—and there is no mention anywhere that their wives became church leaders as well. A pastor's wife is simply that: a pastor's wife. She is there to be his domestic companion. In the church, the pastor works with a team of elders. We need to get back to biblical leadership in the church.

There is also a great need to bring back *servant* leadership into the church. The current spate of demagogues should come to an end. Great orators are manipulating church members to give them their property and finances while they live like chiefs. This is a growing vice particularly in city churches. If thieves were to come into the church car park on a Sunday and steal the most expensive car, it would not be surprising to discover that it is the pastor's car they have stolen! If Judas Iscariot were to be among us today, he would not need to identify us with a kiss. He would simply tell those sent to arrest the pastor to pick out the man with the most expensive suit and perfume. Surely, there is something wrong with all this.

If there is one area of church life that needs serious reform, it is the leadership of the church. There is too much going wrong here. When the head is sick, the rest of the body cannot be well. We need to align our practice of church leadership with the way in which the Bible wants us to practice it. There is so much teaching about it in Scripture that there is no excuse for us to continue with bad practice. Let us ensure that our churches are being led by biblically qualified elders who lead as servant leaders. These should be assisted by biblically qualified deacons as the work in the church grows. This is the biblical norm.

STUDY GUIDE FOR CHAPTER 7
Who Should Lead the Church?

Summary

New Testament churches, following the commands of the apostles and the pattern of Jewish synagogues, were led by elders. Elders are biblically qualified men tasked to shepherd the flock, instructing them in and modeling for them the Lord's commands in Scripture. They should have among them a gifted man who regularly feeds the flock through preaching. Elders are assisted by deacons in the non-pastoral works of service.

Study Questions

1. From the qualifications of an elder in 1 Timothy 3:1–7 and Titus 1:5–9, what are the three general areas in which a person must qualify in order to be an elder in the church?

2. What pitfalls have you observed, or what dangers are there when a person is given a teaching/preaching platform that focuses only on their giftedness as a public speaker?

3. What are the differences between the work of a deacon and that of a pastor? How are these roles confused in churches today?

4. Based on the principles of church leadership taught in this chapter, what is wrong with the common practice of a pastor appointing his wife as an assistant pastor?

5. It has been said that Africans, following the example of the tribal chief, will despise a leader who comes among them and serves them, and instead they will respect the leader who separates himself and waits to be served. How would you respond to this, in light of what we have learned from Jesus's example?

8

Why Practice Baptism and the Lord's Supper?

Apart from the teaching of the word of God, singing, and praying, baptism and the Lord's Supper are the most visible activities in Christian worship. The architecture and furniture of a church building often serve these activities. From that standpoint alone, we can see the importance that the church has placed on the topic of this chapter.

For many Christians, baptism and the Lord's Supper remain a mystery. They undergo baptism because it is commanded in the Bible, but they lack knowledge as to its meaning and significance. Likewise, when a pastor or an elder is praying for the Lord's Supper, and the bread and drink are being passed around, many Christians have no idea how this simple meal benefits them spiritually. They assume that something mystical is happening that impacts them simply by the fact that the bread and drink are swallowed. Due to this wrong perception, they often hold the bread and the cup as if they were holding magic charms in their hands. Such views of the Lord's Supper are superstitious at best and idolatrous at the worst.

In the average African mind, witnessing a pastor or elder praying for the Lord's Supper conjures up thoughts of the village witchdoctor invoking the spirit world as he apparently shatters whatever it is that is causing misery in the lives of those who have come to him for help. They know what it means to watch with awe as a witchdoctor moves a few bones and feathers from dead animals on the floor while he chants some words in an apparent trance. Finally, he puts some concoction together and gives it to them to drink as part of their purification exercise. He may also give the people some roots that they are to put in water the next time they bathe. As they bathe and eat, in obedience to the witchdoctor's instructions, something is supposed to happen in the spirit world. They are supposedly going to be liberated from the mysterious curse and spell that is on their lives.

Is this what really happens when you enter into the baptismal waters, or eat the bread and drink the cup during the Lord's Supper? Let us examine the Scriptures to see what it teaches concerning these two ordinances.[1]

Only Two Ordinances

It is worth stating from the very beginning that the Lord Jesus Christ ordained only baptism and the Lord's Supper as lasting ordinances in the church. Some churches also observe foot-washing as an ordinance, but it is difficult to make a case for its being a command of the Lord.

Concerning baptism, just before his ascension to heaven the Lord Jesus Christ said, "All authority in heaven and on earth has been given to me. Go therefore and make disciples of all nations, baptizing them in the name of the Father and of the Son and of the Holy Spirit . . ." (Matt. 28:18–19).

Concerning the Lord's Supper, the apostle Paul wrote to the Corinthians,

> For I received from the Lord what I also delivered to you, that the Lord Jesus on the night when he was betrayed took bread, and when he had given thanks, he broke it, and said, "This is my body, which is for you. Do this in remembrance of me." In the same way also he took the cup, after supper, saying, "This cup is the new covenant in my blood. Do this, as often as you drink it, in remem-

---

1. I prefer to use the word "ordinance" when referring to baptism and the Lord's Supper rather than "sacrament," although I do not think it wrong to use the latter. "Ordinance" emphasizes the fact that this is something that is commanded, while "sacrament" emphasizes that it conveys holiness to those who partake of it. I suspect that the mysteriousness often connected to these two activities is partly due to the latter emphasis.

brance of me." For as often as you eat this bread and drink the cup, you proclaim the Lord's death until he comes. (1 Cor. 11:23–26)

The command from the Lord Jesus that we should participate in the Lord's Supper is unmistakable. He said, "Do this in remembrance of me."

Whereas both ordinances were commanded by the Lord Jesus and should remain in observance until he returns, individuals undergo baptism only once. This takes place soon after their profession of faith, as we shall see. However, the Lord's Supper is something that we are to participate in regularly. This is one major difference between these two ordinances.

Baptism

I am a Baptist, and my doctrinal convictions on this subject will not go unnoticed. I am writing on the assumption that baptism is only for believers and that it is by immersion. It is beyond the scope of this book to make the case for that position. I simply state it up front.

As we noted in chapter 3, baptism is a command from the Lord Jesus Christ, the head of the church. It is supposed to be the first act of obedience of a new Christian. Even where there are baptismal classes, they should not take so long that a person grows into Christian maturity while waiting for baptism. On one hand, a person being baptized is telling the world that he has now become a follower of the Lord Jesus Christ. On the other, the one baptizing the new convert is adding his own testimony that, from what he has seen and heard, this person's profession of faith is tenable. Let us look at a few features of baptism.

1. Baptism symbolizes what has happened spiritually in the life of the new convert. Paul captured this when he wrote to the Romans,

What shall we say then? Are we to continue in sin that grace may abound? By no means! How can we who died to sin still live in it? Do you not know that all of us who have been baptized into Christ Jesus were baptized into his death? We were buried therefore with him by baptism into death, in order that, just as Christ was raised from the dead by the glory of the Father, we too might walk in newness of life. (Rom. 6:1–4)

The baptism being referred to by Paul was not water baptism but Spirit baptism—the baptism into Christ's death. This is what happens to everyone who becomes a genuine convert, and it happens at the point of their regeneration. They die to sin. How does this happen? Just as Jesus died to this world of sin, was buried, and rose again to newness of life, so also when you become a Christian you are united to Christ by the Holy Spirit, and Christ's experience becomes yours. You too die to sin and are enabled to walk in newness of life. This is why a genuine Christian cannot continue to live a life of sin. This is Paul's argument in Romans 6.

Water baptism symbolizes that reality. When you are immersed in water you are testifying that you have died to the life that you once lived. That life is over. You have been buried with Christ. When you arise out of the water, you are testifying that the person everyone is now relating to is a new, resurrected person, and your one desire now is to glorify God. What a wonderful symbol baptism is! That explains why it should take place soon after a person is converted to Christ rather than later. Through baptism the new convert is testifying about what has happened through his union with Christ.

2. Baptism is closely related to the gospel message. It was the outward way in which those who repented and trusted in Christ made their profession known. On the day of Pentecost, when the people listening to Peter's preaching came under intense conviction and asked him and the rest of the apostles what they should do, Peter said, "Repent and be baptized every one of you in the name of Jesus Christ for the forgiveness of your sins, and you will receive the gift of the Holy Spirit" (Acts 2:38).

When Philip was evangelizing the Ethiopian eunuch in his chariot, the Bible records,

> And as they were going along the road they came to some water, and the eunuch said, "See, here is water! What prevents me from being baptized?" And he commanded the chariot to stop, and they both went down into the water, Philip and the eunuch, and he baptized him. (Acts 8:36–38)

As noted in chapter 3, in the previous verse we are told only that Philip began with Isaiah 53 and told the eunuch the good news about Jesus.

Yet, from this request it is evident that Philip had included in their conversation the fact that the eunuch needed to be baptized immediately following his profession of faith.

3. Baptism is a door into church membership. The phrasing of the Great Commission suggests this: ". . . make disciples of all nations, baptizing them . . ." (Matt. 28:19). Only after that does Jesus say they are to be taught to obey everything that he has commanded. We also see this in the book of Acts. Going back to the day of Pentecost, when Peter had finished preaching, we are told, "So those who received his word were baptized, and there were added that day about three thousand souls" (Acts 2:41).

4. Baptism is not essential for salvation. We are justified before God on the basis of the finished work of Christ. We cannot add to or subtract from that by our own works of righteousness. Baptism is important, but it does not have any saving power in it. You must already be a Christian in order to be baptized. As we have seen, it is merely the first act of obedience by someone who claims that Jesus has now become his master and Lord.

Having stated unequivocally that baptism does not save us, we need to state with equal emphasis that a Christian who resists being baptized is living in disobedience and defiant rebellion. This is a command of the Lord Jesus Christ. Why should you call Jesus your Lord when you are not doing what he so plainly says you should do?

The Lord's Supper

Sometimes the Lord's Supper is called Holy Communion or the Eucharist. I much prefer the designation "Lord's Supper" because it separates it from all other suppers. This one is the *Lord's* supper. He is the one who has given us the menu and has also commanded us to eat and drink of it in remembrance of him. We already noted this from 1 Corinthians 11:23. There, Paul said that the Lord's Supper was not his idea. He simply passed on to the Corinthian church what he had received from the Lord Jesus Christ.

Each of the Gospel writers—Matthew, Mark, Luke, and John—refers to how Jesus instituted this meal. The fact that all of them do so suggests that this was a very significant matter. The sum total of the witness of these writers is that, on the night before our Lord was betrayed, he gathered his twelve disciples in an upper room and had a meal with them. Toward the end of that meal, he gave them instructions about how this meal was to be perpetually celebrated in honor of him until he returns. Let us look at a few of these features.

1. The relationship between the Lord's Supper and the Passover. It is instructive that the Lord's Supper was instituted during the Feast of Unleavened Bread, called the Passover. In fact, Jesus referred to what he was going to eat with his disciples that day as the Passover. The Bible records,

> Now the Feast of Unleavened Bread drew near, which is called the Passover. . . .
>
> Then came the day of Unleavened Bread, on which the Passover lamb had to be sacrificed. So Jesus sent Peter and John, saying, "Go and prepare the Passover for us, that we may eat it." . . . And they went and found it just as he had told them, and they prepared the Passover.
>
> And when the hour came, he reclined at table, and the apostles with him. And he said to them, "I have earnestly desired to eat this Passover with you before I suffer." (Luke 22:1, 7–8, 13–15)

We cannot, therefore, understand the Lord's Supper without looking at the Passover as its backdrop. We see the background of the Passover in Exodus 12. The setting is when Israel was under Egyptian captivity and God was about to deliver them through the heroic and miraculous plagues of Moses. The last of these plagues was to be the death of the firstborn son in every household in Egypt. In order to avoid this happening in the households of the Israelites, they needed to smear the blood of sheep or goats on the door frames of their houses on the day that the angel of death was going to go throughout the land. In the words of God given to Moses we read,

> The blood shall be a sign for you, on the houses where you are. And when I see the blood, I will pass over you, and no plague will befall you to destroy you, when I strike the land of Egypt.

> This day shall be for you a memorial day, and you shall keep it as a feast to the LORD; throughout your generations, as a statute forever, you shall keep it as a feast. (Ex. 12:13–14)

The relationship between the Passover and the Lord's Supper should not be difficult to see. The Israelites survived death in their households through the blood of the animals that was on their door frames. We are saved from the wrath of God through the blood of the Lord Jesus Christ. The Passover was a meal, and so is the Lord's Supper. Both of them speak of God's rescue of his people from enslavement and tyranny. Enslavement in Egypt is a picture of enslavement to sin. The blood of sacrificed animals in the Old Testament is a picture of the blood of Christ in the New Testament. This is the meaning of the Lord's Supper. It is a reminder of the way in which we have been rescued from enslavement to sin and from God's wrath through the atoning sacrifice of the Son of God on the cross.

2. The Lord's Supper is a memorial and not a reenactment. Jesus is not crucified again when we have the Lord's Supper. Nothing mysterious happens when someone prays and breaks bread in full view of the congregation. The bread and the drink are not becoming the literal body and blood of Christ. Those elements remain what they have always been. This is a reminder and not a reenactment. Jesus is currently in heaven. He does not suffer and die again each time we have the Lord's Supper. He died once and for all. God was fully satisfied with the price Jesus paid on the cross for our sin. He will never suffer and die again.

This truth, that we do not repeat the crucifixion of Jesus Christ when we have the Lord's Supper, needs to be emphasized. The Bible says about Jesus's once-for-all and all-sufficient death,

> Christ, having been offered once to bear the sins of many, will appear a second time, not to deal with sin but to save those who are eagerly waiting for him. . . .
>
> But when Christ had offered for all time a single sacrifice for sins, he sat down at the right hand of God, waiting from that time until his enemies should be made a footstool for his feet. For by a single offering he has perfected for all time those who are being sanctified. (Heb. 9:28; 10:12–14)

The Lord's Supper simply portrays the all-sufficient death of Christ as a reminder to us, his disciples.

Elsewhere I have written, "So the Lord's Supper is to us but a memorial. It is not the actual thing. It is like having a memorial service for a family member who passed away about a year ago. We do not expect people to cry because the death took place long ago. We expect the family of the dead person to use the time to recollect what happened a long time ago. That is what we do with the Lord's Supper. We are not re-enacting the death of the Lord Jesus. It took place two thousand years ago. We are merely reminding ourselves of it."[2]

Who Qualifies to Participate in the Lord's Supper?

Baptism and the Lord's Supper are for Christians. We have stated that the only difference is that baptism takes place at the start of the Christian's life, whereas we are to partake of the Lord's Supper regularly throughout our lives.

There is a mistaken notion that only those who are really, really holy should participate in the Lord's Supper. This comes from a wrong understanding of 1 Corinthians 11:27. In the King James Version of the Bible this verse reads, "Wherefore whosoever shall eat this bread, and drink this cup of the Lord, unworthily, shall be guilty of the body and blood of the Lord." The phrase "unworthily" has often been misunderstood as meaning that Christians may on certain occasions be unworthy of partaking of the Lord's Supper and therefore should not participate. So, many people, out of genuine humility and a sense of failure to live up to the dictates of their own consciences, keep away from partaking of this meal. Sometimes, this is exacerbated by the words of the person who is leading in the Lord's Supper. He may say something like, "Examine yourself. If you know that you have not lived right in the eyes of God, then keep away, or else you will be inviting God's judgment upon yourself."

There is also the thinking that the judgment that befell the Corinthians when they took part in the Lord's Supper wrongly (see 1 Cor. 11:30) was because the meal had some mystical powers that caused

2. Conrad Mbewe, *Foundations for the Flock—Truths about the Church for All the Saints* (Hannibal, MO: Granted Ministries Press, 2011), 91.

the "unworthy" participants to suffer mysterious and deathly illnesses. In some churches, women are told to keep away from the Lord's Supper when they are menstruating because, supposedly, they are unclean during that time.

Thankfully, the wrong interpretation of 1 Corinthians 11:27 is more difficult to sustain with the more modern Bible versions. For instance, the English Standard Version says, "Whoever, therefore, eats the bread or drinks the cup of the Lord in an unworthy manner will be guilty concerning the body and blood of the Lord." In other words, it is not that the person is unworthy—we all are! It is the manner in which a person is conducting himself while partaking of the meal that Paul is cautioning about. Every Christian who is in fellowship with other Christians in the church should participate in the Lord's Supper. What is important is one's attitude during the meal. Participants should deliberately meditate on the finished work of Christ on the cross.

Allow for Variations

There will be some variations in the way in which baptism and the Lord's Supper are conducted from church to church. For instance, different words may be used by the person leading in both ordinances. With respect to the Lord's Supper, some may use actual bread, while others may prefer something closer to biscuits than bread. Similarly, some may use any red drink to symbolize the blood of Christ, while others may be dogmatic on the use of red grape juice or even wine. The frequency of these ordinances also varies. Some churches observe the Lord's Supper every week, while others only do so once a month. Ultimately, we cannot pontificate to the minutest details on how these ordinances are to be carried out. Each church will have its own culture and should feel free to follow it as long as it does not contradict the meaning of the ordinance.

Summary

The Lord's Supper and baptism are the only ordinances that Jesus gave to the Christian church. Baptism is practiced by full water immersion of those who have given a credible confession of faith. It symbolizes the reality of the believer's inclusion in Christ. Even though baptism is not essential to salvation, it is closely related to the gospel message and is a door into church membership. The Lord's Supper is a congregational meal of bread and drink that recalls the sacrificial body and blood of Jesus, and it is likewise only for believers. It is not for those who consider themselves "worthy" of it, who have lived righteous lives prior to the meal, but for those who partake of it in a worthy manner, who recognize its value and meaning as they partake.

Study Questions

1. Do you find that the words "ordinance" and "sacrament" bring different thoughts/connotations to mind? What are these differences? Where do you think they come from?

2. "Baptism is a door into church membership" (p. 117). Why do you think a church should not receive into its membership those who are not baptized?

3. What initiation sign does your tribal community practice for men? How do you think baptism compares to such cultural initiation signs, in terms of its meaning?

4. How does your local church practice baptism? What advantages or disadvantages do you think this brings?

5   How does your local church's practice the Lord's Supper? What advantages or disadvantages do you think this brings?

9

What Should Happen during Worship Services?

Visits to chiefs' palaces in tribal regions of Africa are always preceded by a short talk about procedural and protocol matters. You are first taken into a room where a palace officer gives you the dos and don'ts of the place. If you have gone as a group, the group leader is informed specifically where he should go and kneel upon arriving in the chief's presence and where the rest of you should wait. He is told what signal he should wait for before he begins to speak, how he is to greet and address the chief, at what angle his eyes should look, and how to introduce those who have come with him. To visit the chief empty-handed would be an insult, so the visitor is also told at what point it would be appropriate to state what gift he has brought to the chief and how that gift must be presented to him. If you want to bring a request before the chief, you are also told how to present that request. If you are Caucasian, the protocol officer may assure you that the chief may overlook your failures because he knows that they are very foreign to you. However, if you are one of his subjects, the officer will warn you of some of the penalties you may suffer if you fail to observe etiquette in the chief's presence. As the briefing ends and it is time for you to enter the chief's presence, you will be amazed at how all these protocols are taking place just like clockwork. The way in which everyone in the chief's presence stands up or kneels down or claps at appropriate times tells you that you are not in the presence of an ordinary person. You are in the presence of royalty. This is what happens here, and you do well to observe it.

Although God is our Father, he is also the Lord of the universe. In heaven, he is worshiped by thousands upon thousands and ten thousand times ten thousand angels in holy adoration. On earth, he invites us also to worship him collectively as his people. The worship service is not primarily about the worshiper feeling good. It is about worshipers rendering to God what is due his name. He delights in our worship.

There is a special sense in which God is with the gathered church, and so when we go to meet with him we speak in terms of entering his presence. Jesus said, "Where two or three are gathered in my name, there am I among them" (Matt. 18:20). In the context of these words, Jesus was talking about that time when the church collectively meets to excommunicate a stubborn sinner from their midst. The apostle Paul echoed this thought in a similar situation when he wrote to the Corinthians, "When you are assembled in the name of the Lord Jesus and my spirit is present, with the power of our Lord Jesus, you are to deliver this man to Satan for the destruction of the flesh, so that his spirit may be saved in the day of the Lord" (1 Cor. 5:4–5). There is such a thing as the church being assembled in the name of the Lord Jesus Christ.

In one sense, Jesus is always with us because as God he is omnipresent. Yet, this promise suggests a special presence when his people gather in his name. This is especially the case when we meet for what we call "worship services." Every true church will have such times at least once a week. In this chapter we are asking the question, "What should happen during these worship services?" Does the Bible tell us what to do and what not to do, like the protocol officer in the chief's palace, or are we at liberty to simply walk into God's presence and do anything that crosses our minds?

Activities That Should Make Up Our Worship Services

When you read the New Testament, there is ample evidence of a few activities that the gathered church observed literally from the very first day of its existence. Luke describes these activities as follows: "And they devoted themselves to the apostles' teaching and the fellowship, to the breaking of bread and the prayers" (Acts 2:42). From this list we can at least see that the church gathered to listen to the preaching of the word of God, for fellowship with one another, for the breaking of bread, and for prayer. I have referred to this passage a number of times already because it is descriptive not only of the activities of the early church but also of the pattern that we are to follow in the church until Christ returns.

In chapter 1, we noted that the activities of Acts 2:42 help us to see in practice the characteristics of a true church. We called them the church's distinguishing marks. Where these activities are missing, we should doubt whether we are dealing with a real church. In chapter 3, we singled out the first activity in Acts 2:42 as we noted the importance of instructing believers as part of the Great Commission. In chapter 6, we saw from this same passage that believers committed themselves to some describable activities—the apostles' teaching and the fellowship, the breaking of bread and the prayers. So, it is difficult to exaggerate the importance of this passage. Use it to examine what is happening in your church and what you have committed yourself to when you meet with other believers. To refresh our minds, let us briefly walk through each of the activities mentioned in this verse.

Biblical instruction. We are told that the disciples committed themselves to the apostles' teaching. This can also be seen from the Great Commission, where Jesus said that those who were baptized were to be taught to observe or obey everything that he had commanded (Matt. 28:20). To the question of what should happen during worship services, we can state unequivocally that there should be faithful instruction from the word of God.

Fellowship. We are also told that the disciples committed themselves to "the fellowship." This refers to the body life of the gathered church. Believers are not only to be interested in "vertical" worship when they gather together but also in "horizontal" fellowship. They should seek to minister to one another. One way in which they do so is in singing during worship. The songs are often directed to God, but they are also meant to enrich the faith of fellow believers. Paul said, "And do not get drunk with wine, for that is debauchery, but be filled with the Spirit, addressing one another in psalms and hymns and spiritual songs, singing and making melody to the Lord with your heart" (Eph. 5:18–19).

Ordinances. We are also told that the disciples committed themselves to the breaking of bread. This refers to what is called "the Lord's Supper," which is one of the two ordinances that Jesus instituted for the church. The other is baptism (see Acts 2:41 and Matt. 28:19). Baptism is to take place at convenient times whenever individuals have come to Christ in repentance and faith. Some churches have the Lord's Supper every week, while other churches have this meal less frequently. The Bible does not prescribe the frequency, but it is important that this ordinance be observed regularly. It is an important reminder to believers of the price that was paid for their redemption. They need this reminder regularly, if not frequently.

Prayer. We are finally told that the disciples committed themselves to "the prayers." Prayers were a significant part of the meetings of the gathered church. This was over and above the opening and closing prayer. Paul wrote to Timothy as he began to lead the church in Ephesus, saying,

> First of all, then, I urge that supplications, prayers, intercessions, and thanksgivings be made for all people, for kings and all who are in high positions, that we may lead a peaceful and quiet life, godly and dignified in every way. This is good, and it is pleasing in the sight of God our Savior, who desires all people to be saved and to come to the knowledge of the truth. (1 Tim. 2:1–4)

Here's one way to look at these four activities: When the church comes together, God speaks to us through his word as it is preached, taught, studied, and sung. We respond collectively through our mutual care for one another. God speaks to us about his gracious redemption in Christ through his ordinances as we see them acted out and participate in them. Then, because of all this, we sense our need of his help and so we respond to him in praying for ourselves, our family, our church, our communities, our leaders, and the nations of the world. This is what should happen during our worship services. If the New Testament were to act like the protocol officer at the chief's palace, this is what it would be telling us to do when we appear before God as a group.

What about the Taking Up of Tithes and Offerings?

Across history, the church has wrestled with the question of whether we are at liberty to add anything else to this list. One can argue perhaps for adding what we call "the offering" or "the collection." This refers to the opportunity for Christians to give tithes and freewill offerings to God as part of their worship. Since this is often used for the church's welfare, one can see how it fits into the commitment of the disciples to "the fellowship." We are told that "All who believed were together and had all things in common. And they were selling their possessions and belongings and distributing the proceeds to all, as any had need" (Acts 2:44–45). The fact that this was to be done when the church came together can also be seen from Paul's instructions to the Corinthians when he said, "Now concerning the collection for the saints: as I directed the churches of Galatia, so you also are to do. On the first day of every week, each of you is to put something aside and store it up, as he may prosper, so that there will be no collecting when I come" (1 Cor. 16:1–2). Paul wanted this collection for the church in Judea by the church in Achaia to be done weekly as the church met, so that when he came through Corinth on his way to Judea, there would be no need to attempt a larger collection at that time.

Some churches take this collection during the worship service while others prefer to do so at the end of the service through a collection box conveniently placed near the exit doors. These are matters that each church must determine, and it is beyond the scope of this book to help settle this matter one way or the other. Whichever method a church finally decides on, what must be avoided are the twin evils of cajoling the congregation for more and more money, and ostentation on the part of those who are giving. The Bible says that God loves a "cheerful" giver (2 Cor. 9:7), and so, although appeals could be made from time to time, church leaders should not resort to making their members feel guilty for not giving a certain amount. See the example of the wise and sweet appeals of the apostle Paul in 2 Corinthians chapters 8 and 9.

Are There Other Things a Church Can Do in Its Worship Services?

Beyond the possible addition of "the collection," which remains an open question, is there any other legitimate addition to the worship service that is sanctioned by the Bible? This is a very important question, especially today. Let us go back to the illustration of the visit to the chief's palace. Who determines the etiquette to be observed when you enter the presence of the chief and what activities you can engage in while you are there? Is it the subjects of the chief, or the chief himself? It seems rather obvious that it is the chief. You are entering into the presence of royalty, and so you want to know how you are expected to behave. You can neither add to nor subtract from what the chief says.

This was Paul's chief concern in writing his first letter to Timothy. He stated about halfway through the letter, "I hope to come to you soon, but I am writing these things to you so that, if I delay, you may know how one ought to behave in the household of God, which is the church of the living God, a pillar and buttress of the truth" (1 Tim. 3:14–15). We have already looked at this text in chapter 2, where we asserted that church leaders have no right to introduce into the life of the church what God himself has not sanctioned. They should always ask the question, "What does the Bible say?" The Holy Spirit has ensured that we have the mind of the head of the church in the Holy Scriptures. Paul states that this was the reason why he was giving such painstaking instructions to Timothy in this epistle. It was because the church belonged to God. It was "the household of God, which is the church of the living God, a pillar and buttress of the truth." Timothy had no right to introduce practices in the church without divine sanction. The church needed to reflect the activities that God had authorized through his written word. Paul was anxious to get these instructions to Timothy in case he was delayed in getting to him. As you can see, these instructions went beyond the worship service but they certainly included that. This instruction to Timothy is applicable to all church leaders today. God himself has stated what should happen when we meet to worship him. We should neither add to it nor subtract from it.

Should Our Churches Also Have Deliverance Sessions?

In recent years there has been a growing tendency to have "deliverance sessions" in our churches in Africa. They have become a common phenomenon of the gathered church. I saw a sign the other day opposite our church and it read (I leave out the church's name) ". . . invites you all to their Sunday services. A home of signs and wonders. The bound go free, barrenness, HIV, TB, witchcraft terminated, evil dreams, testimonies of jobs by the power of Jesus Christ (John 14:20)." Such signs are very common today. First-time visitors to our church sometimes ask, after the worship service, why there was no deliverance session. These sessions are often viewed as the culmination of everything that takes place earlier in the service. If one asks where in the Bible we are taught to have deliverance sessions in our worship services, one is generally pointed to the book of Acts, where the apostles performed many miracles and healed the sick. One is also pointed to James 5:14–15, where the Bible says,

> Is anyone among you sick? Let him call for the elders of the church, and let them pray over him, anointing him with oil in the name of the Lord. And the prayer of faith will save the one who is sick, and the Lord will raise him up. And if he has committed sins, he will be forgiven.

It needs to be pointed out that nowhere in the book of Acts do we have the apostles performing their many miracles and healing the sick when the church gathered to worship. Rather, the common testimony was that the church gathered to be instructed. Also, notice that in James it is not the elders or pastors calling the sick to come to them (in front of the church) but the sick members asking their elders to go to their homes to pray for them.

Why have deliverance sessions become such a common phenomenon in the churches in Africa? The answer is not difficult to find. It is because church pastors have fast become the equivalent of witchdoctors in the popular African mind. Even Christians come to church not so much thinking in terms of what they should render to God as their divine Benefactor but rather thinking in terms of what they can get from God through his servant, and especially through his powerful intercessions and interventions. As popular as this has become, it is not what should be happening during worship services. There is no biblical warrant for this.

As Africans We Are Very Good Singers, But . . .

Another area that needs to be addressed is our congregational singing. We Africans love to sing. We sing when we marry off our children, we sing when babies are born, and we sing when people die. We sing when we receive important visitors and we sing when we see them off. We sing to welcome the rains and we sing as we bring in the crops. We sing (and dance!) when we are happy and we sing when we are sad. We have a very rich singing culture. There is no doubt about that. Yet, in answering the question about what should happen during worship services, we need to address two areas of this love of singing so that it serves its role in worship as God intended it to.

Our singing should not crowd out the preaching of God's word but must be its handmaid. We noted in the first chapter that in many of our churches we have a lot of choirs. Add to this the fact that each choir has a song as they go forward onto the podium, and then the main song that they have gone forward to sing, and then another song as they make their way back to their seats. By the time all these choirs have sung, there is very little time for the actual preaching of the word of God. We need to arrest this trend and jealously guard the time for preaching, because there is nothing more important in the worship service than for us to quieten our hearts before God while he speaks to us through the faithful exposition of his word.

Our congregational singing needs also to be more effective in capturing the richness of the full menu of Christian doctrine and experience. Too much of the singing in our churches comprises the repetition of a few words over and over again with very little variation. For instance, a song can have the main line set to very good African rhythm and tempo that simply says, "We are going." Whoever is leading the congregation will keep adding different phrases like, "To heaven" or "With my brother" or "With my Jesus" or "With my Bible," while the congregation completes the line with "We are going." This can go on for what feels like forever, and it often passes for the best of congregational singing in our churches. In the light of the lofty truths about God and the unsearchable riches of Christ that we have in the Bible, surely, is this the best we can do in worshiping our great God?

Consider this: Our God is revealed in the Bible as Father, Son, and Holy Spirit. He is three in one and one in three from all eternity to all eternity. He dwells in light unapproachable, and he does not change. He is almighty, present everywhere at the same time, and he already knows all things that will ever happen. He is the sovereign creator and ruler of all things and is in complete control of everything all the time, governing them according to the counsel of his own will. He is an all-wise God who never makes a mistake. All his ways are perfect. He is a holy being who hates sin with perfect hatred, and he is a just God who must punish sin and reward righteousness. He is a good God, full of mercy, love, and grace. He delights in forgiving repentant sinners. He does all this for his own glory. It is this God to whom we owe all our being. It is this God whom angels worship. It is this God who invites us to come and worship him together with the rest of creation. Our songs should reflect these sublime truths as we reflect back to God what he has revealed of himself to us.

Notice, I have not even touched the glorious truths surrounding the person and work of the Lord Jesus in our redemption. Singing of the unsearchable riches of Christ takes us to another level. It reaches notes that even angels cannot sing. Then throw in the truths about the word of God and the church of God and the eternal hope that we have as believers. You begin to realize that, in the immensities and profundities of who God is and what he has done for us in Christ, there are truths that can inspire the most glorious hymns and songs even in our vernacular languages and even in our darkest days. Our singing should, therefore, be a handmaid of the teaching and preaching ministry by reflecting those truths that fill up our Bibles. Simply singing "We are going" over and over again is woefully deficient, even if the music excites us with its beautiful African rhythm. It is one area in which we need to change.

One person whose hymn has captured something of what I am talking about is Emmanuel T. Sibomana (1915–1975), a pastor from Burundi. He wrote a hymn in his own language, titled, "O How the

Grace of God Amazes Me." At the risk of making this chapter too long, I would like to quote it in full for the reader to appreciate its richness:

> O how the grace of God amazes me!
> It loosed me from my bonds and set me free!
> What made it happen so?
> His own will, this much I know,
> Set me, as now I show, at liberty.
>
> My God has chosen me, Though one of nought,
> To sit beside my King in heaven's court.
> Hear what my Lord has done,
> O, the love that made Him run
> To meet His erring son! This has God wrought.
>
> Not for my righteousness, for I have none,
> But for His mercy's sake, Jesus, God's Son,
> Suffered on Calvary's tree;
> Crucified with thieves was He;
> Great was His grace to me, His wayward one.
>
> And when I think of how, at Calvary,
> He bore sin's penalty instead of me,
> Amazed, I wonder why
> He, the sinless One, should die
> For one so vile as I; My Savior He!
>
> Now all my heart's desire is to abide
> In Him, my Savior dear, in Him to hide,
> My shield and buckler He,
> Cov'ring and protecting me;
> From Satan's darts I'll be safe at His side.
>
> Lord Jesus, hear my prayer, Your grace impart;
> When evil thoughts arise through Satan's art,
> O, drive them all away
> And do Thou, from day to day,
> Keep me beneath Thy sway, King of my heart.

Come now, the whole of me, eyes, ears, and voice.
Join me, creation all, with joyful noise:
Praise Him who broke the chain
Holding me in sin's domain
And set me free again! Sing and rejoice![1]

As we conclude this chapter, let us go back to where we began—with the protocol officer at the chief's palace. When we go into God's presence, we are going into the presence of a King. In fact, he is the King of kings and the Lord of lords. What should happen when we are in his presence is revealed in the Bible. As we have already said, let us not add and let us not subtract. We must be careful to heed the words of the wise man in the book of Ecclesiastes. He says, "Guard your steps when you go to the house of God. To draw near to listen is better than to offer the sacrifice of fools, for they do not know that they are doing evil. Be not rash with your mouth, nor let your heart be hasty to utter a word before God, for God is in heaven and you are on earth. Therefore let your words be few" (Eccles. 5:1–2).

---

1. Emmanuel T. Sibomana, "O How the Grace of God Amazes Me," copyright Church Mission Society, all rights reserved. Quoted with the kind permission of the Church Mission Society.

STUDY GUIDE FOR CHAPTER 9
What Should Happen during Worship Services?

Summary

The Bible tells us what to do when we gather together as a church in the name of the Lord Jesus. We see these things in the authoritative commands of the apostles and the corresponding practice of the first churches. We should hear faithful instruction from the word of God, pray together, observe the ordinances, and fellowship together when we gather.

Study Questions

1. What are the elements of worship that the Holy Spirit has given to us in his word? How closely do they reflect the practice in your current church?

2. How would you respond to the suggestion that regularly practicing these elements of worship limits the working of the Holy Spirit?

3. What expectations do you think the average person in your area brings to the church worship service?

4. Why are deliverance services so attractive to some churches in Africa? What harm do you think they do?

5. This chapter calls us to emulate the apostle Paul's wise and sweet appeals in 2 Corinthians 8 and 9 when it comes to asking people to give. What specific things do you notice in these two chapters that you would like to emulate as a leader in your church?

6. Do you sing biblically rich songs in your worship services? Are most of these biblically rich songs written by local African musicians or are most of them from the West? Do you see this necessarily as a problem to be remedied?

10

How Should the Church Raise Its Money?

I mentioned at the start of chapter 6 that my mother died when I was only nine years old. Following the African extended family system, her sister took my two sisters and me from Dad's home to raise us up together with her other children. Mom's other sisters also helped by taking us to their homes during school holidays. That was how I went through my teenage years. It was during one of those memorable school holidays that the incident I am about to narrate happened. My two sisters and I were at the home of one of Mom's younger sisters who was married to a fairly wealthy man in one of Zambia's copper mining towns. The home was in an exclusive area where the top managers of the mining company lived. While playing outside one Saturday afternoon, I noticed a man on a bicycle arrive and begin knocking on the gate. As a teenager, I ran over to him. He asked me if my uncle was around. I told him that he was not. The man proceeded to give me an envelope and asked me to tell my uncle that they had not seen him at church for a very long time but wanted him to handle the matter addressed in the envelope as soon as possible. As the man got on the bicycle, he turned and said to me, "If I do not see him at church tomorrow, I will pass through next week for an answer."

I was just a boy. Curiosity got the better of me. As I took the envelope into the house, I mischievously opened it to see what was inside. It was a record with my uncle's name on it stating how much he owed the church in terms of unpaid tithes and special pledges (perhaps toward a building project). I was still young, but I recall feeling outraged and thinking to myself, my uncle rarely ever went to church. His lifestyle explained why he would not see churchgoing as a priority. Instead of the church people coming to speak to him about his soul, here they were simply being interested in his money. I was either unconverted or a new believer who knew very little about the Bible's teaching on how a church should raise its money, but I could see that there was something drastically wrong with this approach. During the forty years since that happened, I have witnessed many more unjustifiable church fundraising efforts. It is, therefore, only right that in a book on the church at least one chapter should be dedicated to answering the question, "How should a church raise its money?"

There is no doubt that every church needs money and that the primary source of that money will be its own members. The church needs money to pay all those who are in its employment, and especially those who do the work of pastoring the flock and preaching. Such individuals will often also need transport and accommodation, which the church often has to pay for. The church also needs money in order to maintain its buildings and to pay its utility bills and various other fees imposed on it by the municipality and the state. Churches without their own buildings need to pay rent for the place where they meet. The church needs money to underwrite its various activities such as children's work, youth camps, and many other outreach efforts. If the church has begun to support missions work, then there will be need for even more money. In today's technological world, the church will need money to buy and maintain equipment such as public address systems, music systems, computers, and printers. The church also looks after the most economically vulnerable in its ranks, especially those who are orphans and widows, and will need money for that as well. No one can ever doubt that every church needs money. The bigger the church, the more money it needs to keep its systems on the move. The question is, how should the church legitimately raise its money?

The first difficulty with answering this question is simply the fact that the subject of money is always a sensitive one. This is because it deals with a commodity that we toil for most of our lives and never seem to have enough of. We spend a lot of time trying to get more of it from our employers or from our businesses. So, giving it away "just like that" is something we are generally reluctant to do. The moment someone begins to talk about our money and wanting us to part with it, we feel threatened. He must have a very convincing argument before we can accept parting with our money.

The second difficulty with answering this question is the fact that the Bible says very little about how the church should raise its money. That does not mean the Bible is silent about issues to do with money. Rather, most of the teaching in the Bible on the subject of money is about our attitude toward money, including the world-famous verse that says, "The love of money is a root of all kinds of evils" (1 Tim. 6:10). It is this paucity of information that has caused many church leaders to resort to any method that will bring in the money. They use either honey or vinegar to get money out of the pockets of their church members. They say that God will bless you abundantly if you give your money to the church or that he will punish you severely if you do not. Both of those messages tend to bring in the cash. But, surely, that is not the way God wants his people to be inspired to give toward his cause. He wants their giving to be joyful and in truth.

Having acknowledged both the sensitivity of this subject and the paucity of biblical information on it, let's look at the three ways in which the New Testament guides us to raise the much-needed funds for the church and its operations here on earth.

Tithing

Due to the fact that tithing is mainly an Old Testament practice, many Christians sincerely believe and teach that tithing does not apply to the New Testament. They argue that through Christ's death we have been liberated from the law and its demands upon us. Rather, as New Testament believers, we should give much more than Old Testament believers gave in their tithes because we have much, much more to be grateful for in the salvation that Jesus Christ has procured for us on the cross. There is something to be said for that argument. In dealing with the subject of tithing, I accept that some believers will prefer to take this position, and it is not my goal in this book to convince them otherwise.

However, I think there is a good case to be made that tithing is the main way in which God expects his church to raise its money. It is true that tithing is largely taught in the Old Testament. It was a form of tax, in which the heads of homes in the nation of Israel gave a tenth of their income as a way of participating in the sustenance of the priesthood and the religious activities around the tabernacle and later the temple. God's people were to give a tenth of the seed of the land, the fruit of the trees, and the herds and flocks. In Leviticus 27:30–32 we read,

> Every tithe of the land, whether of the seed of the land or of the fruit of the trees, is the LORD's; it is holy to the LORD. If a man wishes to redeem some of his tithe, he shall add a fifth to it. And every tithe of herds and flocks, every tenth animal of all that pass under the herdsman's staff, shall be holy to the LORD.

It is also worth emphasizing that the concept of the tithe did not originate with the law of Moses. There is evidence as far back as Genesis 14:17–20 that it was already a form of personal giving toward those who fulfilled the role of priests. In this passage, Melchizedek blessed Abram, and Abram in return gave him "a tenth of everything" (v. 20). The Bible is careful to give us the reason why this happened. It is because Melchizedek was priest of God Most High (v. 18). So, long before Moses institutionalized tithing into the life of the young nation of Israel, it was already a concept and principle in the lives of the people of God to share "a tenth of everything" with those who ministered to them spiritually.

In the Old Testament, the tithe was given to the Levites (see Num. 18:21 and Heb. 7:5) because they had no other means of income or inheritance. They gave their lives in service to God in the work at the tabernacle and temple. So, it was only fair that the rest of the people shared their income and inheritance with them through this form of tax.

For us in the New Testament, the application of this principle cannot be missed: We do not have priests in the same way that the Old Testament had but we do have pastors who give their lives to the work of preaching and teaching. We must support them in the same way that the Old Testament believers supported the priests. This is what Paul taught the Corinthians. He wrote,

> Do you not know that those who are employed in the temple service get their food from the temple, and those who serve at the altar share in the sacrificial offerings? In the same way, the Lord commanded that those who proclaim the gospel should get their living by the gospel. (1 Cor. 9:13–14)

It is only fair and logical that church members should faithfully set aside a regular percentage of the fruit of their sweat and share it with those who are sweating for them in the context of the church. Through the symbiosis of the tithe system, the New Testament church is sustained in all its ministries just as the Old Testament church was sustained.

Freewill Offerings

The second way in which a church should legitimately raise its money is through freewill offerings or pledges. The apostle Paul taught this to the Corinthian church when he wrote,

> Now concerning the collection for the saints: as I directed the churches of Galatia, so you also are to do. On the first day of every week, each of you is to put something aside and store it up, as he may prosper, so that there will be no collecting when I come. (1 Cor. 16:1–2; see also 2 Cor. 8:1–9:15)

Such a freewill offering is over and above tithing. It is often related to a very specific project in the life of the church. You will notice in the passage we have quoted that this was not the normal collection. It was "the collection for the saints." There was a famine in Judea, so Paul encouraged the churches in Galatia, Macedonia, and Achaia to take up a special collection, which he would later pass through to collect and deliver to the saints affected by that famine.

Whereas tithing relies on our faithfulness, freewill offering relies on our generosity. Although Paul really urged the Corinthians to stretch themselves in giving toward this cause, he quickly added, "Each one must give as he has decided in his heart, not reluctantly or under compulsion, for God loves a cheerful giver" (2 Cor. 9:7).

As stated earlier, freewill offerings and pledges are often related to specific needs and projects. It may be a building project or the support of a missionary. It may be for the purpose of holding a camp for the young people in the church or to help widows in their distress. It may be to purchase a generator for a church building or a car for the pastor. The needs are varied. A need is presented before the church, church members are given time to pray about how much they can give, and at the right time the collection is taken.

Often, Christians end up giving in proportion to their income. Those with "deep pockets" will often give more than those who are eking out a living. No one should despise the coin (i.e., the small amount) that the widow gives out of her poverty (see Luke 21:1–4). What counts is the heart. However, there are times when those who are considered to be poor give surprisingly large sums simply because their hearts have been unusually touched by the cause at hand. This is what Paul testified of concerning the Macedonian believers when they heard about the famine in Judea. He wrote,

> We want you to know, brothers, about the grace of God that has been given among the churches of Macedonia, for in a severe test of affliction, their abundance of joy and their extreme poverty have overflowed in a wealth of generosity on their part. For they gave according to their means, as I can testify, and beyond their means, of their own accord, begging us earnestly for the favor of taking part in the relief of the saints—and this, not as we expected, but they gave themselves first to the Lord and then by the will of God to us. (2 Cor. 8:1–5)

When God touches the hearts of his people, this is what will happen again and again. It is amazing!

Charging for Services

Another way in which the church should raise money is through providing services to people at a legitimate fee. This is one area that we do not normally think about as a form of raising money for the church but we often do it. For instance, we often charge fees for those who want to attend a camp or conference. This helps us to meet some of the costs of organizing such events. We also sell Christian books to those who want to read them. In that way, we are able to continue supplying books to believers to help them in their spiritual walk. A church can provide parking space to a neighboring school or any other institution at a small fee and use those funds toward its own maintenance costs. In Bible days, the apostle Paul joined Priscilla and Aquila in making tents and selling them in order for him to sustain his missionary work for a season (Acts 18:1–5). He was later able to say to the church elders in Ephesus, "I coveted no one's silver or gold or apparel. You yourselves know that these hands ministered to my necessities and to those who were with me" (Acts 20:33–34).

One outstanding historical example of this is William Carey (1761–1834). He is known as the father of modern missions. As a Baptist pastor in England, he looked after his family by making, selling, and repairing shoes. Later, he supplemented his income as a pastor by working part-time as a teacher. The reason he is called the father of modern missions is that, at a time when the church in Europe hardly ever thought of deliberately and purposefully sending missionaries, Carey convinced his fellow Baptist pastors in England to send him as a missionary to India. However, the churches were very poor and raised very little money to support him and his family out in the mission field. So, soon after he arrived in India, Carey found various forms of income to sustain himself there. Over the years, he even mastered many of the Indian languages so that he was employed as a professor of Indian languages at the Fort William College in India. He used his remuneration to support the work of missions that he was doing. William Carey even printed and sold newspapers and dictionaries. The funds raised in these activities were plowed back into the same literature work, which Carey used so effectively to spread the truth of Jesus Christ.

What ought to be discouraged is begging non-Christians to give money to the church. This has become very common especially when churches are raising money toward their building projects. Church members go marching through streets in the city with tins in their hands asking motorists to donate toward their capital campaign.

Whereas this brings in some money, you are not offering a service in exchange for the money you are receiving. Those who have no interest in the cause of Christ are made to feel as if they are doing the church of Christ a favor. Rather than asking for such favors, get your young people to go and wash those cars and get paid for the work done. That is a fair exchange for a service rendered.

The Need to Reform

If there is one area of church life that the African church lags behind in, it is that of faithfully and generously supporting the Lord's work through tithing, freewill offerings, and the provision of services. This is largely because the church in Africa is only one generation away from the pioneering days when international missionaries who were the church planters were supported from Western countries. The financial sustenance of the church and its ministries was not dependent on the financial giving of its members. Their missionary pastor survived—indeed, thrived—pretty well without their help. Thus, however much they were taught about financial stewardship, it became deep-seated in the African psyche that church giving did not really matter. Reversing this way of thinking has proved to be very difficult.

If the church in Africa is to mature and take its place in the missionary movement that will usher in the Lord's return, we must reverse this trend. Our church members must learn to be faithful, generous, and deliberate about financial matters in the context of the church. It is important that church leaders teach young Christians about financial giving so that they develop the habit of giving very early in their Christian lives. The young and the poor in the church should be helped to see that their "small offering" matters to the Lord as much as the abundance that those with "deep pockets" are able to give. In fact, often it is the small giving of the many members of the church that sustains the work of the Lord more than the large giving of the few big givers.

For those of us who believe in tithing, it is also important to remind the church members that the tithe is the Lord's—as God himself kept reminding the children of Israel. It is not theirs. They should learn to faithfully pass it on for the Lord's work as part of their worship.

Because it was a form of tax, you can well understand why the Lord asked the conscience-piercing question and proceeded to promise a great reward to faithful tithing:

> Will man rob God? Yet you are robbing me. But you say, "How have we robbed you?" In your tithes and contributions. You are cursed with a curse, for you are robbing me, the whole nation of you. Bring the full tithe into the storehouse, that there may be food in my house. And thereby put me to the test, says the LORD of hosts, if I will not open the windows of heaven for you and pour down for you a blessing until there is no more need. I will rebuke the devourer for you, so that it will not destroy the fruits of your soil, and your vine in the field shall not fail to bear, says the LORD of hosts. Then all nations will call you blessed, for you will be a land of delight, says the LORD of hosts. (Mal. 3:8–12)

While we ought to teach young believers to develop the habit of regular, faithful, and generous giving to the Lord's work, we must avoid talking about money all the time. This is a source of irritation in many churches today. Pastors are always cajoling their members to give financially to the church. Sermons are tailored to end with an appeal for money. This has reached such epic levels that many people have stopped going to church simply to avoid this annoyance. Churches have become like money-making machines. The kind of promises that God made to the Israelites in Malachi chapter 3 are repeated so much that what was meant to be a general promise to the people of God is made to sound as if it was a promise to each individual who tithes. Church members are told to "sow seeds" into the fertile ground of the ministry of a "man of God" and they will get a bumper harvest in return. God is treated like a banker who promises huge interest on any money that his people give to the church. As a result, some people have given a lot of money to the church or to the ministry of a preacher expecting "miracle money" in return. They have ended up driving their families into poverty because no such financial returns have come their way. It is the preacher and his church who have made themselves rich at the expense of the unwary Christian. This is certainly not the way the church should raise its money.

The financial giving of believers must be the result of their healthy walk with God. It must be the overflow of their spiritual lives. This is what I found upsetting from the story that I told at the start of this chapter. My uncle's church was interested only in his money, and they put together a system to make him feel guilty about meeting his financial obligations. Yet, they did next to nothing to help him spiritually. That is wrong.

Church leaders should prioritize the spiritual growth of their members, and their faithfulness and generosity will grow out of that. Church leaders must also account for the money that they collect. The view that a pastor is not accountable to his fellow church leaders and the rest of the church is foreign to the New Testament. When the apostle Paul was collecting money for the famine relief we mentioned earlier, he put in place checks and balances to ensure transparency, accountability, and integrity in the process. After the words we read in 1 Corinthians 16:1–2, Paul went on to write, "And when I arrive, I will send those whom you accredit by letter to carry your gift to Jerusalem. If it seems advisable that I should go also, they will accompany me" (1 Cor. 16:3–4). In Paul's second letter to the Corinthians he mentioned this matter again. With reference to a man designated to travel with him to Jerusalem, Paul wrote,

> And not only that, but he has been appointed by the churches to travel with us as we carry out this act of grace that is being ministered by us, for the glory of the Lord himself and to show our good will. We take this course so that no one should blame us about this generous gift that is being administered by us, for we aim at what is honorable not only in the Lord's sight but also in the sight of man. (2 Cor. 8:19–21)

I love that last phrase, "we aim at what is honorable not only in the Lord's sight but also in the sight of man. We should have basic accounting systems in the church that make it impossible for us to misappropriate the funds without being immediately found out. This raises the confidence of God's people that their money is going to the end for which they gave it.

A tendency that is becoming popular today, where church members give their weekly offering and it is taken by the pastor to his home, where he decides how the money should be used, is wrong. The reason often given for such a practice is the text in Acts that says that those who had "lands or houses sold them and brought the proceeds of what was sold and laid it at the apostles' feet, and it was distributed to each as any had need" (Acts 4:34–35). The main difference here was that the funds were brought to the apostles collectively. This provided for both the transparency and the checks and balances. The phenomenon that has become common today is that of the money being given to *one man,* who takes it home and gives it out or keeps it for himself as he sees fit. That is wrong.

Let me end on a more positive note by drawing our attention to the order of the money-raising methods. The emphasis should be on faithfulness in tithing, then generosity in freewill offerings, and lastly initiatives in giving out services at a fee. Generosity makes sense only when the minimum has already been given in the form of tithing. And, trying to raise extra funds through the offering of various services should be the "icing on the cake." It should never be the primary method of raising money for the church. If you turn the priority around, you can easily end up inadvertently turning the church into a den of robbers instead of a house of prayer (see Luke 19:45–46). So, in raising money for the church, let us ensure that we keep the spirituality of the church and its members as our first priority.

STUDY GUIDE FOR CHAPTER 10
How Should the Church Raise Its Money?

Summary
Every church needs money to run its internal and external affairs, and the primary source of that money will be its own members. Scripture focuses more on our heart attitudes toward money, yet it still guides the church on how to raise the money it needs, specifically through tithes and offerings. Churches can also lawfully use their facilities to generate income for their God-given mission. In all this, the spirituality of the church and its members should be of first priority.

Study Questions

1. Does the abuse of money that the author describes here show itself in your cultural context? Can you think of a specific example?

2. According to 2 Corinthians 9:7, our giving should be done willingly and cheerfully. Is this different from giving "when you feel like it"? How so?

   How do you think this principle of cheerful willingness relates to the principle of giving regularly to meet the regular needs of the church?

3. The story of the widow (Luke 21:1–4) is at times used to tell people to give all they have. How do you think this relates to 2 Corinthians 8:12, "according to what a person has, not according to what he does not have"?

4. The author shows that the teaching of "sowing seeds" treats God "like a banker who promises huge interests on any money that his people give to the church" (p. 147). What, in your experience, has been the harm caused by the teaching of "sowing seeds"? How can you show from the Bible that this teaching is false?

5. Many new churches in Africa are planted using funds from the West. In your experience, what are the advantages and disadvantages of this patronage?

11

Should Your Church Be Involved in Missions?

"Five, change goal; ten, finish ball." Any young man growing up in an African village or township will understand that statement. That is what often got us in trouble with our parents. It was the way we determined the half-way point in our football matches and how the game would end. The match was not time-bound. No one looked at their watches. Rather, it was determined by how many goals were scored. When one side scored five goals, it was halftime. And when one side scored ten goals, they won. If you were playing against a team that was not as good as yours, the game was over very quickly. However, when you played a team that was as good as yours, the match could go on for what felt like forever. It was brutal. The sun would have gone down, so that you could hardly see the ball, but you had to keep playing because the team that was behind on goals would shout, "We agreed that it is five, change goal; ten, finish ball. We are not yet there!" Finally, in utter desperation, the owner of the ball would suddenly pick it up and head home. That was how the game would end. Then you would suddenly come to the realization that, although you left school long ago, you had not done your homework, had not watered the domestic garden (which would often be a boy's share of the household chores), and were terribly late for dinner. Trouble!

It is this kind of time-less attitude that has prevented the church in Africa from getting involved in the work of missions. We have given ourselves a kind of "five, change goal; ten, finish ball" expectation, which keeps us away from doing what the head of the church has told us to do. I recall when our church elders first presented the need for our local church to get involved in church planting. It was an uphill battle because every excuse conceivable was brought up. We only had two elders. We did not have a church building. We did not have enough money. We were only a young church. If it were not for the resolve of my fellow elder and I, any hope of getting involved in missions would have ended that day. However, we kept arguing that the work of missions was our responsibility and that there was nowhere in the Bible where we read that we need more elders or a church building or a lot of money in order to get involved in missions. There was no Scriptural warrant that a young church was excused from participating in the work of missions. That was how we convinced a reluctant Kabwata Baptist Church to start what has now become a most glorious and fulfilling journey.

What Do We Mean by the Word "Missions"?

The word "missions" refers to what Jesus commanded his church to do before he left for heaven in what has come to be called the Great Commission. He said,

> All authority in heaven and on earth has been given to me. Go therefore and make disciples of all nations, baptizing them in the name of the Father and of the Son and of the Holy Spirit, teaching them to observe all that I have commanded you. And behold, I am with you always, to the end of the age. (Matt. 28:18–20; see also Mark 16:15–16; Luke 24:45–49; John 20:21)

It is the work of going to people who have not heard the gospel and sharing the gospel with them, with a hope that they repent of their sins and put their trust in the Lord Jesus Christ as their Savior. These converts are to be gathered into local churches and taught how to live in order to please God and worship him. Through this multiplication process, the gospel is to enter every people and language and tribe and nation before Jesus Christ returns to wrap up history. There are many details to the work of missions, but this is the most basic definition.

The fact that all the Gospel writers wrote about this Great Commission emphasizes that missions was a great priority to the Lord Jesus Christ before he returned to heaven. Any casual reading of the book of Acts soon shows that it was the one main agenda of the church from the day of Pentecost onwards. The apostles went around Asia and Europe preaching the gospel and planting churches. Although it was initially the persecution that broke out in Jerusalem that forced them to spread out, the preaching of the gospel and the planting of churches soon became their chief work. They were willing to sacrifice anything and even to die rather than cut short this work. They understood that this was a duty that the Lord Jesus Christ had left with them. Not to do this was to sin against him.

It is worth emphasizing that although evangelism is part of missions, the two are not the same thing. In this chapter, I want to emphasize the aspect of a church reaching out to another community or people group with a view to establishing the Christian faith there by the avenue of planting a viable local church. It may even involve the learning of a new language. Sometimes we call evangelistic outreach a "missions" outreach. As long as we end there, we are not doing what Jesus said must be done in the passages we listed earlier. In the mind of Christ, missions is about the church being his "witnesses in Jerusalem and in all Judea and Samaria, and to the end of the earth" (Acts 1:8). Notice, the extension from the local community to the furthest ends of the earth. This is the agenda that our churches should be involved in intentionally and perseveringly. It will not be easy.

It is also worth stating that acts of benevolence carried out in a poorer community may be a good way to express the love of God that he has put in our hearts as his people, but it is not the primary work that Jesus had in mind in the Great Commission. It is true that sin has brought suffering with it in this world. We ought to be concerned about all human suffering and should do all we can—if we have the means—to alleviate it. In the Gospels we see a number of times when Jesus was moved with pity and as a result healed the sick and fed the hungry and even raised the dead. His love in our hearts should cause us to do what we can as well. However, that is not the primary task of missions. Missions is about preaching or sharing the gospel with one aim, namely, to bring people to repentance and faith in the Lord Jesus Christ. Those who respond to the gospel in this way should be brought together into local churches, where they are to be instructed in the ways of God. We must never lose sight of this focus.

Having clarified that missions work is primarily about preaching the gospel and planting new churches in areas and communities that do not have such a witness, I must hurry to say that this often includes a lot of supportive workers who come alongside missionary pastors to lighten the work and to handle other areas of need. It may involve other missionaries who are majoring in language study, Bible translation work, and literature development and distribution. It may also involve individuals trained as teachers or medical workers who can teach in schools and work in clinics associated with the missions work. Some of the teaching may even go as far as tertiary education, depending on the situation in the field. In cases where there are high levels of poverty or deadly diseases that wipe out the parental age-group, there may be a need to open orphanages or feeding programs for children. In today's technological world, missions work may need those who can handle computers so that they develop internet-based outreach programs. In the end, as missions work grows, you will find that the primary missionary pastor has quite a huge team working alongside him, as was the case with the apostle Paul. Look at his team in Acts 20:4. All the individuals named in this verse were playing different supporting roles to Paul's ministry as the main church planter.

How Do Churches Participate in Missions?

In order to best appreciate how churches should be involved in missions today, we should go back to the New Testament and see how churches participated in the work of missions then. There are at least four ways in which they did so.

1. They sent out missionaries. A typical example of this in the book of Acts was when the leaders of the church in Antioch were praying together in a leadership meeting. We are told, "While they were worshiping the Lord and fasting, the Holy Spirit said, 'Set apart for me

Barnabas and Saul for the work to which I have called them.' Then after fasting and praying they laid their hands on them and sent them off" (Acts 13:2–3). What is amazing about this text is that Barnabas and Saul were the founding missionaries of this church. Yet, in obedience to the Holy Spirit, the church's leadership set them apart and sent them out to go and do further missions work. From this we see that it is the responsibility of church leaders to prayerfully identify those whom God is calling to this all-important work and to send them off. The calling goes with areas of giftedness. This may involve ensuring that they undergo appropriate training for the work at hand.

2. They prayed for missionaries. They prayed that God would provide more and more missionaries. This is what Jesus meant when he said, "The harvest is plentiful, but the laborers are few. Therefore pray earnestly to the Lord of the harvest to send out laborers into his harvest" (Luke 10:2). They also prayed for those who were currently serving in missions. The apostle Paul, who was almost always involved in planting churches, often pleaded with Christians in already established churches to pray for him. On one occasion he wrote,

> I appeal to you, brothers, by our Lord Jesus Christ and by the love of the Spirit, to strive together with me in your prayers to God on my behalf, that I may be delivered from the unbelievers in Judea, and that my service for Jerusalem may be acceptable to the saints, so that by God's will I may come to you with joy and be refreshed in your company. (Rom. 15:30–32)

3. They raised and sent support for missionaries. One example of this was the church in Philippi that supported Paul in his missions work in Europe. He was able to write back to them on one occasion saying,

> And you Philippians yourselves know that in the beginning of the gospel, when I left Macedonia, no church entered into partnership with me in giving and receiving, except you only. Even in Thessalonica you sent me help for my needs once and again. Not that I seek the gift, but I seek the fruit that increases to your credit. I have received full payment, and more. I am well supplied, having

received from Epaphroditus the gifts you sent, a fragrant offering, a sacrifice acceptable and pleasing to God. (Phil. 4:15–18)

This partly explains why, although the letter of Paul to the Philippians was written from prison, it is the most joyful of all his letters. The church in Philippi played a very important role in raising and sending his much-needed support, even when he was in prison.

4. They heard reports from missionaries. This was through reports that the missionaries sent to them or through visits by missionaries. You may not realize this, but the letters that we read in the New Testament by the apostle Paul served partly as avenues through which the churches would know what was happening in his life and ministry. Most of the information was not in the letters themselves but in the instructions he gave to those who delivered the letters. Hence, he wrote to the Colossians,

Tychicus will tell you all about my activities. He is a beloved brother and faithful minister and fellow servant in the Lord. I have sent him to you for this very purpose, that you may know how we are and that he may encourage your hearts, and with him Onesimus, our faithful and beloved brother, who is one of you. They will tell you of everything that has taken place here. (Col. 4:7–9)

That was how the churches participated in missions in the days of the early church. Two thousand years later, missions is still the responsibility of the church and of every Christian. We should either be sending and supporting missionaries with our prayers and finances or we should be in the mission field ourselves. There is no place for indifference. It is God's agenda across history, and we should be actively involved in it.

That was how the gospel came to Africa. Missionaries came from Europe and America to live and die on this continent to share the gospel with us. Many of them died soon after arrival because of malaria and other diseases. That did not stop the flow of missionaries to this continent. As news of the death of missionaries reached Europe and America, more and more of them came. They learned our many African languages, they taught us to read and write, they translated the Bible into our languages, and they preached the gospel and taught us the word of God. Churches were planted by them in many of our villages, and through them our forefathers were discipled into the Christian life. By the middle of the last century, the pioneer missionaries were handing over the churches to indigenous African leaders. It is now our turn to obey the Great Commission and get involved in missions.

Our churches today should be setting aside missionaries and sending them out to evangelize and plant churches in new communities and villages and towns and countries, especially in those places where the gospel has never been heard. The work of missions should be at the heart of our church prayer meetings. Expenses involved in the work of missions should take a prominent place in our church budgets. We should be challenging believers in our churches to seriously consider going out as missionaries or personally pledging to regularly pray for and consistently give financially to the work of missions.

Why Are Many Churches Not Involved in Missions?

Sadly, very few African churches are actively and intentionally involved in missions. I rarely ever hear of what we have seen happening in the New Testament churches taking place in our churches today. Why is that the case? There are a number of deep-seated, unconscious beliefs that prevent the church in Africa from playing its role in the Great Commission. Here are a few of them:

1. **We tend to think that we are at the end of the missions process.** The missionaries came from somewhere else to establish Christianity here in Africa. The work has been done. All we need to do now is to ensure that we are evangelizing our own people and our neighbors so that our churches can continue to grow in number. We do not realize that the baton has actually been passed on to us, and that we must now be the ones sending out missionaries farther afield, to regions that desperately need to hear the gospel.

2. **We think that missionaries are "white" people.** This is because almost all the pioneer missionaries whose pictures we have seen are Caucasians. William Carey, Mary Slessor, David Livingstone, Stanley Moffat, Olive Doke, and so on, were all Caucasians. Also, for many of

us, the only missionaries we know are non-Africans. When missionaries come to our churches to preach or to share with us what they are doing or to simply worship with us, they are invariably non-Africans. So, the concept that we can have "one of us" as a *bona fide* missionary is very strange. Yet, the only reason why it is strange is because we have not begun sending out missionaries ourselves. The sooner we start doing so the better, and we will soon get used to seeing missionaries of every skin color.

3. We think that missions is only for extraordinary people. They have heard an audible voice calling them to leave everything they are doing and go to the most dangerous and needy parts of the world to share the gospel. We assume that they are not like us. They have extraordinary courage and strength. The sooner we realize that missionaries are as ordinary as we are and suffer from the same anxieties that we all suffer from, the better it will be for the church in Africa. The call to the work of missions comes to ordinary Christians and ordinary struggling churches. It is the sense of obedience that overcomes the hurdles.

4. What is worse is that we think only people and churches with a lot of money should support missions work. We think that our church must be able to raise the full support of a missionary before we can get involved in missions work. Almost every church I know on our continent is struggling financially because of the poor economies of our countries. Paying pastors' salaries and meeting other demands of the church and its members proves very difficult for many of our churches. Therefore, the work of missions is treated as expendable. The excuse is that we cannot afford it. But we actually *can.* You see, the secret to the large number of missionaries that have come out to Africa from the West was not that they were supported by wealthy churches. No. Many poor Christians and poor churches gave the little they had, and it added up to such amounts that missionaries could have their needs met on the field. It was a collective effort. If each of our churches in Africa gave a little to the work of missions, you would be surprised how much this would come to in total and how much work could be accomplished in the furtherance of the gospel on the continent and farther afield. In missions, a little goes a long, long way!

5. **We assume that because our church has not sent out any missionary, therefore we should not bother about the work of missions.** It is only those churches who have missionary families laboring out there who should make the subject of missions part of their regular announcements, prayers, and giving. It is interesting that Paul could write to the church in Rome, saying,

> But now, since I no longer have any room for work in these regions, and since I have longed for many years to come to you, I hope to see you in passing as I go to Spain, and to be helped on my journey there by you, once I have enjoyed your company for a while. (Rom. 15:23–24)

Paul was not a missionary of the church in Rome, but he still assumed that they would assist him in his missions work as he headed on to Spain. Our churches should do the same. We should develop relationships with missionaries sent out from other churches and see how we can be a blessing to their work as well.

6. **Finally, we think our time has not yet come to get our hands dirty in the work of missions.** Remember, "five, change goal; ten, finish ball"? We think we are still in the first half. We have not yet scored the five goals. There is an assumption that something will happen that will trigger the right time for us to get involved in missions. Whatever it is has not yet happened. Therefore, we suffer no pangs of conscience about the fact that missions is totally missing from our church budgets and our prayers. We think that our time has not yet come. That was also the general belief in churches in Europe and America before the great missionary movement of the eighteenth and nineteenth centuries that is associated with William Carey and Adoniram Judson. The general belief was best encapsulated in the words spoken to the young William Carey by an older pastor when Carey was advocating for missions. Carey was told, "Young man, sit down; when God is pleased to convert the heathen world, he will do it without your help or mine." William Carey did not agree. He instead preached the most famous missionary sermon in human history, based on Isaiah 54:2–3 and titled, "Expect Great Things from God; Attempt Great Things for God." In that sermon, Carey pleaded with his fellow pastors that

it was time to get involved in foreign missions because it was God's perpetual demand upon the church. Finally, he achieved his goal and so was born the Baptist Missionary Society. It is now time for the church in Africa to rise to the challenge of missions, because God demands it of us.

Our Churches Should Be Involved in Missions

We must get rid of the "receiving" mentality in the African church and get into a "giving" one. When they see the tremendous growth of Christianity across our great continent, missiologists say that Africa is poised to be the next major sender of missionaries to the rest of the world. But if this is to happen, churches across the continent must stop thinking in the ways we have seen in the six points above. There must be a recognition that the Great Commission that the Lord Jesus Christ gave his disciples was not only for them but also for us today. We are not the end of a process but are right in the midst of it. The gospel that has come to us at such great cost to others must now be passed on to those who need to hear it in other regions—at great cost to us!

The second coming of Christ is tied up with the spread of the gospel. Jesus said, "And this gospel of the kingdom will be proclaimed throughout the whole world as a testimony to all nations, and then the end will come" (Matt. 24:14). Should your church be involved in the work of missions? The answer is a resounding "Yes!" If your church is to be truly pleasing to Christ, the head of the church, you should be doing everything you can in an intentional and persevering way to see to it that missionaries are being identified, commissioned, supported (through prayer and finances), and encouraged while they labor in the mission field. You should be working toward ensuring that gospel-centered churches, where God's word is faithfully preached, are being established in new places in God's world until all the nations are reached. Then Jesus will return and usher in the final consummation of all things.

STUDY GUIDE FOR CHAPTER 11
Should Your Church Be Involved in Missions?

Summary

"Missions" is about fulfilling the Great Commission. Preaching the gospel, making disciples, training leaders, and planting other churches was the one main agenda of churches from the beginning onward. Works of mercy can support the work of missions but are not themselves missions. Churches should send, pray for, support financially, and sustain fellowship with missionaries.

Study Questions

1. In what way is evangelism different from missions?

2. What reasons does the author give when he argues that acts of mercy (giving to the poor, digging wells, conducting medical camps, helping orphans, etc.) are not the same as the work of missions?

3. How can these works of mercy support the work of missions?

4. How many tribes or people groups around you or in your country are currently unreached with the good news of Jesus Christ? (Ask around, or where possible, do an internet search to answer this question.)

   What reasons does the author suggest for why we as Africans have been slow to take up the work of missions.

5. Does your local church have missionaries you support or partner with? How consistent is this support?

   What can you do as an individual or as a church to strengthen your support for missionaries?

12

Should Your Church Be Involved in Training Pastors?

If you drive past an average African village, you will often find that each homestead has an open shelter conspicuously placed somewhere in the middle of the homestead, and then there is another one that is often bigger in the middle of the village. To the uninitiated, this open shelter is simply a place where people can sit and shelter from the heat of the sunshine or from getting drenched by the rains. To those who have grown up in the village, this simple structure is the place where the culture of the family or the tribe is passed on from generation to generation. This is often through the heads of homes, and even more importantly it is through the village storyteller. In West Africa, these storytellers are called "griots." They tell stories interspaced with simple choruses that the hearers often join in to sing. The village storyteller is the depository of the history of the tribe and the village itself. He is gifted with a brilliant memory. He would have received many of these stories from a previous generation and knows that he is responsible to pass these stories on. So, on certain days, the village drums invite the younger generation to the central open shelter and they eagerly gather around this man to hear the next captivating and enchanting story from the past. Each story is craftily woven together and has some important lesson meant to instill cultural and moral values in the generation that will soon be the adults of the village. Important events that shaped the history of the tribe are recounted and thus passed on to the next generation. Leaders for the village and the tribe are nurtured as the storyteller teaches, influences, and inspires these young minds and hearts.

The task of passing on the knowledge and values of an older generation to a younger generation for the purpose of laying a strong foundation for generations to come is not only fundamental to our communities generally but is even more fundamental for the future of the church. This happens every week when the church gathers and listens to the preaching of God's word. In a special way, this is what happens when young men who sense the call to the preaching and pastoral ministry are gathered for instructions to prepare them for that work.

Precedents of Pastoral Training

There is nothing new about the training of preachers in Christianity. In the Old Testament, you had the schools of the prophets. These schools were instituted for the purpose of training young men for the prophetic office in Israel. Those who were being trained were often referred to as the "sons of the prophets" (2 Kings 2:3–15).

In the New Testament, we have the excellent example of our Lord Jesus Christ, who invested about three years of his life preparing twelve men for the work of ministry that they would carry out after he was gone. These were men carefully chosen by Jesus very early in his ministry. He taught them the truth of God and about God in contrast to the current notions in the days in which they lived. He counseled them with God-centered wisdom when they showed worldliness in the area of jostling for position and when they were overexcited about demons obeying their commands. He opened his life up to them so that they could see what true godliness looks like. He labored with them and sent them out in pairs to preach the gospel in nearby towns and villages. He was preparing them to take his message of salvation to the very ends of the earth. Just before he left earth for heaven, Jesus prayed to the Father, saying,

I glorified you on earth, having accomplished the work that you gave me to do. . . .

I have manifested your name to the people whom you gave me out of the world. . . . For I have given them the words that you gave me, and they have received them and have come to know in truth that I came from you; and they have believed that you sent me. (John 17:4, 6, 8)

Earlier, he had said to them, "No longer do I call you servants, for the servant does not know what his master is doing; but I have called you friends, for all that I have heard from my Father I have made known to you" (John 15:15). In other words, these men had matured significantly under his instructions. They were now ready to take up the task of leadership—and they would be even more ready once the Holy Spirit had come upon them on the day of Pentecost. This is what we do even today when we are involved in training pastors. We give them the full body of Christian truth and help them to mature spiritually at the same time.

In the New Testament, we also have the example of the apostles who took younger men under their wings not only to help them in ministry but also to mentor them and pass the baton of ministry to them. It is in this context that Paul wrote those famous words to Timothy: "What you have heard from me in the presence of many witnesses entrust to faithful men, who will be able to teach others also" (2 Tim. 2:2). In due season, Paul sent Timothy to pastor the church in Ephesus and left Titus in Crete to pastor the church there. These men had been trained and were now capable to handle these church situations.

This is one area in which our African churches are very weak. We all know the importance of having a well-trained pastor in charge of the regular ministry in the pulpit and also in spearheading the work of pastoral counseling in the church. We want a pastor who is knowledgeable in doctrine, who is skilled in handling the word of God and in managing the church, and who is disciplined and mature in character. When our pastor moves on to another church or retires, we are quick to start searching for a replacement. We know that the church needs a pastor. However, very few churches actually participate in the work of training the next generation of pastors. Our general attitude is that this is the work of Bible colleges. As to how the Bible colleges are being financially supported, we do not know, and we do not want to know. It is this attitude that needs to change if we are going to have good and strong churches in the years ahead. Our churches must invest in the training of pastors.

Identifying Potential Pastors

The first role that a church should play in the training of pastors is that of identifying individuals who manifest God's calling upon their lives for pastoral ministry. What often happens is that individuals who fail to do anything else in life will be the first to apply to Bible college because they see it as a place where they can easily get a job. Because many Bible colleges are trying to increase their enrollments, they tend to accept almost anyone who applies. They end up bringing individuals into the college who are not really serious about being pastors.

The local church is best placed to do the screening. This is because the leaders and members of the church know from experience how credible a person's testimony of salvation is. They also know whether the person has matured in the things of God and is serious about serving the Lord. They know whether he is a humble team player or is most likely simply wanting to fulfill his own personal dreams of greatness. They will know how teachable he is and how he has been progressing in his knowledge of the Bible. They will know how healthy his personal relationships are with members of the opposite sex.

The local church is also best placed to prepare a person for Bible college training. Unlike most professions, where a person can practice only when they have a licence, skill in pastoral ministry is something one can develop even before receiving formal training. The context of the church enables the person to exercise his gifts, and these gifts become evident to the people around them. It is in the local church that the leaders notice this and begin to ask whether the person senses a call to the preaching ministry. This helps him to confirm his own sense of call. His pastor may even suggest some books to read about pastoral ministry, so that by the time he is applying to go to college, he is fully aware of what to expect there. This is an important part of a church's involvement in the training of pastors—the screening and the preparation.

Having a Pastoral Internship Program

Another way in which your church can be involved in training pastors is to provide an internship program. In such a program, a younger man who is aspiring to become a pastor comes alongside a more seasoned pastor for an extended period of time, the same way that the apostles were with Jesus or the way in which Timothy was with the apostle Paul.

The pastoral interns get to see how a pastor uses his time during the week and how he prepares his sermons. They see how he relates to his wife and children. They see how he relates to church members and his fellow church leaders. They are also given some reading assignments that help them to appreciate the theory behind what they are seeing happening in the pastor's life and ministry. The pastor spends time with them discussing various issues arising from their observations and reading. He challenges their presuppositions so that they can think more clearly about their own beliefs and practices. They follow along as the pastor visits the sick and sorrowing. They also have the opportunity to sit in leadership meetings and see how these are handled in order to produce the well-oiled church programs that they often admire. They participate in the visitation program of the church, especially where it involves following up with first-time visitors to the church. As their levels of giftedness are appreciated, they may be asked to lead Bible studies, prayer meetings, and worship services. They may even be asked to preach!

Such exposure and experience is absolutely important for those who are training to be pastors. It enables them to have a three-dimensional view of church and pastoral life. In that way, they are not lost when they take up a pastoral charge. It is the same in the training of doctors. Despite the hands-on training that medical students receive, especially toward the end of their training, they are expected to work under a seasoned doctor for a while before they can get their license to practice on their own. This is because there are lives at stake. For instance, would you allow someone who has only trained to be a surgeon by studying from books to operate on you? Of course not! If you cannot get a very seasoned doctor to conduct an operation on you, you will at least want one who has done similar operations successfully under the watchful eye of a seasoned doctor. If this is so important for those who are merely looking after our bodies, how much more important should it be for those who are watching over our souls?

· In order to have such a pastoral internship program, a church will need to invest time and money. The pastoral interns will need to be accommodated and fed. They will need to be provided for in terms of a small stipend to enable them to meet other needs in their lives. Our churches should set aside some money for this purpose if we are going to see good and strong churches in years to come.

Supporting Bible Colleges

Another way in which your church can participate actively in raising up the next generation of church pastors is by financial giving toward one or more Bible colleges. These institutions are important because they give specialized training to those who will soon be regularly preaching and teaching in churches. The health of the churches will depend on this.

Some of the major courses taught in Bible college are:

1. Church history. This course explains what has happened in the history of the church from the time recorded in the Bible to the present day. The students learn about how some of the doctrines we cherish were forged in the furnace of controversy. They learn about some of the mistakes that previous church leaders made so that they do not make the same mistakes in their own ministries. They also learn how Christianity came to their area and the price that was paid by the pioneer missionaries. Like the village storyteller, church history lecturers ensure that students capture the values that propelled Christianity across history until today. As the saying goes, "If you do not know where you are coming from, you are not likely to know where you are going."

2. Christian doctrine. The big word for this is "systematic theology." This course explains the main teachings of Christianity. When a student has gone through this course he knows what the Bible teaches about God, about ourselves as human beings, about Jesus Christ as our Redeemer, about how one becomes a Christian, about the church, and about the future—including the second coming of Christ, and heaven and hell. Pastors well-schooled in true doctrine will be able to smell false doctrine when it is still a mile away!

3. Biblical studies. The main book from which any pastor gets his teaching is the Bible. It is vital that he knows how to handle this precious book. In Bible college, students are taught who wrote the various books of the Bible, how the whole of the Bible came together, what the various books of the Bible are by way of content, and how to teach from them in such a way that the original intent of the author is not violated. The students may also be taught Hebrew or Greek—the languages in which the Old and New Testaments were written. Too many people who are not trained to properly handle the Scriptures end up teaching error while they are quoting the Bible.

4. Practical theology. Finally, pastors need to be trained in the practical aspects of the work they are called to do. In this course, students are taught about how to prepare sermons, how to work with other leaders in the church, how to organize church life, how to conduct baptisms and the Lord's Supper, how to counsel those who are going through difficult situations, how to conduct weddings and funerals, and so on.

You can see from all this that Bible college training is important for men who are going to labor among us for any meaningful length of time in the work of pastoring. We must encourage those who want to take up this charge in the church to take time out of their busy schedules for such studies.

Running a Bible college is very expensive. Some of the lecturers will need to be in full-time employment in the college for it to be effective. The college will also need other administrative and auxiliary workers. Then there is the cost of hosting the students who are studying with the college. Often, the students do not have funds to meet the real cost of their training. Even churches that do not have their own students in a Bible college should consider being regular financial supporters of the college—simply because they want to see future pastors being trained with the kind of depth that Bible colleges are able to give. Who knows, perhaps one day one of those pastors will succeed their own current pastor!

There are two other ways in which churches should help in the training of pastors.

1. Pastors should participate in lecturing. Pastors have accumulated a lot of experience in ministry, and so they should be the primary instructors of those who want to join their ranks one day. Whereas some of the lecturers will be fully employed by the training colleges, some pastors who are currently in active pastoral ministry should supplement their efforts.

2. Churches should participate in governing these colleges. Strictly speaking, such colleges ought to be owned by the churches even if they report to the higher bodies of the church denominations. When churches, and especially church pastors, sit on the governing bodies of the colleges, it helps them to keep to their initial purpose and doctrinal position. Churches can function like anchors for these institutions, keeping them from going off on tangents.

The Lack of Finances

The main excuse in Africa as to why so many churches are not involved in the training of pastors is the lack of money—imagined or real. But have you noticed how we find money for things that we consider very important for us? Churches will find money to send young people to camp or to have a married couples' outing or to refurbish their church building but will claim that they have no money to invest in the training of pastors. This is because, in the minds of those who are in charge of the church's finances, the young people and married couples in the church and the church building itself are more important than preparing people whom they might not even know for future ministry. This mindset needs to change.

As we have noted, the church in Africa is enjoying strong and steady growth. Statisticians say that at the start of the twentieth century there were less than 9 million Christians on the continent of Africa. By the start of the twenty-first century, 100 years later, there were about 380 million Christians on this continent. Granted, most of these are nominal Christians, but still this is phenomenal growth. It is estimated that by the middle of this century, the number of professing Christians in Africa will be around 600–700 million. All these Christians will need to be in churches, under well-trained church leaders and pastors. If our churches are truly forward-looking, they ought to be preparing for this windfall by putting in time and money to train these future leaders. This is not the time to claim that we do not have money. Pastoral training is not an optional extra. It is an essential part of every church's ministry if it is to participate responsibly in the Great Commission that Jesus left with the church.

Much of the chaos and confusion that we have in the churches across the African continent today are due to ignorance. Again, statisticians tell us that 90 percent of the people who are currently functioning as pastors on this continent are untrained. They were simply set apart for the work of ministry. Thus, you have men who are ministering in churches but who do not know the history of the church, have not been taught Christian doctrine systematically, have not developed the skills of rightly handling the word of God, and who have not been schooled in doing ministry work in and through the church. Does it surprise you, then, that there is so much confusion in the churches? In no other profession would this be allowed. In fact, governments of African countries have noticed this confusion and are beginning to demand that pastors should be trained before they are allowed to take charge of churches. If this situation is going to be turned around, then the church in Africa will need to pay the price of time and money to support the work of training pastors.

STUDY GUIDE FOR CHAPTER 12
Should Your Church Be Involved in Training Pastors?

Summary
It is fundamental for the future of the church that it lay a strong foundation for generations to come. This happens through the regular, weekly preaching but should also be done by identifying potential pastors and focusing on them either through local programs or Bible college training. Churches should therefore be involved with Bible colleges to lead in raising the next generation of pastors.

Study Questions

1. How is the task of training modeled in the Old Testament and in Jesus's, Paul's, and Timothy's ministries in the New Testament?

2. Does your pastor have opportunities where he too can be taught and sharpened in his capacity? What can you do as a church to serve him in this way?

3. It is observed that when young men go abroad to train as pastors, most of them finish and choose to serve there, instead of returning to be pastors in Africa. Why do you think this is so? What can we do to encourage these highly skilled men to return to Africa and serve here?

4. Prior to reading this chapter, was it obvious to you that training future preachers and pastors is part of fulfilling the Great Commission? If not, why do you think we forget this?

5. What criteria do you use, or have you used in the past, to identify potential pastors?

Does this criteria line up with 1 Timothy 3?

Make some time to talk with some of the men in your church who aspire to be pastors. Find out what encouragement or frustrations they might have and how you can serve them.

13

What about Church Discipline?

One aspect of life on our continent that I really cherish is our sense of community. Although we all live in separate homes, there is a sense of belonging to one another that I do not readily see elsewhere. Neighbors not only know one another but they are also interested in the way their children behave. I recall when growing up that it was not uncommon for my parents to go and visit a home in the neighborhood primarily to report to their fellow parents in that home about some serious misdemeanor that they may have observed in their neighbor's child. In the same way, if an adult in the neighborhood saw me misbehaving, I knew that my parents would soon know about it and I would be in big trouble. This sense of community helped us a lot when we were growing up. We knew that we needed to be on our best behavior whether our parents were around or not. The entire community considered it their business to help our parents raise us up to be good citizens. I can well understand the saying that "it takes a village to raise a child."

What is true in society generally is also true in the life of the church, especially when it comes to the whole question of discipline. The whole church must be involved in watching over one another as the process of sanctification takes place in our individual lives. Let us admit it. The subject of discipline is not a popular one. It is as difficult as going into the hospital for surgery. You know that there will be a lot of pain. Yet it is a necessary part of life in this fallen world. We must never be tolerant of sin. When church members see fellow Christians in the church doing what is patently wrong and then look elsewhere as if it were none of their business, then that church will soon be in a downward tailspin as far as true godliness and spirituality is concerned. Church discipline is the responsibility of the whole church.

Formative Discipline

One reason we tend to be negatively disposed toward church discipline is that we always begin with its negative aspect. We think of restorative discipline as the only form of discipline. But there is also formative discipline. In fact, as we engage more and more in formative discipline, we will find that we will need less and less restorative discipline. It is the equivalent of what happens in the natural world. If you are disciplined in doing your physical exercises and maintaining a good diet, you will find that your visits to the doctors will be less frequent. But if you neglect this positive form of discipline, your body easily gives way to all kinds of diseases and your medical bills pile up.

Formative discipline refers to the kind of discipline that directly produces positive spiritual qualities in the lives of God's people. It refers to the teaching and training ministry of the church that nurtures the inner spiritual beings of believers. Part of this teaching and training comes through the regular instruction from God's word, and part of it happens as believers participate in the common life of the church. As members have fellowship with one another, they help one another as iron sharpens iron (Prov. 27:17). As they serve together in various departments and ministries of the church, they learn to be godly in their humility and their zeal for Christ.

Formative discipline produces good order in the church. This is because most church members get to know how they are supposed to live and what they are supposed to do in terms of the use of their gifts in the life of the church. This can be illustrated by a well-ordered home. When visitors come, the children in the home know that they are supposed to come out and greet them and then leave the parents space to talk with the visitors. All the children in the home know that they are supposed to keep their bedrooms tidy and they are supposed to participate in household chores. Even when they go visiting, they know how to behave when they are far away from home and they know when it is time to return home. The fact that they are doing so on a regular basis without constantly being asked to do so means that they are disciplined children.

A church should be like that. It should be well-ordered. The apostle Paul wrote to the Corinthians, "All things should be done decently and in order" (1 Cor. 14:40). And to the Colossians he wrote, "Though I am absent in body, yet I am with you in spirit, rejoicing to see your good order and the firmness of your faith in Christ" (Col. 2:5). Formative discipline produces a well-ordered church.

Restorative Discipline

That brings us to the form of discipline that we often dread to speak about. Restorative discipline, as the name suggests, is that form of discipline that seeks to restore Christians to true spiritual health. It can also be called corrective discipline. This is applied where there is stubborn sin. This needs further explanation, because there is the mistaken belief in the minds of many church leaders and ordinary church members that, whenever it is known that a Christian committed a sin, especially sexual or scandalous sin, he or she must be disciplined. That is a wrong view.

It is wrong because all of us are sinners and we sin every day. We commit sins of commission and sins of omission. We sin in thought, in word, and in deed. If we are to discipline Christians simply because we have come to know that they have sinned, then the whole church—including its eldership—would have to undergo restorative discipline all the time! If we say that it is only for some sins and not for others, we must still answer the question "Where do we draw the line?" Which passages of Scripture will we use to justify, for instance, disciplining a man who commits adultery and not the man who in anger beat up his wife? Why should we discipline a young person for stealing church money and not another one for telling lies?

Things get complicated when we start using church discipline the way judges in law courts mete out punishment. In court, the judge simply wants to know if the accused is guilty of an offense according to the law of the land. If he is guilty, the judge then punishes him according to what is written in the penal code. Whether the person is a first-time offender or a perpetual offender will only add to or subtract from the severity of the punishment. Church leaders do not primarily function as judges but as doctors. They do not think in terms of whether a person has sinned but rather whether the person is stubbornly continuing in unrepentant sin. The aim of the church leaders is to cure their member rather than to simply punish him for what he has done.

That is a very important distinction. If church leaders fail to make this distinction, their members will be afraid of coming to see them for counsel when they are struggling with sin due to their own weaknesses and failings. They will see their church leaders as policemen who will quickly drag them to the courtroom instead of seeing them as doctors who will wheel them into the operating theater only if there is need for surgery to remove the life-threating cancer. It is crucial that church members understand that we are all sinners who are in the process of being sanctified day by day. They should see that it is only when a Christian is refusing to yield to the plain teaching of Scripture about how he should live that Christ expects and demands that restorative discipline be used. In fact, restorative discipline is one of God's tools in sanctifying his people on earth.

Strictly speaking, there are only two forms of restorative discipline that are taught in the Bible:

1. Private or public admonition. This is the exhortation that is given to a member so that he repents of the sin that he wants to continue living in. It may be in the form of a rebuke or a warning. Paul wrote to Titus about both of these. He said, "Declare these things; exhort and rebuke with all authority. Let no one disregard you" (Titus 2:15). He also said, "As for a person who stirs up division, after warning him once and then twice, have nothing more to do with him, knowing that such a person is warped and sinful; he is self-condemned" (Titus 3:10–11).

Private admonition is often the final warning before excommunication takes place. It is that private rebuke or warning in which the stubborn sinner is exhorted about the dire consequences of the sinful lifestyle that he has chosen. Sometimes, it may also be done where someone's cycle of sin and repentance is now becoming like a circus. You want to believe that the person is again genuinely repentant but you realize that he needs some "shock treatment" so that he does not take the Lord's pardoning grace for granted. So, the church leaders admonish the member to instill the fear of the Lord in his heart.

Public rebuke is often given in instances where a member's sin has become public or has the potential of becoming public. So, although the member has confessed the sin to the church leaders and is evidently repentant, it is important that those who know or will know about the sin should be equally convinced that the church leaders have not turned their eyes the other way. Hence, the need for this public rebuke. An obvious example is where there has been sexual sin and a pregnancy has resulted. The pregnancy may not be evident yet, but it is only a matter of time. Although the individuals involved may be genuinely repentant, it is important for the church to know about this sin and for the individuals to be admonished publicly. That way, the church knows that the leaders do not condone this lifestyle. It also means that, when the pregnancy becomes visible, and outsiders begin to ask members about it, they can say, "Yes, we know about it. They confessed their sin to the church and our leaders admonished them about it." This preserves the honor of the church of Christ.

2. Excommunication. This is the exclusion of a member from the fellowship of believers in the church. It is the withdrawal of all the privileges that the person was enjoying as a church member. It certainly includes an exclusion from the Lord's Supper, though the person may still be welcome to attend worship services if he is not being disruptive. We see the apostle Paul exhorting the church in Corinth to use this form of discipline when he wrote,

> But now I am writing to you not to associate with anyone who bears the name of brother if he is guilty of sexual immorality or greed, or is an idolater, reviler, drunkard, or swindler—not even to eat with such a one. For what have I to do with judging outsiders? Is it not those inside the church whom you are to judge? God judges those outside. "Purge the evil person from among you." (1 Cor. 5:11–13)

We see from this text that excommunication is not for those who merely attend church but for those who claim to be Christians but are living a sinful life. Paul speaks about a person "who bears the name of brother." Later, he says that God will judge those who are outside the church; it is the business of those who are *in* the church to "purge the evil person" from within the church. This is particularly important to stress because of the popular belief that Christians should not judge. Since we are all sinners, why should we condemn other people and even ask them to leave the church? We do not discipline people because they have sinned; we discipline them because they are stubbornly continuing in sin. We want to help them start fighting sin in their lives, which is what every Christian should be doing, instead of embracing sin and nursing it in their hearts and lives.

We also see from 1 Corinthians 5:11–13 that it is those whose way of life can be described as being sinful who should be disciplined with excommunication. Paul does not say that everyone who has committed any sexual sin or who has stolen money or who has gotten drunk must be excommunicated. If he had said that, it would mean that as long as someone was guilty of any of those offenses they would need to be excommunicated. Rather, he uses words that suggest a way of life. He says, ". . . if he is guilty of sexual immorality or greed, or is an idolater, reviler, drunkard, or swindler. . . ." As you can see, it is sin as a lifestyle. It is such individuals who should be excommunicated. And the goal of excommunication is that such people will come to see that the head of the church, Jesus Christ, wants them to seek to be holy because he is holy (1 Pet. 1:14–16).

For how long should a person remain under excommunication? It should be only for as long as the person stubbornly continues in sin. Therefore, it is wrong to set a definite period. You cannot say that you are excommunicating someone for one year or two years. What if the person becomes repentant before that period is over? Or what if the person continues in stubborn sin well beyond that period? When the case of excommunication mentioned in 1 Corinthians 5:1–5 took place and the individual being disciplined truly repented of his misdeeds, the apostle Paul immediately asked the church in Corinth to restore that individual to the full rights of membership. He wrote,

Now if anyone has caused pain, he has caused it . . . to all of you. For such a one, this punishment by the majority is enough, so you should rather turn to forgive and comfort him, or he may be overwhelmed by excessive sorrow. So I beg you to reaffirm your love for him. . . . Anyone whom you forgive, I also forgive. Indeed, what I have forgiven, if I have forgiven anything, has been for your sake in the presence of Christ, so that we would not be outwitted by Satan; for we are not ignorant of his designs. (2 Cor. 2:5–8, 10–11)

What causes people to come to repentance when they are under excommunication is when their fellow church members withdraw their fellowship from them. A few may still want to associate with the excommunicated person. Others who are related to them either in the family or in the school or workplace will still have to continue associating with them, but purely for the purpose of that relationship and not by fraternizing with them. But they will notice that the majority of the members who were dear to them will have withdrawn their fellowship from them and they will feel the pain keenly. The message will be very clear to them. They cannot dance with the devil all week and expect to be welcomed among God's people on the Lord's Day, or on any other day for that matter. The people of God are grieved by this stubborn, sinful lifestyle. The excommunicated person must choose to either continue in sin and be denied fellowship with God's dear people, or deny the sin and be restored to fellowship. Excommunication keeps them at this T-junction. If they turn to the left, they remain outside the church. If they finally turn to the right, the church is willing to receive them back.

When a person has become genuinely repentant of a sinful way of life, they can be under a lot of grief. They realize that they not only have wronged specific individuals in the church but, above all, they have wronged the great head of the church, the Lord Jesus Christ. It is vital not to delay their restoration because they can be overwhelmed with this grief and Satan can use it to destroy them even further by causing them to become bitter toward God's people. The restoration should not only be an announcement of the lifting of excommunication. It should be real. Those who were once close to the individual should go the extra mile to reassure the person of their love and desire to restore fellowship. Paul wrote, "I beg you to reaffirm your love for him" (2 Cor. 2:8).

The Disciplinary Process

It is beyond the scope of this book to go into the details of the exact procedures that churches should go through in order to ensure that restorative discipline takes place. Depending on whether your form of church government is Congregational, Presbyterian, or Episcopal, you will find that you will have different ways of processing church discipline. Some forms of church government allow a greater involvement of church members in arriving at the discipline to be meted out, while others involve only elders.

Jesus said,

> If your brother sins against you, go and tell him his fault, between you and him alone. If he listens to you, you have gained your brother. But if he does not listen, take one or two others along with you, that every charge may be established by the evidence of two or three witnesses. If he refuses to listen to them, tell it to the church. And if he refuses to listen even to the church, let him be to you as a Gentile and a tax collector. (Matt. 18:15–17)

There seem to be three stages of handling a disciplinary matter in this text. The first stage is private because it is a personal offense. You confront an offending brother and, if he accepts his fault and apologizes for it, you should pardon him and close the matter. If he does not accept his fault, you take the matter to the second stage and bring in one or two others to listen. This is semiprivate and it brings objectivity. The matter is being established by two or three witnesses. If the offender is persuaded by these witnesses and apologizes, then the matter ends there. If he still refuses and you are still convinced that he was wrong and needs to repent of this matter, Jesus says, "Tell it to the church." This is the third stage. It is usually at this point that churches that equally respect the authority of the Bible do not totally agree. For some, "the church" means all the members of the church, who will then take up the matter. For others, it means the church as an institution, and so you tell it to the leaders of the church, who will then take up the matter. Finally, when this last stage is done and the person is still stubbornly hanging on to their sin and showing a lack of repentance, then "the church" treats that person with the disgust that the Jews had for Gentiles and tax collectors.

Although we will never fully agree on the mechanics and process because of our different forms of church government, we must still see that it is our responsibility to ensure that those who are hanging on to sin are disciplined (whether through admonition or excommunication) in order to seek their restoration to spiritual wholeness. In the book of Revelation, the Lord Jesus Christ warned the churches that he would punish them himself if they did not discipline those in their midst who were living in stubborn sin. Often this immediate punishment by the Lord Jesus involved temporal judgments and even death. For instance, we read,

> But I have this against you, that you tolerate that woman Jezebel, who calls herself a prophetess and is teaching and seducing my servants to practice sexual immorality and to eat food sacrificed to idols. I gave her time to repent, but she refuses to repent of her sexual immorality. Behold, I will throw her onto a sickbed, and those who commit adultery with her I will throw into great tribulation, unless they repent of her works, and I will strike her children dead. And all the churches will know that I am he who searches mind and heart, and I will give to each of you according to your works. (Rev. 2:20–23)

In the light of this sobering account, we need to see that church discipline is an act of love and not an act of hatred. When we exercise church discipline, we are seeking to prevent God's judgment upon his people. Sadly, however, many people see any such discipline as an act of hatred. They tend to sympathize with the stubborn sinner. This is often seen when a person under discipline by one church simply moves to another church. The leaders of the new church tend to hear only the offender's side of the story. In sheltering him, they feel as if they are expressing love toward him over and against the hatred he experienced in his previous church. In the end, the sin in that person continues to grow like a cancer until he is destroyed. That is not love.

Our greatest hindrance to church discipline in the African context is our sense of *ubuntu*. We have very strong social, tribal, family, and cultural ties, which spill over into the church. When church leaders present a case of stubborn sin, we lose sight of all that has been mentioned above and our strongest emotion is that we must express solidarity with that person. In the end, we undermine church discipline because we secretly continue to have fellowship with him . . . until God's judgment falls on him or on the rest of the church. We need to be biblical and ensure that both formative and restorative discipline are exercised in the church so that we can have healthy churches to the glory of God.

STUDY GUIDE FOR CHAPTER 13
What about Church Discipline?

Summary

Church discipline is both formative and restorative. Formative discipline is the teaching, training, and mutual discipleship ministry of the church that matures the Christian. In restorative or corrective discipline, the church seeks to restore Christians who stray from the faith. When members cooperate with the elders in a biblically based process of excommunication, they show love for the individual, the church, and Christ.

Study Questions

1. In your own words, where is the difference between using church discipline for punishment and using it for restoration?

2. What are the two forms of corrective/restorative discipline that the Bible teaches?

   From your experience with churches, how have you seen these two forms of corrective discipline done?

3. The author mentions the questions that "outsiders begin to ask members about" (p. 181). How would you respond to the view that we should not care what outsiders think as long we know what the truth is?

4. How can our communal nature as Africans tempt us to disregard the importance and application of restorative discipline?

   In view of God's judgment, is this truly loving the sinning party?

5. How easy do you think other Christians would find it to approach you if you were walking in sin? What can you do to improve this?

14

Does It Matter What Your Church Believes?

You have probably heard a variant of this story, which is typical of life on our continent. A worker goes to his employer to ask for time off from work. Let us imagine that this man's name is Chanda. Chanda says that his father has died. He is given leave to go and mourn his father. A year later, he again applies for compassionate leave. Reason? His father has died. The leave is granted. A few months later, Chanda walks into his manager's office looking very sad. His manager asks what has happened. He says, "I am devastated. I got a call from my sister telling me that my father has died in a car accident." By this time, the manager, who is of European descent, is thinking that Chanda is playing games and thinks he has a bad memory. He finally asks with exasperation, "Chanda, how many fathers have you got? Last year your father died. Six months ago, again your father died. Here you are again telling me that your father has died. If it were not for the fact that you look so miserable, I would have chased you out of my office thinking you were cheating me. Tell me, how many fathers have you got?" Chanda, still looking miserable, replies, "I had five, sir. Three have now died. It is very sad. I am only remaining with two."

The story may sound funny, but the scene represents reality. In many African tribes, your father's brothers are also your fathers, while your father's sisters are your aunts. Similarly, your mother's sisters are also your mothers, while your mother's brothers are your uncles. It also follows that your father's brothers' children and your mother's sisters' children are your brothers and sisters. They are not your cousins. It is your father's sisters' children and your mother's brothers' children who are your cousins. This culture is so deeply ingrained in the mind that it is even deep-seated in the emotions. Chanda was truly affected at the death of what to the Western mind would have been an uncle. It was as if his actual biological father had died. In short, what you believe really affects the way you live.

It is the same in the church and in the Christian life. What you believe determines how you live. This is why doctrine matters. Since I will be using the word "doctrine" a lot in this chapter, let me explain what it means. Doctrine refers to a set of beliefs that are held by a group of people. In this case, we are talking about a set of beliefs that are held by the church. The beliefs are clear enough to be taught by or to them. Doctrine can also refer to one of those beliefs, e.g., the doctrine of justification by faith. Again, it is sufficiently clear that it can be taught to people. Churches are historically understood to be based on particular teachings, which are purported to be from the Bible. These teachings are called doctrines. Those who belong to those churches will be understood to believe those teachings.

Doctrine is important because if a Christian believes error, he will live an erroneous life. This is even worse for a church because it comprises many people. When a church believes in erroneous teaching, its practice will also be wrong. By its wrong practice it will dishonor the Lord. This logical deduction is obvious. Yet there is a very strong resistance to doctrinal instruction today. Many people feel as if, when you teach Christians doctrine, you cause them to be divisive and unloving. There is a strong push away from that. What is wrong is not Christian doctrine but wrong doctrine and wrong practice.

Let me illustrate the importance of correct doctrine this way. On one occasion, while Jesus was with his disciples, he told them, "They will put you out of the synagogues. Indeed, the hour is coming when whoever kills you will think he is offering service to God"

(John 16:2). The worst enemies of the Christian church have often been religious people. In the early days of the church, it was the Jews who failed to see that, with the coming of Christ, the old covenant was giving way to a new covenant. Therefore, the church was not an enemy of God; it was the fulfillment of his promises to the nation of Israel. If the Jewish leaders had understood this, they would have welcomed the birth of the Christian church. However, they did not. They wrongly believed that the church was an enemy of God, and as a result they went about persecuting Christians. Those who professed faith in Christ were booted out of the synagogues. Some of them were even killed, as was the case with Stephen in Acts 7. In fact, the apostle Paul, who earlier had been a persecutor of the church and then later became one of its foremost champions, wrote to the Corinthians, saying, "We impart a secret and hidden wisdom of God, which God decreed before the ages for our glory. None of the rulers of this age understood this, for if they had, they would not have crucified the Lord of glory" (1 Cor. 2:7–8). The reason the rulers crucified Christ was because they had the wrong belief. So, what you believe determines how you live. This is why what Christians believe and what churches believe matters. It determines how they will live.

A Pillar and Foundation of the Truth

An important God-given duty of the church is that of preserving and propagating the truth. Your church can fulfill this responsibility only if the members and leaders of the church know what that truth is. We saw in chapter 2 that the apostle Paul wrote to Timothy, who was functioning as a young pastor, "I hope to come to you soon, but I am writing these things to you so that, if I delay, you may know how one ought to behave in the household of God, which is the church of the living God, a pillar and buttress of the truth" (1 Tim. 3:14–15). In that chapter we were seeing from these verses how Timothy was not to use his own pragmatic reasoning on how the church should run, because he was merely a steward of it. The church belonged to God. He was to organize it according to the mind of God. We also saw this text coming in very handy in chapter 9 when we considered what should happen during our worship services. We needed to be reminded of it because of our tendency to introduce into our worship services anything that people seem to enjoy. Again, the church belongs to God, and he wants us to organize it according to his mind.

What I did not emphasize in those two chapters was the last part of Paul's description of the church, as "a pillar and buttress of the truth." What did Paul mean by this? He was using words from the world of concrete buildings to reinforce an important truth about the role of the church in the world. A pillar is a concrete column that holds up the roof of a building. A buttress is anything that supports, strengthens, or stabilizes a structure. The picture emerging is that the church holds up the truth for all people to hear it amid the howling winds of error in the world. The truth remains constant and unshakable when the church faithfully discharges its duty. It is a pillar and buttress of the truth.

Paul was concerned that Timothy should organize the church in such a way that it is not hindered in fulfilling this mandate. The issue we are dealing with in this chapter is even more fundamental than that. We are saying that, if the church does not know what the truth is, how can it uphold it in a world that is full of error? It is of utmost importance that church leaders know the truth and pass it on to the rest of the members, especially to those who are new converts. This is why Paul insisted to Titus that one of the qualifications for church elders was that they must know the truth about Jesus Christ. He wrote about an elder that "he must hold firm to the trustworthy word as taught, so that he may be able to give instruction in sound doctrine and also to rebuke those who contradict it" (Titus 1:9). Elders should be men who are grounded in the truth.

Notice the phrase "the trustworthy word as taught." This suggests that there should be no novel teaching in the church. Our role is that of being faithful stewards of God's revealed truth. Your church should not come up with fanciful teachings in line with the new age in which you live. Neither should it try to blend its teachings with cultural teachings, such as African traditional religions, in order to be more acceptable to the people. It should propagate only "the trustworthy word as taught." Yes, as taught throughout the Scriptures.

Sanctification Is through the Truth

The spiritual lives of believers depend on their knowledge of the truth. We have already stated that erroneous belief can only lead to erroneous living, because we live what we believe. Here I want to go further and state that the Holy Spirit uses the truth of Scripture in order to make believers more and more like the Lord Jesus Christ in character, to the glory of God the Father. Jesus prayed to the Father, saying, "Sanctify them in the truth; your word is truth" (John 17:17). The truth is the instrument that God uses to make his people holy.

Sadly, there is a prevalent view today that emotionalism is what will draw people closer to God. Many individuals think that some emotional high, perhaps as a result of an emotionally charged sermon or due to the stirring music played during worship, is what will take God's people to the next level of spirituality. For a very limited time, such tactics will make people feel a greater emotional attachment to Christianity, but that never lasts. Trials and temptations soon cause such people to turn away from their obedience to Christ. It is those who are deeply grounded in the truths of the gospel who tend to overcome these onslaughts upon the soul and go on to greater heights of godliness. The mind must be filled with truth in order for the heart to truly embrace Christ despite the trials and temptations of life. This is why it matters what your church believes. If it believes and teaches the truth concerning Christ, then the lives of its members will soon show maturity that truly glorifies God.

Paul also said this to the Thessalonians: "But we ought always to give thanks to God for you, brothers beloved by the Lord, because God chose you as the firstfruits to be saved, through sanctification by the Spirit and belief in the truth" (2 Thess. 2:13). Belief in the truth is an essential component of our salvation and sanctification. The church should jealously guard the truth and ensure it is taught regularly so that more and more people can be saved and sanctified. God's electing grace is confirmed in individuals who are plucked out from the world as the truth of God grips their hearts. It is the chief means of calling them out of the world and keeping them unstained by the world. When a church loses the truth and peddles error, especially in soul-damning heresies, it no longer produces the fruit of salvation and sanctification. That is a tragedy.

Paul also stated this truth to the Ephesians. Referring to the ascended Lord Jesus Christ, he wrote,

> And he gave the apostles, the prophets, the evangelists, the shepherds and teachers, to equip the saints for the work of ministry, for building up the body of Christ, until we all attain to the unity of the faith and of the knowledge of the Son of God, to mature manhood, to the measure of the stature of the fullness of Christ, so that we may no longer be children, tossed to and fro by the waves and carried about by every wind of doctrine, by human cunning, by craftiness in deceitful schemes. (Eph. 4:11–14)

Without the teaching of the truth in the church, believers will remain vulnerable to false teachers. When the truth is taught by teachers whom Jesus has gifted to the church, the believers become more united, grow in spiritual maturity, and labor together to serve Christ in the world. That is how church was meant to be. That is what Jesus, the head of the church, wants to see.

Some Important Church Doctrines

In the light of the foregoing, it makes sense that the evil one should be opposed to the church of Jesus Christ being clear about its beliefs. This is why it is important for every church to have a well-defined, biblically based doctrinal statement. The leaders of the church should from time to time draw the attention of the members to that statement. Churches that are grounded in the truth will do great exploits for God in this world, a world that is full of error and sin. What are the great truths that your church should believe in and teach? Some of them are the following (I will be very brief):

The Bible. It comprises sixty-six books and is the only inspired word of God. It has no errors. Although it does not address every detail about life, all that we need to know about God's ways and the way to be reconciled to him through Jesus Christ is clearly addressed in it. It is a sufficient book. You do not need any extra revelations to deal with situations in your life. All you need to do is to study the

Bible. It should be the final authority in settling any questions related to God, his will for our lives, and how the church is to be governed.

God. There is only one eternal God, who is the creator and ruler of the entire universe. Everything exists for his glory. God is infinite in all his characteristics and he subsists in three persons—the Father, the Son, and the Holy Spirit. He is all-powerful and all-knowing. He is a God of holiness, truth, love, and justice. These are essential aspects of his being. He has revealed himself in creation, through his prophets across history, and finally through his Son, the Lord Jesus Christ. This God alone is to be worshiped, both now and forever.

Human beings. When God made the universe at the beginning of time, he also created human beings as the apex of his creation. They are the only creatures that he made in his own image—both male and female. Although they were made upright, they sinned and incurred the punishment that God had warned them about, which is death. They lost their innocence and their fellowship with God. They also became corrupted in their minds, hearts, and wills. This corruption has been passed on to all generations to the present day. We are all born sinners and deserving of God's wrath, both in this life and in eternity in hell fire.

Salvation. God is merciful, loving, and gracious. Although he owes us nothing, he has provided a Savior from sin in the person of his own Son, Jesus Christ. The Bible summarizes this in those well-known words, "For God so loved the world, that he gave his only Son, that whoever believes in him should not perish but have eternal life" (John 3:16). Jesus was born sinless and lived a perfectly righteous life. In this way, he provided the gift of righteousness for us. He then willingly died on the cross as our substitute. In this way, God could remain righteous while at the same time freely welcoming sinners into his heaven. The only condition he gives is that of repentance from sin and trust in his Son, Jesus Christ. Those who repent and believe are declared righteous by God and become his children. The Holy Spirit who brings about the work of salvation in the human soul also takes residence in the hearts of those who are converted and begins a process of sanctification (i.e., growth in holiness). This reaches perfection when they arrive in heaven. This is the heart of the Christian message. It is the gospel that must be proclaimed to the ends of the earth.

The church. (This doctrine is the subject of this whole book, so I will be very brief.) All those who repent and believe in the Lord Jesus Christ should be baptized and should become members of a local church, where they should worship and actively serve together with other believers. The local church is an expression of the one universal body of Christ that comprises true believers everywhere on earth, as well as those who have already gone to heaven. Since church leaders are not all-knowing, they will inadvertently welcome into membership individuals who may not be converted, and some true believers will backslide. As a result of this, churches on earth will never be perfect (e.g., the churches of Asia Minor in Revelation 2 and 3). They will, however, strive toward this perfection through regular instruction from God's word and through church discipline.

There are other areas of belief where churches will continue to differ. Some of these areas of difference involve deep theological subjects such as election and predestination. Then there will be issues having to do with how much of the Old Testament we are expected to practice in the New Testament era. There will also be thorny matters such as in what circumstances Christians can legitimately divorce and remarry. We can also throw in church-related questions like modes of baptism and how open the Lord's Supper should be. Other topics will have to do with the future, especially the thousand-year reign of Christ. What matters is that each church should work toward having a position on these matters as a fruit of their study of the Bible. They should also recognize that these are secondary matters over which they should not break fellowship with other believers who see things differently.

Your Church Should Be a School of Doctrine

Since it matters what your church believes, you must ensure that your church is intentionally turned into a school of Christian doctrine. That was the first observable trait of the early church. "They devoted themselves to the apostles' teaching" (Acts 2:42). This was because the apostles knew that these new believers would live what they believed. They wanted them to believe the truth. We should emulate them. The sermons that are preached regularly in the life of our churches should not only be devotionally inspiring, helping people to live energetically for Christ. They should also be doctrinally rich, bringing out the truths of Scripture to help Christians grow in their understanding of God and his ways. Our churches should also hold Bible studies and seminars where Christian doctrine is taught with greater depth and where believers have the opportunity to ask and to receive answers to their pertinent questions. Devotional sermons alone are like trying to cook a meal on a fire where the firewood consists of nothing but twigs. They burn quickly and make a lot of noise, but you will soon discover that your meal is not well cooked. Get logs instead. They take longer to catch the fire, but they burn longer too and result in a well-cooked meal. As we have seen, doctrinally rich teachings are what will produce strong Christians who will in turn lead their families and communities into godly living.

Once upon a time, it was normal to refer to churches by their doctrinal distinctives. They were either Roman Catholic, Presbyterian, Baptist, or Methodist churches. They also had church constitutions with fairly well-articulated doctrinal statements, including supporting Bible verses. That is slowly becoming the exception to the rule. The tendency today is to build churches around personalities, with the charismatic personality of the leader being the primary attraction to the people. If you were to ask the members of such churches what their church believed, they would most likely not know how to answer that question. What matters to them is that their pastor is a good preacher who prays for them when they are sick. This explains why our churches are having such little impact on our societies.

Another tendency today, especially here in Africa, is that of basing church distinctives on tribes. Even when these churches operate in the country's official language (like English or French) and are situated in big cities where there are people from many tribes, you still find that the people in that church are almost all from the same tribe. What matters in the minds of the people is not what the church believes but what tribe the people belong to. That is wrong, because the church ought to comprise people "from every tribe and language and people and nation" (Rev. 5:9). At the most, what ought to separate us should be what the church believes. In other words, it should be Christian doctrine.

One tragic consequence of our failure to emphasize doctrinal instruction has been the proliferation of "Christian" cults on the continent of Africa. Almost every day a new "church" starts and soon draws large crowds. Usually, these are not new converts. They are church members who are abandoning their old churches for new ones. The vulnerability of the people is soon exploited by wolves in sheep's clothing. They are financially defrauded and sexually abused. Despite the fact that their leaders are doing what is patently wrong, they still give them the honor that should be given only to Jesus Christ. Some of the victims are real Christians who had not learned to discern truth from error because they lived on a perennial diet of devotional sermons. The only way to reverse this trend is when church leaders start taking seriously the need to turn their churches into schools of sound Christian doctrine.

STUDY GUIDE FOR CHAPTER 14
Does It Matter What Your Church Believes?

Summary

A church's doctrine (the set of beliefs it holds) determines what it practices and even how the members will be taught to live. The Scriptures contain a trustworthy system of beliefs that has been taught and passed down, that churches and their elders must know and teach. These truths, and not emotionalism, are God's instrument to call his people and make them holy. Churches should therefore have doctrinally instructive preaching and so be built on truth, not on their pastors or tribes.

Study Questions

1. The author makes reference to the charge that Christian doctrine causes people to be divisive and unloving (p. 190). Is it possible for Christians to have no doctrine? Why or why not?

2. How do you think it benefits a congregation to have their doctrines formalized in a "statement of faith"?

3. What does it mean that the church is a "pillar and buttress of the truth" (1 Tim. 3:15)?

4. Does your church have a defined statement or confession of the truth it stands for and preaches?

If yes, is the regular preaching in theological agreement with this statement?

5. Given our tribal rules in Africa, what should a Christian do when biblical doctrines oppose the rules of our tribes? If we took a stand against the tribal rules, would we be ready to bear the burden of persecution that might result?

15

How Should Your Church Grow Spiritually?

Chola was perplexed. He said that he was thinking of writing a blog post about the subject of his perplexity. The theme was that in Africa you do not need to achieve anything to gain people's respect; you simply need to remain alive long enough to be among the oldest in your family or community. Why was this such an important matter for Chola, and so important that he wanted to write about it? He told me of an uncle in his family who was a complete failure in life. He was jobless and homeless. His attempt at marriage had failed. His wife had divorced him. He was addicted to alcohol and gambling. Everyone in the family knew this. Yet, because he was the oldest surviving uncle, he was often given a place of honor and even asked to give speeches at family functions. Chola said that there were a number of admirable uncles and aunts in the family who had proven themselves in maturity and wisdom. Yet, when this good-for-nothing uncle was around, they would be left in the shadows while this man got center stage. No wonder Chola was incensed about this. To borrow his words again: In Africa you do not need to achieve anything to gain people's respect; you simply need to remain alive long enough!

I often find the same attitude in church circles. Church pastors gain the respect of society simply because they have been around long enough. Their churches can be well-known for sexual indignities and financial scandals. Yet, once there is a public event and they show up, everyone else must bend backwards like reeds on a windy day and give them center stage. The outrage that Chola felt in the family circle ought to be felt in church circles too. It is not enough to simply occupy space in church leadership; we must help the church to grow into God-glorifying spiritual maturity. That was why Jesus gave teaching gifts to his church. It was so that God's people could

> . . . attain to the unity of the faith and of the knowledge of the Son of God, to mature manhood, to the measure of the stature of the fullness of Christ, so that we may no longer be children, tossed to and fro by the waves and carried about by every wind of doctrine, by human cunning, by craftiness in deceitful schemes. (Eph. 4:13–14)

If you have not heard the phrase "The church in Africa is a mile wide but only an inch deep," then welcome to Planet Earth. I hear it everywhere I go, both on the continent of Africa and in other parts of the world. It is a well-known fact, albeit a painful one. On one hand, it celebrates how widely Christianity has spread across Africa. On the other hand, it bemoans the lack of spiritual depth in the African church. The two stand in stark contrast. In terms of numbers, we are seeing steady growth. In terms of maturity, however, we still lack the depth that can enable us to impact the continent for good. That is the burden that is being addressed in this chapter.

Strictly speaking, this chapter should have been titled, "Should you be concerned about your church growing in spiritual maturity?" This is because, if we can get that concern right, we would have solved our biggest challenge. Very few church leaders are concerned about church growth in terms of growth in spirituality. When the matter of church growth is being addressed in church leaders' meetings, it is often in terms of quantitative growth. It is as though God is interested only in how many people there are in his church. Nothing can be further from the truth. God seeks to be glorified by the way in which his people live. Sadly, what the apostle Paul said about the Jews is often true about the church in Africa today, namely that, "The name of God is blasphemed among the Gentiles because of you"

(Rom. 2:24). Every church leader ought to be concerned about the kind of lives church members live in the church, in the home, and in society at large.

In a sense, the subject of Christian maturity has already been addressed in this book, so this chapter may be seen as unnecessary. If all Christians can understand and practice what has been taught in the previous chapters, it would catapult the spirituality of the church to another level. For instance, if church members understood what the church really is, what it means to have Christ as the head of the church, and what the primary task of the church is in the world, that in itself would transform the church completely. Add to this the impact that would take place across the continent if professing Christians really understood the glorious gospel of Christ, became members of the church only upon responding to the true gospel, and lived gospel-saturated lives of service in the church. There is no doubt that this would result in the kind of revival never seen before anywhere in the world. All these subjects have been covered in previous chapters. Understanding them and applying them would certainly give us a mature and fruitful church that is pleasing in the eyes of God.

Yet this chapter is not a mere repetition of what has been covered in the previous chapters but a crystalizing of the necessity of spiritual growth. It is also a stating of the main activities that should be put in place in the life of the church to secure this growth. If you can be persuaded as a pastor or an elder that the growth of your people in holiness is your primary goal as a church leader, and if you can be persuaded to ensure that the biblical means for their growth are conspicuously in place in your church, then this chapter will have accomplished its purpose.

The Necessity of Spiritual Growth

A brief study of the New Testament shows that both the Lord Jesus Christ and the apostles were concerned about the spiritual growth of those who became followers of Christ. It was not enough that individuals made a profession of faith and were added to the number of disciples. They wanted those individuals to press on toward spiritual maturity.

Soon after Jesus began his public ministry, he preached the famous Sermon on the Mount. That sermon argued for spiritual growth in ways that should have knocked all the listeners out of their sandals. He said, "For I tell you, unless your righteousness exceeds that of the scribes and Pharisees, you will never enter the kingdom of heaven" (Matt. 5:20). The scribes and Pharisees were known for their outward righteousness. They were seen as righteousness itself walking on two feet. So, to be told that only those who exceeded their righteousness would be welcomed in heaven must have been quite a blow to the hearers. What did Jesus mean? You have only to read the rest of Matthew chapters 5 and 6 to realize that when Jesus looked at the righteousness of the Pharisees, he largely saw an outward and hypocritical righteousness. It was not real holiness. It was like a ring made of gold plating over a piece of aluminum compared to the whole ring being made of gold. So, in chapters 5 and 6 of Matthew's Gospel, Jesus spoke about the necessity of inner godliness by giving examples of the need to control anger and lust, the permanence of marriage, integrity with vows, and not seeking revenge but instead loving one's enemies. He ended chapter 5 by saying, "You therefore must be perfect, as your heavenly Father is perfect" (Matt. 5:48).

In chapter 6, Jesus went further to condemn the ostentation of the Pharisees in terms of their almsgiving, their prayers, and their fasting. He appealed for true godliness that does not seek the praises of men but the approbation of God. Over and over again he said, "And your Father who sees in secret will reward you" (Matt. 6:4, 6, 18). It is a truly godly soul who will live for the eye of God alone, and yet that is what Jesus is demanding of those who are truly God's children. It must be clear to anyone reading this that such a life is impossible. It demands serious spiritual growth. That is precisely what Jesus urges. With the help of the Holy Spirit, such a life is possible to a very large degree. All of God's people should intentionally aim for it. Those of us who are church leaders should be helping them realize this more and more in their lives.

One church that gave the apostle Paul a lot of anguish was the Corinthian church. It was characterized by immaturity. There were divisions over the personalities of their past leaders and preachers, sexual immorality, lawsuits against fellow believers, selfish insensitivities to personal qualms and scruples, the scandalizing of the Lord's Supper, worldly competition over spiritual gifts, and acceptance of false doctrines, especially about the resurrection. Paul was very grieved about all this. Early in his first letter to the Corinthians, he put his finger on where the real problem was. It was the fact that most believers in the church had not grown in maturity. He wrote, "But I, brothers, could not address you as spiritual people, but as people of the flesh, as infants in Christ. I fed you with milk, not solid food, for you were not ready for it. And even now you are not yet ready" (1 Cor. 3:1–2). As Paul had planted the church, he had taught the believers the basics of the Christian life. He had expected that by now they would be ready for the deeper truths of the faith. In the light of what he was hearing about the confusion there, he concluded they were still infants in Christ. They still needed to be helped to mature out of their worldly thinking.

Toward the end of this first letter to the Corinthians, Paul again brought up their lack of maturity. He wrote, "Brothers, do not be children in your thinking. Be infants in evil, but in your thinking be mature" (1 Cor. 14:20). True spiritual maturity would have enabled them to overcome their worldly and sinful tendencies, especially those of using their spiritual gifts to compete with one another. The same can be said of the scandals that continue to rock so many churches today. If only believers would be spiritually mature in their thinking, these scandals would be nipped in the bud. Interpersonal relationships in the church would be less selfish, more loving, and more God-glorifying. It was for this purpose that Paul wrote his letters to churches, including 1 Corinthians. All the teachings in the New Testament epistles were meant to foster spiritual growth in believers, because maturity is not an optional extra to Christian living. Pastors should urge Christians to grow toward maturity.

The unknown author of the epistle to the Hebrews had a similar concern, that the recipients of his letter should move on to Christian maturity. He wrote,

> Therefore let us leave the elementary doctrine of Christ and go
> on to maturity, not laying again a foundation of repentance from

dead works and of faith toward God, and of instruction about washings, the laying on of hands, the resurrection of the dead, and eternal judgment. (Heb. 6:1–2)

Anyone who reads the epistle to the Hebrews soon sees that it must have been written to Jewish believers to enable them to see the supremacy of Christ as compared to the prophets and priests of Israel. The author felt constrained to lay again this foundational teaching. Yet he really wanted the recipients of his letter to "go on to maturity." They needed to move on from perpetually dealing with issues related to spiritual infancy, to doctrines and practices of mature adulthood in Christ. This should not remain the concern of this man alone. It should be the concern of every Christian leader. The church should be like a ladder, with young believers at the bottom rung of the ladder and more mature ones making their way to the top. The church leaders should be on top and should be urging everyone to keep climbing toward spiritual maturity.

The Means of Growth in Maturity

Spiritual maturity is not attained by one event in a Christian's life. It is a lifelong process. It is the equivalent of physical growth. While you can speed up physical growth by good nutrition, you cannot produce it overnight. Where there is life there must be growth, but it takes time. What we should be asking is, "What do we need to put in place in the life of the church and in the lives of believers to ensure that they continue to grow at an optimum pace toward spiritual maturity?" This is the responsibility of church leadership. If I were to give one answer to this question, it would be that church leaders should ensure a regular and comprehensive diet of preaching and teaching God's word. This is the food that enables true spiritual growth.

In chapter 3, we learned that one of the primary responsibilities of the church here on earth was that of instructing believers through regular teaching from God's word. We saw how Jesus prayed to the Father, "Sanctify them in the truth; your word is truth" (John 17:17). We also saw from Ephesians 5:25–27 how Jesus washes his church through the word so that in the end he may present the church to himself "in splendor, without spot or wrinkle or any such thing, that she might be holy and without blemish." The emphasis in that chapter was that the church should be an educational institution where God's people are being regularly instructed in the whole counsel of God. This alone is what will ensure that they grow to maturity. It is the responsibility of the church to do this. If the preaching and teaching of God's word is to produce spiritual maturity it must be (a) faithful to the text of Scripture, (b) doctrinally rich, and (c) relevant in application. Let us look at each of these in a little more detail.

The teaching must be conspicuously faithful to the text of Scripture. When Paul wrote his last epistle to Timothy, he said,

> All Scripture is breathed out by God and profitable for teaching, for reproof, for correction, and for training in righteousness, that the man of God may be complete, equipped for every good work.
>
> I charge you in the presence of God and of Christ Jesus, who is to judge the living and the dead, and by his appearing and his kingdom: preach the word. (2 Tim. 3:16–4:2)

Paul wanted Timothy to intentionally use the Bible in his teaching ministry because Timothy was not an inspired apostle. He was to get his teaching directly from the Scriptures. We call this "biblical" or "expository" preaching and teaching. The people listening to the preaching or teaching should be able to see how what is being taught is legitimately being derived from the text of Scripture. Christians grow in their appreciation of the Bible and its teachings when those who teach them in the church show that what they are saying is what God actually said.

I cannot emphasize this enough. This approach to teaching God's people allows God himself, rather than mere human authors, to speak to his people. They sense that the authority of the preacher is really divine authority because they can see the truth in the text itself. They learn to respect you as a preacher for your integrity in preaching. You do not try to force your own personal opinions on them in a sly way. They learn God's lessons in the pattern of words that the Holy Spirit himself preserved for their instruction.

Where this teaching also encompasses the whole of the Bible, the effect on the believers in the church is incalculable. It transforms an entire congregation as God's people hear God's voice from Genesis to Revelation. They learn from the Law and the Prophets in the Old Testament and from the Gospels and Acts and the Epistles in the New Testament. Some passages in the Bible have truths that are like low-hanging mangoes on the tree, which even little children are able to pick. Other passages have truths that only giraffes can reach. Such passages demand the best, even from the best of men. As your church members see their pastor doing his utmost to handle such texts of Scripture, they grow in their appreciation of the Bible. Some passages have very unpleasant truths, which believers will learn and apply because the pastor has reached those texts of Scripture in his preaching schedule. Preaching through the whole Bible in an expository way will give your church a balanced spiritual diet.

One fruit of this kind of ministry is that believers become biblically literate. They are exposed to the full breadth of Scripture and learn from the pastor's example how to dig into the Bible to get spiritual food for their own souls. As they engage in inductive Bible study together with others, they can see the spiritual truths being taught in the Bible and share their insights with their friends.

By far the most popular form of preaching today is what we call "topical" preaching. This is where a pastor comes up with a topic to preach about and then goes to the Bible to find a good place to begin. He teaches on that topic, and every so often goes to the Bible for proof texts to augment his arguments. In the end, people go home more with what the pastor said about the topic rather than with what the Bible says in the text of Scripture. This has its place in a pastor's teaching ministry, but it must never be the main form of teaching in the church. One major shortcoming of this type of preaching is that the pastor remains within the limited orbit of the topics he loves and can more easily handle. The comprehensiveness of the truths of Scripture, meant to mold the lives of believers in a more holistic fashion, is missed. If we are going to see well-rounded and spiritually mature Christians in our churches, we must deliberately and intentionally teach and preach in an expository fashion.

The teaching must be doctrinally rich. In the last chapter, I dealt with the subject of doctrine. We saw that it matters what your church believes and what Christians in your church believe. Take it as a maxim: Without doctrinal soundness, Christians cannot grow into strong believers. They must be taught Christian doctrine through the regular exposition of God's word so that they can see for themselves that these are truths of God himself.

The tendency today is that of merely drawing out devotional lessons from the Bible instead of rich doctrinal truths. We are too quick to tell our people what they should do without first laying before them what they should believe. That deprives them of sinking deep spiritual roots. We must be like the apostle Paul. When he wrote his letter to the Romans, he did not tell them how to live until he reached chapter 12. In the first eleven chapters, he opened up many doctrines, including the two natures of Christ, total depravity, justification by faith alone, the grace of God, positional and progressive sanctification, spiritual adoption, the final perseverance of the saints, and eternal election. It was only after this, and based on these doctrines, that he then launched out on how they should live as believers in Christ. We should teach the "imperatives" of Scripture—how we should live—on the back of the "indicatives" of Scripture—what we should believe.

It is beyond the scope of this book to teach pastors how to do this. All I am doing here is to urge everyone who has a teaching ministry in the church to ensure that the doctrines of Christianity are intentionally brought out from the texts of Scripture. We will never have strong and spiritually mature Christians in our churches if they are not grounded in "the faith . . . once for all delivered to the saints" (Jude 3).

The teaching must be relevantly applied. We have already seen this from the example of Paul. After he taught Christian doctrine in the first eleven chapters of Romans, he went on to teach Christian practice in the remaining five chapters. He applied doctrine to practice so that Christians can live in a way that pleases God. He dealt with the need for Roman believers to be totally dedicated to God, to use their gifts to minister to one another, to live in love and not retaliate when offended, to submit to those who are in positions of authority over them, to accept one another in the church despite their different religious scruples, and so on. These were all relevant issues in the context of life in Rome, and Paul was concerned that the believers in that city conform their lives to what the Bible says and not necessarily to their own cultural practices.

There are many issues in our own African context that need to have the torch of Scripture shone on them. As God's word is taught and the doctrines of Scripture are enunciated, we must apply God's word to those areas. Think of areas like ancestor worship, tribalism, corruption, funeral and burial rites, initiation rites, marriage and family relationships, human sexuality, servant leadership, relating to refugees and foreigners, culture and traditions, superstition and witchcraft, the world of the spirits (ancestral spirits, Satan, demons, and angels), taboos, polygamy, traditional sacrifices, bride price and weddings, widows and orphans, religious syncretism, disease and healing, and so on. As you can see, the list is endless. If Christians are going to grow in maturity, they should be taught how to think through these issues from God's perspective so that they can know how to live in society in a way that truly glorifies the God of the Bible. These teachings should be Bible-based and must grow out of doctrines of Christianity that are drawn out of Scripture.

One more appeal as I draw this chapter to a close: If our churches are to grow spiritually, we need to help our members to develop a *reading* culture. You have no doubt heard the saying, "If you want to hide something from an African, put it in a book." It is a painful truth. Our people do not really appreciate the benefit of reading. Reading should not be simply for the purpose of passing exams. The mind needs to be fed as much as the body is fed. A pastor who inspires his members to read good Christian books will soon reap the benefits as this becomes a powerful handmaid to his teaching ministry. Many servants of God have put their knowledge of God and his ways in print. Some of them have since died, and some live far away, across lands and seas. Through their books, however, Christians in our churches can still access those teachings and benefit immensely from them. So, if your church is going to grow to spiritual maturity, help your members to develop a reading culture.

Our churches need to grow spiritually. As I said at the beginning of this chapter, in accordance with Romans 2:24, "The name of God is blasphemed among the Gentiles because of you." We know that too well. It is primarily because of the lack of maturity in the lives of believers in our churches. The blame lies squarely on those of us who occupy the teaching role in our churches. There is need for a major seismic shift in how we do ministry. We should teach in a way that is faithful to the text of Scripture, bringing out the rich doctrines of the Christian faith and applying those truths relevantly to the lives of God's people. We must also engender in God's people a love for reading good, sound Christian books. If we can do this consistently enough, we will see our churches producing spiritually mature believers who will in turn impact our continent to the glory of God.

STUDY GUIDE FOR CHAPTER 15
How Should Your Church Grow Spiritually?

Summary

A church should judge its growth and maturity not by how long it has existed, how much it owns, or how many members attend, but by the spiritual maturity of its people. This is the burden of the authors of the epistles to the churches. Church leaders should lead and rally the church toward spiritual growth by modeling it, patiently pursuing the biblical church practices we have looked at so far, and preaching sermons that are faithful to the text, doctrinally rich, and relevant in application.

Study Questions

1. How does the observation that "The church in Africa is a mile wide but only an inch deep" show itself in your cultural context?

2. The author identifies a number of benefits that both the pastor and the congregation enjoy when the pastor faithfully preaches the texts of Scripture book by book ("expository preaching"), instead of coming up with topics to preach ("topical" preaching). Which of these benefits have been the weightiest for you?

3. A majority of African countries are believed to be overwhelmingly
   Christian (80 percent in South Africa, 85 percent in Zambia, 70 percent in Kenya, and Nigeria is said to have the sixth-largest Christian
   population in the world). Most faithful pastors on the ground strongly
   reject these numbers. What is the generally assumed percentage of
   Christians in your country? How would you respond to these numbers, and why?

4. What are the pressing cultural issues in your country (consider the list
   given on p. 210) that need to have the torch of Scripture shone on
   them?

5. How can your local church build the culture of reading good Christian
   books to help in the congregation's maturity?

16

How Should Your Church Grow Numerically?

One issue that upsets me about politics in Africa is the way in which politicians win numbers to their political parties. There is very little said and understood about the policies that those parties intend to actualize if they are voted into office. The appeal is often to tribal groupings. In such cases, the parties that belong to the largest tribes are likely to remain in power unless some genocide takes place and a tribe loses its obvious majority. Sometimes, the appeal is on the basis of a charismatic personality. I recall one such leader who won an election in my own country. He promised to lower taxes and at the same time build three-bedroom houses for the people and give them out freely. When asked how he was going to do that with lower taxes, he simply responded, "Vote for me and you shall see." Well, as meaningless as that answer might be, he still won the election because of his magnetic personality. The three-bedroomed houses have never been built. Perhaps the most degrading method of building up the numbers are the free items that are given out during electioneering—free clothing, free food, and free opaque beer. Numbers swell in political parties and even at campaign meetings because of this. You find individuals who have party cards and clothes for all the major political parties. Whichever party is coming to campaign in the community, they quickly go into the house and put on the correct clothing and carry the right card.

The leaders of that political party do not even need to explain how they hope to develop the nation when voted into power. They simply take off their jackets, tie them around their waists, and dance to the excitement of the crowds while free opaque beer is distributed—and the votes come pouring in. The people have no convictions about policies. It is all built on the politics of hunger. With this mindset, it is difficult to see how we will ever have mature politics on the continent.

Sadly, this is increasingly the mindset among growing churches as well. It is about tribes, it is about charismatic leaders, and it is about consumerism. There is very little being taught that challenges our thinking. This is why, whenever a new church comes into town, they are hardly winning any new converts from the world. When you visit those churches, you find that it is the same people who were once in the other churches who have now flocked there. Perhaps it is because their tribal church has now come into the area. It could also be because they have had enough of their previous charismatic leader and now they want to try out the new one. Perhaps it is that the free things from their old church have dried up and they are hoping to get them from the new church. That was not how churches grew in the New Testament.

There is nothing more exhilarating than reading through the book of the Acts of the Apostles. It oozes with energy as men on a mission turn the world upside down through the preaching of the gospel. It begins with a few men and women hidden away in a room in Jerusalem due to fear of the Jews, and with only the instruction of Jesus that they should wait for the promised Holy Spirit. In due season, the Holy Spirit comes upon them on the day of Pentecost and they are never the same again. Jerusalem, Judea, Samaria, and the known world of the day are transformed. In fact, on the day of Pentecost itself, the church grows from a handful of people to about three thousand souls (Acts 2:41). The church in Jerusalem was growing daily. We are told that "the Lord added to their number day by day those who were being saved" (Acts 2:47). By the time we reach chapter 4 of Acts, we are told that the numbers have shot up from three thousand to five thousand. The Bible says, "But many of those who had heard the word believed, and the number of the men came to about five thousand" (Acts 4:4). The growth was so much that by chapter 6 the apostles were failing to cope with looking after the widows. They had to appoint their first deacons to take care of this. Talk about a church growing numerically? This was it!

Should we be seeking such phenomenal growth today? This question seems superfluous when one realizes that the church in Africa is already growing rapidly. Even churches that meet under trees in villages are growing. Those who own church buildings are often having to break down a few walls and expand their buildings in order to accommodate their growing congregations. Although there are not many congregations as large as the church in Jerusalem, there is no doubt that everywhere you look our churches are continuing to grow. Shrinking or stagnant churches are the exception to the rule. So, why should we bother to address the issue of numerical church growth?

The most important question we should be asking is not whether we should seek numerical growth in our churches. As we have seen, that is already happening all around us. Rather, the question we should be asking is, "*How* should your church grow numerically?" This question is not merely about whether it should happen, but about the method by which we can have numerical growth that is truly pleasing to God.

It Should Be through People Responding to the Gospel

In looking at the book of Acts, it is evident that the church in Jerusalem grew as people responded to the gospel. The initial three thousand came into the church on the day of Pentecost as they responded to the gospel:

> And Peter said to them, "Repent and be baptized every one of you in the name of Jesus Christ for the forgiveness of your sins, and you will receive the gift of the Holy Spirit . . ." And with many other words he bore witness and continued to exhort them, saying, "Save yourselves from this crooked generation." So those who received his word were baptized, and there were added that day about three thousand souls. (Acts 2:38, 40–41)

We find precisely the same testimony when the church grew to five thousand. The Bible says,

And as they were speaking to the people, the priests and the captain of the temple and the Sadducees came upon them, greatly annoyed because they were teaching the people and proclaiming in Jesus the resurrection from the dead. And they arrested them and put them in custody until the next day, for it was already evening. But many of those who had heard the word believed, and the number of the men came to about five thousand. (Acts 4:1–4)

Notice that what annoyed the Sadducees was the gospel message that the apostles were proclaiming. Their message was that in Jesus Christ there was the resurrection from the dead, which went against what the Sadducees believed and taught. It was those who believed this message of the gospel who were then added to the church in Jerusalem.

We need to emphasize this afresh today. Church growth should be through the preaching of the gospel. Only those who respond to the gospel through repentance and faith should be added to the church. We already handled this matter when we dealt with why the gospel is so important to the church (in chapter 4) and who should be in church membership (in chapter 5). We saw in chapter 4 that the gospel was important to the church because it was through this message that the church got its new members. In that chapter we also defined what the gospel is; that is to say, just what do people need to respond to in order to be saved and to become members of the church? We also noted there that it is the Holy Spirit who uses this message to give spiritual life to those who are otherwise spiritually dead and under the wrath of almighty God. In chapter 5 we saw that non-Christians cannot rightly be made members of the church because they are spiritually dead, enslaved to the world, to the devil, and to their own sinful natures. It is only when they respond to the gospel that this is changed and they become new creatures in Christ. Only people with this spiritual and moral change should be welcomed into church membership. So, we cannot overemphasize the importance of ensuring an accurate presentation of the gospel in order to ensure the church's numerical growth.

The modern trend of using "miracles" to increase membership is worrying, to say the least. Whether or not those miracles actually happen is not the issue here. The point is that the individuals who join churches because they are seeking or have found anything other than salvation in Christ will still be lost in sin and on their way to hell. Nothing short of the regenerating work of the Holy Spirit, which results in repentance toward God and faith in the Lord Jesus Christ, can make a person a real Christian. There is no doubt that claims about miracles bring great numbers of people into the church. The attitude of the Lord Jesus Christ toward those who were following him because of his miracles was one of caution and not excitement. He said to them, "Do not work for the food that perishes, but for the food that endures to eternal life, which the Son of Man will give to you" (John 6:27). He wanted them to seek salvation from him and not physical food. That should be our attitude as well when we are seeking numerical growth in our church. We must encourage the people to genuinely seek the salvation of their souls. Seeing or experiencing miracles does not automatically translate into faith for the forgiveness of sins. In fact, it often becomes a distraction. All people want to see is that which will benefit them materially or physically. That is temporal. Their greatest need is spiritual.

It Should Be through the Holy Spirit's Work

There is no doubt that we should be actively evangelizing if we are going to see numerical growth in our churches. That is what we saw in Acts. The gospel was actively being preached everywhere, and people were being converted as they responded to the message. They were being added to the church, and the church was growing. However, behind all this fruitfulness was the work of the Holy Spirit. He alone converts stony hearts and makes them soft. He alone opens spiritually blind eyes so that they can trust in the crucified Savior.

The Holy Spirit is the third person in the blessed Holy Trinity. He cannot be manipulated. He is sovereign and does whatever he pleases. We can never calculate whom he will convert and when he will do so. This is what Jesus taught Nicodemus. He said,

> Truly, truly, I say to you, unless one is born of water and the Spirit, he cannot enter the kingdom of God. That which is born of the flesh is flesh, and that which is born of the Spirit is spirit. Do not

marvel that I said to you, "You must be born again." The wind blows where it wishes, and you hear its sound, but you do not know where it comes from or where it goes. So it is with everyone who is born of the Spirit. (John 3:5–8)

In this passage, Jesus taught Nicodemus two very important lessons.

The first was that human beings are totally unable to produce spiritual conversions. He said, "That which is born of the flesh is flesh, and that which is born of the Spirit is spirit" (v. 6). As human beings, we can only produce other human beings in the most natural process of childbirth. It is only the Holy Spirit who is able to give birth spiritually. In considering the subject of church growth, we need to be reminded of this truth. It is only the Holy Spirit who is able to give us fresh recruits from the world and bring them in as newly regenerated souls. He is the life-giving Spirit. He is able to raise the spiritually dead and make them God's children. We should thank God that he is currently in the world doing precisely that.

The second lesson Jesus was teaching Nicodemus was that, in the work of regeneration, the Holy Spirit is totally sovereign. He does as he pleases. Jesus said, "The wind blows where it wishes, and you hear its sound, but you do not know where it comes from or where it goes. So it is with everyone who is born of the Spirit" (v. 8). In the Greek, the word "spirit" and the word "wind" are really the same word. You can only tell which sense the author means when you read the context. The translators have opted to use the word as "wind" in the first part of this verse and as "Spirit" in the last part of it. Whichever way you opt to translate the word in the first part of the verse, the emphasis in the mind of our Lord was on the way in which this is out of human control. The wind blows where it wishes. You can only hear its sound. You cannot direct where it should go and when it should do so. You are but a recipient of its sovereign activity. Then he concluded by saying that it is the same with everyone who is born of the Spirit. Human beings cannot manipulate this process. The Holy Spirit is absolutely sovereign as to whom he regenerates.

Having said this, we also need to address a misconception that often justifies perpetually small numbers in a church by the claim that the Holy Spirit is holding back his blessings. This kind of reasoning is suspect, when the church next door is experiencing the blessing of the same Holy Spirit through the salvation of many souls. The tendency is to assume that the church which is growing must be using worldly means while the church that is stagnant or dwindling is the one that is truly spiritual. That is not necessarily the case. It could be lack of evangelistic fervor and spiritual laziness. It is important to do some serious heart-searching in such situations.

At the same time, because the Holy Spirit gives the new birth to whomsoever he wills, there might be seasons when he will withhold that blessing and conversions will become very rare. During such seasons, the church stagnates as far as numbers go. In fact, the numbers may even dwindle during such a time. We must not give up the work of evangelism during such seasons. We must not resort to pressure tactics and tricks to simply bring in the people. We must remain faithful in spreading the gospel. The planting of the seed should continue. It is that same seed that the Holy Spirit will germinate in the souls of his people when he is pleased to give life to the dead.

It Should Be a Fruit of Prayer

Our role in this matter of numerical growth is that of preaching and praying. In preaching, we sow the seed. In praying, we ask the Holy Spirit to give life to those who hear so that the seed that is sown can germinate in their hearts. The sowing of the seed is nothing if the Holy Spirit does not infuse life where there is death. This is what the apostle Paul alluded to when he wrote, "I planted, Apollos watered, but God gave the growth. So neither he who plants nor he who waters is anything, but only God who gives the growth" (1 Cor. 3:6–7). If we are interested in our church growing numerically in a God-honoring way, we must be a praying church. That does not guarantee growth, but it certainly shows that we understand that we are utterly dependent on God to grow our church.

Praying also keeps us spiritual in our perspective. We see growth as a side effect of people being saved and coming into God's kingdom, which is our primary desire. When we are praying, we are not asking God to grow our church. Rather, we are asking him to grow his kingdom so that he may be glorified. We are saying, "Our Father in heaven, hallowed be your name. Your kingdom come, your will be done, on earth as it is in heaven" (Matt. 6:9–10). That was how the church in the New Testament grew. The apostles were not church growth specialists. They were fulfilling the Great Commission that Jesus gave them. We have seen again and again how crucial the marching orders of Jesus are to our understanding of the church. We should always get back there if we are to avoid losing direction. Jesus had commanded his apostles, "All authority in heaven and on earth has been given to me. Go therefore and make disciples of all nations, baptizing them in the name of the Father and of the Son and of the Holy Spirit . . ." (Matt. 28:18–19). Those to whom the apostles preached the gospel, and who consequently repented and believed, were baptized and in that way they became a part of the church, and the church grew. We must follow their example. We should not merely be interested in having big churches. Our prayer and heart's desire to God should be for the salvation of those with whom we share the gospel. Our church should grow because people are responding to the gospel that we are sharing by the power of the Holy Spirit. This is the only kind of church growth that is truly pleasing to God, because it focuses on his glory and not on us.

It Must Never Be at the Expense of Godliness

When people are consumed with zeal to see their church grow numerically, they can fall into the trap of wanting to see huge numbers at the expense of godliness. It is interesting to note how the church in Jerusalem grew while the apostles were exercising church discipline. Soon after the church hit the five thousand mark, a man named Ananias and his wife Sapphira sold a piece of property, and when they brought the money to the apostles they claimed that it was the total money that they had received for the property, which was a lie. The apostle Peter confronted both of them about it and they both died on the spot, one after the other. We are told that as a result of this, "great fear came upon the whole church and upon all who heard of these things" (Acts 5:11). Quantity must never replace quality in the church. This was the message from God and his apostles by this unusual discipline.

Church leaders are often afraid of exercising discipline for fear that they will lose some people. The first time I ever witnessed this fear was before I became a pastor. I was working as an engineer in the Zambian copper mines. One day, I witnessed a female neighbor who was a single parent entertain a married man for the night. As she escorted him to the car the following morning, I saw every evidence in the car park that this was an adulterous affair. I went and confronted the lady on the same day, and she simply warned me that she would pour boiling oil on my head if I ever told her church leaders about what I had seen. As I left her home, I advised her to put the oil on the stove because she was going to need it! Well, my major disappointment came when I told her church leaders. They told me, "We cannot confront her. If we do, we will lose her." I was shocked. I never thought I would ever hear that from church leaders. Well, that was more than thirty years ago. I have since known better. Many church leaders hide sin under the carpet in the church because they are afraid of losing members. The truth is that, where church discipline is handled correctly and stubborn sin is punished, the church may lose people for a season but the blessing of God often visits the church before long. Hidden sin grieves the Holy Spirit, and thus he withdraws his gracious influences from a church. The number of people in the church may grow, but it is often not from truly converted people. The church soon becomes more of a "synagogue of Satan" (Rev. 2:9; 3:9) than a church of Jesus Christ.

The church is supposed to be the "salt of the earth" and the "light of the world" (Matt. 5:13–16). What is the point of having thousands of church members if it is because the salt has lost its saltiness and it is being "trampled under people's feet"? (v. 13). Why should we celebrate great numbers in our church if there are no good works to shine before men so that they may see them and "give glory to [our] Father who is in heaven"? (v. 16). Big congregations alone without godliness mean nothing in the eyes of God. Church leaders should be willing to lose their positions in the church rather than allow blatant sin to remain unchallenged in the church.

Once you emphasize godliness, you will find that in most cases your church will not be the fastest-growing one. Jesus said, "For the gate is wide and the way is easy that leads to destruction, and those who enter by it are many. For the gate is narrow and the way is hard that leads to life, and those who find it are few" (Matt. 7:13–14). People want to belong to a church where they are allowed to live as they please, rather than being challenged to live as God's word says they should live. Paul warned Timothy about this phenomenon in the last days. He said, "For the time is coming when people will not endure sound teaching, but having itching ears they will accumulate for themselves teachers to suit their own passions, and will turn away from listening to the truth and wander off into myths" (2 Tim. 4:3–4). So, the fact that a church is full to overflowing does not necessarily mean that it is being blessed by God the Holy Spirit. Often, it is because sin is being allowed to flourish. Do not follow such examples. They contradict the purpose of the existence of the church.

While seeking true spiritual growth, we should not necessarily look down on churches that have many non-Christians in attendance, because it does provide an opportunity for these nonbelievers to hear the gospel. As long as those churches do not turn worship into entertainment, we should thank God for the spiritual thirst in the community that causes them to go to church long before they are converted. We can welcome these large crowds as long as the unconverted people are not made church members in an effort to keep them coming. Only converted people should be added to the church's membership.

The tragedy today is that most of the growth of the church in Africa comprises unconverted people. This is a sad phenomenon. It has resulted in serious spiritual compromise. Churches have become social or tribal clubs rather than "the church of the living God, a pillar and buttress of the truth" (1 Tim. 3:15). This must change if the church is to truly glorify God. Our thirst for numbers is causing us to use underhanded ways to increase the membership roll. There is a wrong and worldly sense of competition between churches that is fueling this. We must stop trying to impress people and seek the glory of God alone. That is what will make us seek the salvation of individuals before we bring them into church membership.

We live in a day when high numbers matter a lot. Quality is sacrificed on the altar of quantity. Companies are doing it and often getting away with it. This attitude in the world seems to have crept into the church as well. Although large numbers are what is most emphasized today, they are not what is most important in the eyes of God. The church's budget does not necessarily reflect its spirituality. So, as we seek numerical growth, let us not do it at the expense of spiritual growth. The two must go together. Where faithfulness to the truth causes the church to go through a lengthy period of little or no growth, God's people should be encouraged to remain faithful to God. That is what ultimately matters.

STUDY GUIDE FOR CHAPTER 16
How Should Your Church Grow Numerically?

Summary

Many churches in Africa are growing numerically. The real concern is not whether we will get people in but whether the methods we use to get them in will be faithful to God's word. Since only those who respond to the gospel should be added to the church as members, we should pursue growth by preaching the gospel. We should expect the growth to come by the Holy Spirit's work and so we should seek this growth prayerfully, yet never pursuing growth above spiritual maturity.

Study Questions

1. In our context here in Africa, where churches are growing quickly regardless of whether they uphold the truth or not, how can we make sure that we remain faithful even in seasons when the Lord does not appear to be increasing the numbers of those being saved?

2. In what ways do you think we can manipulate people and end up with numerical growth that is not a supernatural work of the Holy Spirit but a work of human wisdom?

3. "The attitude of the Lord Jesus Christ toward those who were following him because of his miracles was one of caution and not excitement" (p. 219). How does Jesus's attitude in John 2:23–25 reflect the statement above? What is Jesus's concern?

4. How have you been tempted in your local church to cut corners so as to draw in more people? What temptations have you seen other churches fall into?

5. The author advises us to be more concerned in our prayers for the growth of God's kingdom than for the growth of our particular church (pp. 221–222). How does your concern for your local church compare to your concern for God's wider kingdom (see Matt. 6:10)?

17

How Should Your Church Relate to Other Churches?

A few years ago, my family lived in a neighborhood that was very close to a poorer, crime-ridden residential area. The economic difference between the two residential areas was like night and day, which is a common feature in many of our African cities. A week did not pass by without us getting the news that a home in our neighborhood had been broken into, especially at night. Finally, one man asked for a meeting for heads of homes in our residential area. He asked us to form a neighborhood watch group. Men took turns driving around the neighborhood at night with an armed policeman. Usually, this involved three men at any one time. Homes that could not participate in this helped by providing some snacks to those who were on night patrol duty. Donations were also made so that a cell phone was purchased to use as a hotline. If there was any news of a theft, the people in the car would be notified and they would rush there very quickly. Usually, this was from about midnight to the early hours of the morning before sunrise. I participated a few times. Most of our time was spent patrolling the road between that poorer residential area and our neighborhood. This was because the thieves did not use cars. They walked. They carried the stolen goods on their heads. So, as long as we got the news of a theft in the area and patrolled that road, it was not long before we caught up with the thieves as they tried to cross over to the side where they lived. The neighborhood watch group did not last long. Word made the rounds in the crime-ridden residential area that many of their friends were being caught, and so the number of thefts drastically went down. It was a joint effort that bore lasting fruit. Individual homes on their own could not have managed to arrest this trend, but by working together the level of crime was reduced. Churches are also like that when it comes to fulfilling what has now come to be called the Great Commission.

Why Churches Should Relate to Other Churches

The Lord Jesus Christ left us with the Great Commission. It has been referred to in this book a number of times: "Go therefore and make disciples of all nations . . ." (Matt. 28:19). It is impossible for any one church to accomplish this on its own. Churches need to work together in order to accomplish this worldwide task. This is because Jesus tends to distribute his gifts and resources differently in different churches. Some churches will have plenty of human resources, while others will have funds that can help to accomplish major missions work. Some churches may be particularly burdened to pray while others may be close enough to the needy situation to travel there and help in practical ways. Churches that are always inward looking will never do much for Christ. It is those churches that are conscious of the magnitude of the task that Jesus left with the church who see the need to not only relate to other churches but also to cooperate with them. What does this cooperation look like in practice?

Before we answer that question, it is important to give yet another reason why your church should intentionally relate to other local churches. It is the fact that the body of Christ does not start or end with your local church. The body of Christ comprises believers in your church and also in other local churches around the world—wherever the gospel has borne fruit. According to the Bible, we are all one body and one family. It only makes sense that we should relate to one another, because we are truly brothers and sisters in Christ despite our different geographical locations, cultures, tribes, and languages.

The apostle Paul wrote to the Romans, saying, "For as in one body we have many members, and the members do not all have the same function, so we, though many, are one body in Christ, and individually members one of another" (Rom. 12:4–5). The very fact that he included himself in this "one body in Christ" suggests that he was not limiting it to the church in Rome alone. He must have been referring to all the believers in Christ, because he was not a member of the church in Rome. In the same way, before the Lord Jesus Christ ascended to heaven, he specifically prayed that his people on earth would express something of the unity that exists in the Godhead. He prayed,

> I do not ask for these only, but also for those who will believe in me through their word, that they may all be one, just as you, Father, are in me, and I in you, that they also may be in us, so that the world may believe that you have sent me. The glory that you have given me I have given to them, that they may be one even as we are one. (John 17:20–22)

Jesus prayed not only for those whom he had called to himself while he was on the earth but also for all those who would become believers through their ministry. What was his prayer? He prayed that all his people may be one, even as God is one in the Trinity. This to some extent has been realized by the work of the Holy Spirit when he baptizes us into Christ at our conversion. However, it needs to be worked out in practice as believers learn to relate to one another in the local church and beyond that local church.

Another Bible passage that teaches this unity of believers beyond the local church is 1 Corinthians 12. There we read,

> For just as the body is one and has many members, and all the members of the body, though many, are one body, so it is with Christ. For in one Spirit we were all baptized into one body—Jews or Greeks, slaves or free—and all were made to drink of one Spirit. (1 Cor. 12:12–13)

When we become Christians we are not only immersed into one body, the body of Christ, but we are also indwelt by one Spirit, the Spirit of the living God. The result of this is that we sense a real sympathy with those who are Christians wherever they might be. We are one family in Christ.

Perhaps one more passage and we should be convinced that our local church does not draw boundaries for us in terms of relating to other believers. It is John chapter 10. There the Lord Jesus Christ said,

> I am the good shepherd. I know my own and my own know me, just as the Father knows me and I know the Father; and I lay down my life for the sheep. And I have other sheep that are not of this fold. I must bring them also, and they will listen to my voice. So, there will be one flock, one shepherd. (John 10:14–16)

Just as we have only one shepherd, he also has only one flock. Yes, we are located in different places around the globe and we gather in different church buildings, but in the eyes of the Lord Jesus Christ we are one flock. We must never lose sight of that.

What Churches Can Partner Together In

It must be obvious from the Great Commission that churches should relate to other churches in order to achieve the work of helping one another and also in order to push the agenda of world evangelization forward. Everything else grows out of this. A good example of this is in 2 Corinthians 8 and 9. Famine had broken out in Judea. Paul was concerned that the churches in Europe (in the provinces of Macedonia and Achaia) should participate in helping their brothers and sisters in Judea to survive this very difficult time. You would need to read the whole of 2 Corinthians 8 and 9 to appreciate the entire context. However, the following statement best summarizes what was going on as the churches were relating to one another concerning this project:

> For the ministry of this service is not only supplying the needs of the saints but is also overflowing in many thanksgivings to God. By their approval of this service, they will glorify God because of your submission that comes from your confession of the gospel of Christ, and the generosity of your contribution for them and for

all others, while they long for you and pray for you, because of the surpassing grace of God upon you. (2 Cor. 9:12–14)

We see from this passage of Scripture some areas of inter-church cooperation.

First, the churches engaged together in "the ministry of this service," which was supplying the needs of the saints. Paul refers to it as "the generosity of your contribution for them." The churches in Macedonia and Achaia were contributing generously toward this famine relief project. Earlier, in 2 Corinthians 8, Paul wrote about an individual whom the churches together chose so that he could accompany Paul as he took the finances from Europe to Asia. He wrote,

> With him we are sending the brother who is famous among all the churches for his preaching of the gospel. And not only that, but he has been appointed by the churches to travel with us as we carry out this act of grace that is being ministered by us, for the glory of the Lord himself and to show our good will. (2 Cor. 8:18–19)

So, the churches were not only working together to raise funds, but they also ensured accountability for the funds by collectively choosing a person who would accompany the money that was being raised.

Churches should not only work on projects that are of a social nature but should also work together to support the work of church planting missions. Anyone who reads the New Testament soon discovers that the churches worked well together in this. A good example is that of the apostle Paul himself. He was initially supported by the church in Antioch when he set out on his first missionary journey with Barnabas in Acts 13. However, when he later went on his second missionary journey with Silas, after the planting of the church in Philippi, it was this latter church that took over much of his support, as he points out in Philippians 4:15. Yet there were times when other churches, like the church in Rome, also supported him (Rom. 15:24).

Second, the churches cooperated in the area of prayer. This grew out of the activities the churches were doing together. The generosity of the church in Macedonia and Achaia resulted in "many thanksgivings to God" by the churches in Judea. It also resulted in the churches in Judea longing for them and praying for them, as Paul says in the passage quoted above (2 Cor. 9:12–14). Churches should not only pray for what is happening in their own midst. They should pray for other churches as well, especially those churches that they are relating to regularly. As they work together in the cause of the gospel, they should also uphold one another before the throne of God.

We should pray for other churches and other Christians. Paul wrote to the Ephesians about our spiritual warfare as believers. He said they should be "praying at all times in the Spirit, with all prayer and supplication. To that end, keep alert with all perseverance, making supplication for all the saints" (Eph. 6:18). Notice that this is "for all the saints." He did not specify whether those saints were only those in the church in Ephesus. This is because all the saints need the prayers of other saints. For instance, the churches outside the Muslim world should be praying for the churches in the Muslim world because of the persecution that the brothers and sisters are undergoing there. They need the grace of God to enable them to persevere amid these difficult times.

In order for churches to work together in projects, in missions, and in prayer, there is need for consistent communication. The days in which the New Testament was being written were days in which communication was very difficult. There was no post office system. There were telegraphs or telephones. There was no internet or email. Yet, the churches did their best to keep each other informed about what was going on among them. Whenever a brother or sister traveled from one town to another, they ensured that the church in that town would be informed about the church where that person was coming from. And when that person returned, they brought back news from the church where they had gone.

Similarly, if you read the epistles of the apostle Paul, you soon discover that they speak about individuals who were specifically sent to tell the churches about his own circumstances as a missionary. He knew that, if the churches did not know what was happening to him, they would not send him any assistance and they would not pray for him. Regular communication makes this possible. He wrote, for instance,

> Tychicus will tell you all about my activities. He is a beloved brother and faithful minister and fellow servant in the Lord. I have sent him to you for this very purpose, that you may know how we are and that he may encourage your hearts, and with him Onesimus, our faithful and beloved brother, who is one of you. They will tell you of everything that has taken place here. (Col. 4:7–9)

He also wrote to the Romans a letter of commendation for Phoebe. He said,

> I commend to you our sister Phoebe, a servant of the church at Cenchreae, that you may welcome her in the Lord in a way worthy of the saints, and help her in whatever she may need from you, for she has been a patron of many and of myself as well. (Rom. 16:1–2)

That is how important communication was to the apostle Paul. That is how important it must be to us as well. In these days of cell phone technology that enables texting, and internet services that enable emails and social media, our churches and missionaries have no excuse for not communicating with sister churches. This is what will fuel our prayer lives for one another and increase our sense of fellowship with one another as churches.

There is no doubt that denominational structures are a great help in inter-church cooperation and communication. Through such structures, churches can get involved in common ventures together. This could be ventures like organizing joint conferences, church planting, running a Bible college to train pastors or an ordinary school or college, developing a literature ministry, running a health institution like a clinic or even a hospital, doing disaster relief, opening an orphanage, developing a pension fund for pastors and other church workers, managing a broadcasting station for radio or television, and so on. The list is endless. Yet, even churches that are not in denominational structures should learn to work together with other churches to do what is otherwise impossible for most single churches to do on their own.

Where We Should Draw the Line

Although we are one body in Christ and have a common "Great Commission" to accomplish in Christ, it is not long before you find that your church cannot relate to and cooperate with all other churches. So, the question that we need to answer is, "Where should we draw the line in a practical way?"

One obvious boundary is a doctrinal one. We have emphasized throughout this book that doctrine matters. The church is described as ". . . the household of God, which is the church of the living God, a pillar and buttress of the truth" (1 Tim. 3:15). The teaching of the truth about Jesus Christ and the spreading of this truth is one of the primary functions of the church on earth. Therefore, you will find that churches that have a common understanding of what the Bible teaches concerning salvation and other areas of divine revelation will associate together more closely. This only makes sense.

When Paul and Barnabas returned to Antioch from their missionary journey and found that individuals who had come to that church from Jerusalem were teaching something contrary to what they had taught the church, they did not overlook this matter for the sake of maintaining skin-deep unity and fellowship. The Bible says,

> But some men came down from Judea and were teaching the brothers, "Unless you are circumcised according to the custom of Moses, you cannot be saved." And after Paul and Barnabas had no small dissension and debate with them, Paul and Barnabas and some of the others were appointed to go up to Jerusalem to the apostles and the elders about this question. (Acts 15:1–2)

This doctrinal matter needed to be settled before meaningful fellowship could continue.

It must be the same with us today. Although we will never have exactly the same beliefs in everything between one Christian and another, or between one church and another, it is still important that we associate only with churches that hold on to the same doctrinal beliefs as we do on the most important things, especially on the question of how a person becomes a Christian. Churches that have lost the gospel are to be evangelized instead of being embraced as fellow churches in Christ, just as those who profess to be Christians but teach a salvation by works should be evangelized rather than related to as fellow Christians.

Inter-church cooperation may also be affected by the way in which different churches conduct their worship. The truth that we believe in determines how we live as individual believers and also as local churches. Remember that, before the apostle Paul described the church as the pillar and buttress of the truth, he had been telling Timothy of the need for the church to conduct itself in a particular way. He had written, "I hope to come to you soon, but I am writing these things to you so that, if I delay, you may know how one ought to behave in the household of God" (1 Tim. 3:14–15). It mattered to Paul how the church that Timothy was pastoring in Ephesus conducted itself and so he sent him this letter, which was full of practical instructions. So, you will find that churches that have what is called a common "church order" will tend to relate more closely together. It only makes sense, and is a very practical matter.

An example of this practical outworking of belief was how women were to function in the New Testament church. Paul did not leave this issue to the initiative of the various churches. For instance, to the Corinthians he wrote,

> For God is not a God of confusion but of peace.
>
> As in all the churches of the saints, the women should keep silent in the churches. For they are not permitted to speak, but should be in submission, as the Law also says. If there is anything they desire to learn, let them ask their husbands at home. For it is shameful for a woman to speak in church.
>
> Or was it from you that the word of God came? Or are you the only ones it has reached? If anyone thinks that he is a prophet, or spiritual, he should acknowledge that the things I am writing to you are a command of the Lord. If anyone does not recognize this, he is not recognized. (1 Cor. 14:33–38)

My interest in citing this text is not to attempt to settle the contentious issue of the role of women in the church today, but rather to draw your attention to the way in which the apostle Paul said that this must be the same "in all the churches of the saints." He wanted the same understanding of female roles to be held by all the churches. This would enable the churches to relate to one another and work together without contention on this subject.

This explains why churches that are in the same denomination tend to relate to each other more than those across denominational barriers. It is because those churches have a common set of beliefs and a common church order. These are written in their constitutions and carried out in practice in individual churches and also when the churches gather together.

As we think about inter-church cooperation, we also need to be wary of the tendency to build ecclesiastical empires with many churches reporting to one church. With the "founder" mentality that we addressed in earlier chapters, the empires are built not around one church but around one person. We have already shown that this is wrong. Even where we have denominational structures with Episcopal or Presbyterian systems of government, the individual churches themselves must still see themselves as equal with one another, if they are to have any meaningful cooperation.

We must also be wary of the spirit of competition. There are church leaders who fear exposing their members to the ministry of leaders and preachers in other churches lest they lose their members to them. They have a sense of ownership over the flock of the Lord Jesus Christ that is not warranted by Scripture. As stated earlier, church members of a number of churches coming together in inter-church conferences can have an enriching effect on their lives. The gifts that Jesus gives to other churches should also bless the members of your church. It is part of belonging to one body, the body of Christ.

How Should Your Church Relate to Other Churches?

Summary

It is impossible for any church to accomplish the Great Commission on its own. Not only are all churches part of the same body of Christ, the Lord Christ has given to them varying resources, burdens, and opportunities. He expects there to be unity among his people, for we are all only one flock. Churches can partner in caring for each other's material needs, in supporting gospel work, and in prayer.

Study Questions

1. What reasons does the author give for why churches need to cooperate together to fulfill the Great Commission?

2. Is it possible to relate to our own local church so much that we forget our spiritual and Christian union with those in other churches? How can this be overcome?

3. Is your church presently cooperating with another church (in prayer, missions, finances, practical help, etc.)? What do you think has contributed to the success or lack of success in your attempts to cooperate?

4. What resources, blessings, and opportunities does your church currently have that another church can benefit from to fulfill the Great Commission?

5. As a leader or member of the church, do you find it easier to receive free support than to offer free support to other congregations? If so, what does this reveal about your heart?

18

How Should Your Church Relate to the State?

Life in a typical African village is quite different from life in the city, especially with respect to male and female roles. Both fathers and mothers go out to bring food to the household, but men often do so by hunting animals, while women do this by gathering wild foods. The wild foods may comprise fruits, nuts, roots, grains, and so on. Women also normally draw water either from a well or from a nearby flowing stream or river and bring it to the house for the family to use for drinking, cooking, and bathing. Village households also have some land for basic subsistence farming. Often, the ax is the man's tool for clearing the land, while the hoe is the woman's tool for ploughing the land. When it comes to firewood, the women normally bring in the dry branches that are used for cooking meals, while the men bring in the larger logs that light up the meeting place for evening socializing activities. The men also use the ax to splinter the logs into smaller pieces that can be used for cooking. Activities such as cooking food, sweeping the home and the surrounding grounds, washing clothes, and nursing babies and toddlers are left to the women. Men tend to be in charge of overall management of the home and the discipline of older children. As the children grow older, women take charge of the older girls and men take charge of the older boys to prepare them for adulthood and marriage. Whereas there might be some exceptions to this description, this is life in a typical African village even today. The saying, "The place of the woman is in the kitchen" does not have the negative connotations it has when repeated in the more urban context. Men know their roles and women know their roles. There is hardly any conflict. As each side plays its role, the village household goes forward with great harmony and joy.

In a sense, that is how God expects the church and the state to function in his world. The two have different spheres of responsibility in ensuring that human existence in God's world is harmonious. When one steps into or interferes with the role of the other this balance is disturbed, with disastrous consequences. Let us go to the beginning of human existence in order to understand this.

Where Church and State Came From

A study of the first few chapters of the Bible shows us a time when there was neither church nor state. This was the time before Adam and Eve fell into sin in Genesis 3. Prior to that, it looked like the family was to be the unit of gathering for human beings. God said to Adam and Eve, "Be fruitful and multiply and fill the earth and subdue it, and have dominion over the fish of the sea and over the birds of the heavens and over every living thing that moves on the earth" (Gen. 1:28). As long as there was no sin in the world, this harmonious living was possible. Humans would have continued to exploit and develop God's world without needing the church and the state.

Sadly, in Genesis 3, Eve listened to the lies of Satan through the serpent. She disobeyed God's instructions and ate the fruit from the forbidden tree. She gave some of the fruit to her husband, who also ate of it. Immediately their natures became corrupted. God came onto the scene and pronounced judgment on both of them (and on the serpent as well), and the worst form of that punishment was death. Genesis 3 is perhaps the most sobering chapter in the whole Bible—and rightly so. We have been paying the consequences of what Adam and Eve did in that chapter from that point to this very day. To borrow the words of the apostle Paul, "Therefore, just as sin came into the world through one man, and death through sin, and so death spread to all men because all sinned . . ." (Rom. 5:12).

The need for redemption was immediate, and that was why the church became necessary. We have the promise of the Savior stated in Genesis 3. God said to the serpent, "I will put enmity between you and the woman, and between your offspring and her offspring; he shall bruise your head, and you shall bruise his heel" (Gen. 3:15). With hindsight, in view of the full revelation of both the Old and the New Testament, we know that this was a promise referring to the death of Jesus Christ on the cross for the forgiveness of our sins (see, e.g., Heb. 2:14). There is also a hint of this in God's clothing of Adam and Eve with garments of skin (Gen. 3:21). Our spiritual nakedness is covered by the righteousness of Jesus, which was procured for us by his perfect life and his death on the cross. There is no doubt that part of the reason Abel's sacrifice was accepted was that it was a blood offering (Gen. 4:4). It took cognizance of the fact that he had sinned against God and needed to be reconciled to him through the death of a substitute. The study of what is called biblical theology shows how God's redemptive plan is interwoven with and develops through the stories of the Bible until it reaches its climax with the actual death and resurrection of Jesus Christ. This is the message at the heart of the nation of Israel in the Old Testament and the heart of the church of Jesus Christ in the New Testament. The need for redemption and reconciliation with God is what necessitated the church.

So, what necessitated the state? It was again the ugly consequences of the fall. The corruption that entered human nature at the fall made human beings chronically selfish and self-centered. The most blessed relationship between a man and his wife was not spared. The rift in the marriage relationship between Adam and Eve is sensed from the way Adam reported to God how he ended up disobeying him. Adam said, "The woman whom you gave to be with me, she gave me fruit of the tree, and I ate" (Gen. 3:12). He blamed his wife for his own disobedience! The human family was not spared either. The first two brothers who ever lived should have related to each other in brotherly affection for the rest of their days on earth. Alas, Cain murdered Abel purely out of jealousy because the offering made by Abel was accepted by God while his was not. As Cain was banished to live as a fugitive for the rest of his life, he feared that those who found him would kill him. The need for security and justice was already being felt. God said to Cain, "If anyone kills Cain, vengeance shall be taken on him sevenfold" (Gen. 4:15). Later, after the flood, God instituted the death penalty for those who committed murder. This was not meant to be done as individual revenge but rather by organized society. He said,

> And for your lifeblood I will require a reckoning: from every beast I will require it and from man. From his fellow man I will require a reckoning for the life of man.
>
> Whoever sheds the blood of man,
>   by man shall his blood be shed,
> for God made man in his own image. (Gen. 9:5–6)

It is evident in these first chapters of Genesis that human beings organized themselves beyond families. They formed clans, which were groupings of families from one grandparent. Then these formed themselves into nations, and these nations spread out across the earth. The Bible says, "These are the clans of the sons of Noah, according to their genealogies, in their nations, and from these the nations spread abroad on the earth after the flood" (Gen. 10:32). Within these nations, people organized themselves under kings. They also had armies that fulfilled their sense of need for defense and their appetite to acquire more land and property from others. This explains the battles that took place in Genesis 14 between various kings, which resulted in Abram rescuing his nephew and his possessions. The state system not only ensured protection from external aggression but it also ensured security and justice for individuals and families within. In today's language, we say that the state ensures "law and order." Without this, human existence on the earth would be impossible because of human fallenness.

The Roles of Church and State

From the preceding, we see that the church and the state play different roles. Putting it loosely, the church plays a more vertical role, ensuring a right relationship between human beings and God, while the state plays a more horizontal role, ensuring a right relationship between us as human beings. As we shall see later, this might be an oversimplification, because the two areas feed into each other. You cannot love God whom you cannot see if you do not love other human beings whom you can see (1 John 4:20). However, as we saw with life in the African village, by being well-defined about the different roles of the institutions, we reduce the conflicts between them and we increase their working in harmony with each other. Even when Jesus was on earth, and the Jews were under the Roman government, he said, "Render to Caesar the things that are Caesar's, and to God the things that are God's" (Mark 12:17). He was not willing to confuse these spheres of God's rule—the state and the church.

What is the role of the state? It is primarily that of enacting laws and upholding them so as to ensure the proper ordering of society and especially the protection of the weak and vulnerable. It is also that of ensuring security from external aggression, as we have already seen. Inevitably, because of the shared life of people in a nation, the state also provides various goods and services, such as clean water, good sanitation, efficient transport, and so on. With further developments, the state has tended to ensure the provision of electricity, banking services, postal systems, and so on. Bearing in mind the needs of the poor, the state has also tended to provide education and health facilities. This is often in terms of infrastructure and regulations, while the citizens may provide the actual means. The state funds its operations through taxing its citizens.

While all this is going on, what is the role of the church? We have already seen that the role of the church is evangelism and edification, or salvation and sanctification. As the church remains faithful in teaching and preaching the word of God, it not only brings the citizens of the nation to Christ but also indirectly improves the moral standards of the nation. Human beings have consciences. So, even when they do not respond to the gospel, when they hear the word of God they know that it is the truth. This, in due season, causes a higher moral standard among the general citizenry of a nation. Of course, the goal of the church is to see individuals coming to repentance and faith in Christ. As they do so and become a part of the church, the individual Christians are discipled into being responsible citizens of God's world. One major benefit that the church has on the nation is that of making marriages stronger through the conversion and instruction of its citizens about God's plan for marriage and family life. Broken homes weaken society, and strong families strengthen a nation. So, in whichever station in life those impacted by the gospel might be, they seek the good of other people and the glory of God. They use their gifts and training in order to fulfill the cultural mandate of Genesis 1:28 to multiply, fill the earth, and subdue it. Those Christians who are in government also ensure that godly principles dictate the enacting and implementing of the laws of the land. As we have already seen, just as the state raises its funds through taxation, the church funds its operations through the tithes and offerings of its members. Yes, those who belong to the church render to Caesar what is Caesar's and to God what is God's!

The church should also teach its members about their responsibility to the state. As Paul said to the Roman Christians,

> Let every person be subject to the governing authorities. For there is no authority except from God, and those that exist have been instituted by God. Therefore whoever resists the authorities resists what God has appointed, and those who resist will incur judgment. . . . Pay to all what is owed to them: taxes to whom taxes are owed, revenue to whom revenue is owed, respect to whom respect is owed, honor to whom honor is owed. (Rom. 13:1–2, 7)

Christians should obey all the laws of the land, unless those laws are directly opposed to the laws of God. Where that is the case, they should say, "We must obey God rather than men" (Acts 5:29). Christians should also be taught to be faithful in paying their taxes, just as they are taught to be faithful in paying their tithes. They live under two realms, and they should be faithful in both.

Church leaders should lead by example in showing the responsibility of Christians to the state. They should not only obey the laws of the land and be faithful in paying their taxes, but they should also be respectful to civic and government leaders.

The Conflict and Cooperation between Church and State

Due to the reality of fallen human beings ruling nations, there will be times when the church will be forced to rebel against the state. It is like life in the African village when it becomes evident that, to save the children from relentless abuse, the innocent party must rise against the spouse to defend the children. There are times when remaining silent is equal to a conspiracy in evil. As we have already seen, there will be times when the church will have to say, "We must obey God rather than men." This is often the case when the state enacts laws that make worshiping God impossible.

There will also be times when the state will see it as its responsibility to interfere with the church. This is normally when church leaders begin to abuse church members physically, financially, or sexually. In other words, it is in circumstances where the laws of the land that seek to protect the vulnerable in society are being broken under the guise of religious freedom. In such situations, the state may have to come in to protect its citizens. There have been cases where pastors and priests have been arrested for sexually abusing minors. On the African continent, governments are very concerned about the many pastors who are defrauding their church members and impregnating young ladies in the church. Although the state cannot tell the church how to run its affairs, a number of African governments are coming up with legislation to arrest this trend. This happens when the church loses its "saltiness" (see Matt. 5:13). The church should not wait for this to happen. It should have mechanisms to stop such abuses and mechanisms to discipline those who are guilty of such mischief.

The church also cooperates with the state especially in the area of meeting the needs of the most vulnerable in society. It tends to help the poor with food, clothing, health, and education. This is because Christians are concerned about all human suffering and not just about eternal suffering. The state tends to see the church as a partner because, as a result of its efforts, there are higher living standards among those citizens who would never have had any hope to attain such standards. The state also allows church leaders to handle some civic duties like conducting weddings, especially the weddings of its own church members. This fits in well with the fact that the church is also involved in the families of its members when they have babies born among them and when they suffer illnesses and death.

The worst danger in this cooperation seems to be when church leaders and political leaders join hands for the purposes of political gain. This is usually around political election times. Usually, the politicians entice those pastors who have huge congregations to support them in exchange for financial favors or government favors if they win the elections. Sometimes the politicians woo entire pastors' fellowships to their side in this way, and these pastors then try to convince their church members to support the candidates who have done them such favors. This is very common, but the fact that it is happening everywhere does not make it right. Remember what we learned in the earlier chapters: The church does not belong to us. It belongs to the Lord Jesus Christ. He has given it the Great Commission that defines its role in this world. To take the church and start using it for our own political ends is to invite upon ourselves the judgment of the Lord Jesus Christ. We are playing where angels fear to tread. Church leaders should be wary of gifts from politicians around election times. Those gifts often have strings attached.

STUDY GUIDE FOR CHAPTER 18
How Should Your Church Relate to the State?

Summary

The church and the state each have their function in the world. Both are made necessary by the fall, because people have turned against God and against each other. The state enacts laws and upholds them to ensure the proper ordering and well-being of society, whereas the church works to see individuals coming to repentance and faith in Christ. Churches should teach their members to be faithful citizens, in obedience to God. The church may at times be forced to resist the state, and the state may at times need to interfere with the church. In some cases, the two institutions can also cooperate, as when church leaders handle civic duties like conducting weddings.

Study Questions

1. How do the church and the state differ in how they find the funds to do their duties?

2. Many African politicians like to use church podiums to campaign for their parties. What would you say to a pastor who says that, by allowing the politicians to address the church and solicit votes, they are honoring authority?

3. During the coronavirus epidemic, the state in most countries ordered churches not to gather, in order to reduce cases of the spread of the disease. Was this a case of the state interfering with the church?

Were the churches that resisted justified in resisting the state order and having their Sunday gatherings?

4. Under what circumstances is it right for Christians to resist the state?

5. The church eventually "causes a higher moral standard among the general citizenry" and contributes to there being stronger marriages and families, which strengthens society (p. 245). Can you think of any other ways in which the state benefits from having churches within it?

19

How Does the Church Offend or Please God?

A few years ago, I attended a workshop for theologians at a Bible college in Lusaka, Zambia. Someone presented a paper whose title I cannot remember. However, he stated something that I had never quite thought about until then. He recalled how during his school days they were asked in class to state the first names of their mothers. He realized for the first time that he did not know his mother's first name! That was because she was always called "Amake Jeff," which means, "the mother of Jeff." The teacher gave him the homework that when he came back to school the following term he should tell the class his mother's first name. When he was back home, he asked his mother and she told him her name. He rejoiced in the fact that he now knew her first name. However, when they returned to school the following term and his teacher asked for his mother's name, he said he could not get himself to say her first name in class. It was too "heavy" on his tongue. He felt as if he was demeaning or dishonoring her. He finally mentioned her first name and felt really bad afterwards. She was "Amake Jeff." That was her honorable name, her respectful title.

As a fellow African, I can identify with that speaker. Although I could have mentioned my mother's name to other people, I could never have gotten myself to call my mother or my father by their first names. Never! That would have been too disrespectful. What I had never thought about until the day I was listening to this lecture was how this can be likened to the way in which the Jews over the centuries lost the vowels in God's name. It was because they never mentioned his name. It was too sacred to be mentioned, and in the long haul only the consonants were retained in the Hebrew spelling.

Our relationship with our parents and our relationship with God are both vertical relationships. In the fifth commandment God says, "Honor your father and your mother, that your days may be long in the land that the Lord your God is giving you" (Ex. 20:12). He gave this command-ment because of this same vertical relationship. If you dishonor your parents whom you see, how can you claim to honor God whom you do not see? The way we show respect to our parents may differ slightly from culture to culture, but it is still our God-given responsibility as children growing up together in a home to genuinely respect our parents. Our parents represent the role of God in our lives as we are growing up. We learn to pray to God saying, "Our Father who is in heaven," because we had been saying, "Our father," to our earthly fathers for a long time. Hence, we simply pass on to God something of the respect that we have for our earthly father. That parallel shows why, as a church, one of our greatest responsibilities is to ensure that we are honoring God. As mem-bers of the church we are like children growing up in a home. When we honor God, he is pleased; when we dishonor God, he is offended. We must make sure we are always honoring him. In what ways do we therefore honor God and thus please him?

The Way We Relate to the Glory of God

The most important way in which we please God is when we keep our focus as a church, and especially as church leaders, on the glory of God in our worship and in all other areas of church life. Nothing can be more important than this. We must seek to relate to God with reverence and submission. His word should be supreme in our lives and in our church. Serving him should be our number one joy. Our goal should be to love God with all our heart, mind, soul, and strength (Deut. 6:5; Mark 12:30). He should be our chief delight. But it must be a reverential delight, as in the presence of majesty, and not a frivolous one. Let us look at this in a little more detail.

In the Old Testament, God commanded his people through Moses, "You shall have no other gods before me" (Ex. 20:3). God was to have the supreme position in their lives and in their worship. In the New Testament, the apostle Paul wrote to the Corinthians saying, "So, whether you eat or drink, or whatever you do, do all to the glory of God" (1 Cor. 10:31). That ought to be the primary motivating factor in all areas of the Christian life, including worship. That was what we were made for. As human beings, we were created as the pinnacle of God's creation so that we could manifest the excellency of God through all that we do. As we shall see, sin ruined all this and made us self-centered. In salvation, God seeks to restore this rightful relationship in those he regenerates individually and collectively in the church. That is why God is pleased when his children understand this and intentionally do everything with an eye on his glory and pleasure. When the church preaches the gospel of God's glorious grace in Christ, showing what it cost God to purchase our free salvation, those who are in regular attendance in that church respond in love for God and willing submission to his will for their lives (Rom. 12:1–2). Their obedience to God's word comes from the heart.

We sin when we take the glory that belongs to the only God and bestow it on any creature, including ourselves. All sin is offensive to God, yet the sin of idolatry is the most offensive because it steals God's glory from him. He is a jealous God, who will share his glory with no one else (Ex. 34:14; Deut. 5:9; etc.). Paul described idolatry in these words: "Claiming to be wise, they became fools, and exchanged the glory of the immortal God for images resembling mortal man and birds and animals and creeping things" (Rom. 1:22–23). The ancient world made images out of marble and metal and bowed down to them in worship. Others worshiped large trees and mountains. Today, the tendency in the church is to elevate human beings to the position that ought to be occupied by God alone. So, you find that churches are thinking more about impressing and entertaining people than about honoring God. The songs chosen for "worship" are really chosen for their entertaining content and tunes. The focus on music (and dancing!) becomes more prominent than the preaching of God's word. Also, instead of seeing pastors and preachers as channels through whom we learn God's word, we tend to elevate them to the point where their personal opinions are believed without question. Church life revolves around them instead of revolving around God. They can introduce anything they want into the worship of God and his church, and we do not question them at all. Yet, as we saw earlier in this book, God has stipulated how he is to be worshiped. We dare not allow anyone to bring in his own innovations, even if he is the church pastor.

The Way We Relate to the Truth of God

One of the ways in which we honor God is by preserving and propagating his truth in the world. God has revealed himself in creation, but due to the fall recorded in Genesis 3 and its resulting effect of spiritual blindness, God also ensured that his truth was proclaimed by prophets across history and preserved for us in the Bible. This truth includes the only way in which human beings can find pardon with God. It is through the life and work of the Lord Jesus Christ, especially his death and resurrection. We must come to God in repentance, trusting in the finished work of Christ for our acceptance with God. This truth must be proclaimed to the whole world through the church. The church that is given to the preservation and proclamation of this truth pleases God.

When the church fails to preserve God's truth and instead yields to the half-truths and lies propagated by the world, it displeases the Lord. One of the ways in which this happens is through syncretistic beliefs and practices. In Africa, it is seen in the way we mix Christianity with traditional African beliefs and practices. You hear people say, "But we are Africans, and this is what our ancestors always believed!" If what our ancestors believed does not line up with what the Bible teaches, then we should put aside those beliefs and only believe and live by what the Bible teaches. If we mix the two, we not only confuse young believers but we also incur the judgment of God. Even our worship should be dictated by what the Bible teaches about worship and not by how our ancestors worshiped. The Scriptures should inform and form our beliefs and practices.

Another way in which the church dishonors and displeases God in this area is when it succumbs to what is falsely called Western education today. The Bible teaches that God created the world in six days and then rested on the seventh. When the Christian church fails to preserve and propagate this truth and instead embraces the belief that is most popular in the world today—that the world merely evolved over millions and millions of years—it dishonors and displeases God. The world is in darkness; the church is supposed to shine its light into this darkness. Out of this darkness, the world has come up with many other false teachings—about human sexuality, for instance. Marriage is being redefined. It is no longer confined to one man and one woman for life. In fact, the Western world is fast getting to the stage where there is no objective truth. What you believe is truth to you. The church should not succumb to this. It must continue to teach the biblical norm or else face the wrath of its Lord.

There are many other compromises making the church fail to hold its own as far as truth is concerned. One pressure comes from the ever-increasing trend toward religious inclusiveness. The idea that salvation is to be found only in the finished work of Christ is increasingly seen as a view held only by a few religious bigots. The popular view is that all religions lead to God. As long as those who advocate their religious beliefs are sincere, the popular view claims, God will accept them. Yet our Bible says, "And there is salvation in no one else, for there is no other name under heaven given among men by which we must be saved" (Acts 4:12). We must proclaim this truth with genuine humility and love. It is the only gospel that saves from sin and hell. The church that takes the Great Commission seriously through evangelistic efforts and missions endeavors is the church that pleases God. When a church abandons the gospel, God comes and removes its lampstand (Rev. 2:5). The building will still be there, and people may still be gathering there, but death and decay begins. The judgment of God cannot be missed.

The Way We Relate to Sin in Our Midst

We have stated that God is holy. The Bible says, "As obedient children, do not be conformed to the passions of your former ignorance, but as he who called you is holy, you also be holy in all your conduct, since it is written, 'You shall be holy, for I am holy'" (1 Pet. 1:14–16). This is a nonnegotiable in the church, because it is God's essential nature to be holy. He hates every form of sin. Whenever God's people have stubbornly continued in sin, at some point God has come down to punish them. He has withdrawn his Spirit from their midst and they have become nothing more than a social club.

In many churches, stubborn sin is dealt with quickly when the culprit is a young person who is not connected to any "powerful" personality or family in the church. However, when the culprit is the son or daughter of a church leader or a very rich person in the church or some politically powerful person in the community, church leaders tend to want to hide that person's sin. It is even worse when the offender is himself a church leader. The temptation is to sweep such a person's sin under the carpet. That is wrong. God is no respecter of persons. In fact, those who are in leadership should be held to an even higher standard. The qualifications set out in 1 Timothy 3 and Titus 1 suggest that leaders must be "a cut above" others in the church in their godliness. They must lead by word and deed. If they are walking in sin, they must be removed from office.

Hypocrisy stinks in the nostrils of God. Hidden sin is hidden only from human eyes. It is not hidden from God. The God whom we worship is an all-seeing God. In the Old Testament, he punished the whole nation of Israel when Achan secretly hid in his tent the looted treasures from Jericho (Joshua 7). In the New Testament, he punished Ananias and Sapphira when they lied in claiming that the money they brought to the apostles to be given to the poor was the total amount that they had received for the sale of their land (see Acts 5). When Jesus was on earth, the greatest denunciations he made were against the scribes and Pharisees because of their hypocrisy. He preached against this with a pungency not heard in any of his other sermons. He said,

> Woe to you, scribes and Pharisees, hypocrites! For you clean the outside of the cup and the plate, but inside they are full of greed and self-indulgence. You blind Pharisee! First clean the inside of the cup and the plate, that the outside also may be clean.
>
> Woe to you, scribes and Pharisees, hypocrites! For you are like whitewashed tombs, which outwardly appear beautiful, but within are full of dead people's bones and all uncleanness. So you

also outwardly appear righteous to others, but within you are full
of hypocrisy and lawlessness. (Matt. 23:25–28)

In the light of such cutting words from our Savior's lips, church leaders should do everything possible to ensure that there is no sin kept
hidden in their ranks and in the church as a whole. Where there is no
repentance from sin, church discipline should be the next course of
action. There should be no sacred cows.

We must encourage a spirit of humble repentance in the church by
pointing to the free and full pardon available to us in Christ's atoning
sacrifice. Not every sin must be brought before the whole church for
discipline, but every known sin should be repented of. We are all sinners. We sin in various ways every day. When we become conscious
of sin, especially as it is brought before our eyes through the regular
teaching of God's word, we should not hide or deny the sin. Rather,
we should confess it in genuine repentance of heart. The Bible says,
"If we say we have no sin, we deceive ourselves, and the truth is not in
us. If we confess our sins, he is faithful and just to forgive us our sins
and to cleanse us from all unrighteousness" (1 John 1:8–9). Ongoing
humble and heartfelt repentance should characterize our church if it
is to be pleasing in God's sight.

The Way We Relate to One Another

Sometimes Christians can have the right belief and practice but have
the wrong heart attitude, especially toward other believers. This is
very displeasing to God. When Jesus was asked what the greatest
commandment was, he said,

> You shall love the Lord your God with all your heart and with all
> your soul and with all your mind. This is the great and first com-
> mandment. And a second is like it: You shall love your neighbor
> as yourself. On these two commandments depend all the Law and
> the Prophets. (Matt. 22:37–40)

Notice that Jesus was not content to end with the commandment
that speaks about our love for God. He included our love for fellow
human beings. You cannot love God whom you cannot see, when you

are failing to love your brother who is sitting right next to you (see 1 John 4:20). Obviously, few believers would ever claim not to love their fellow Christians, but they often fail to do it in practice. Lack of love in the church is very common and has destroyed many churches.

This is nothing new. Look at the church in Corinth, for example. It was a church highly gifted and doctrinally knowledgeable. Yet it was also a church full of quarrels. They quarreled over their leaders. They sued each other in court. They rode roughshod over one another's religious qualms and ethical scruples. They fought over which gifts were better than others. Paul was so concerned about this that, in the end, he gave them the best description of the nature of love found anywhere in Scripture. He wrote,

> Love is patient and kind; love does not envy or boast; it is not arrogant or rude. It does not insist on its own way; it is not irritable or resentful; it does not rejoice at wrongdoing, but rejoices with the truth. Love bears all things, believes all things, hopes all things, endures all things.
>
> Love never ends. As for prophecies, they will pass away; as for tongues, they will cease; as for knowledge, it will pass away. . . .
>
> So now faith, hope, and love abide, these three; but the greatest of these is love. (1 Cor. 13:4–8, 13)

Paul wanted the Corinthian believers to prioritize love above all the things they were fighting over. It is when love is at center stage that we are better able to handle our interpersonal challenges.

Love for one another should be the hallmark of the Christian church. Jesus said, "A new commandment I give to you, that you love one another: just as I have loved you, you also are to love one another. By this all people will know that you are my disciples, if you have love for one another" (John 13:34–35). This love is not only a command; it is "birthed" in believers when they are born again. The Holy Spirit fills them with himself, and love is a fruit of the Spirit. So it only makes sense that, when those who are indwelt by the Holy Spirit come together, love will be conspicuous among them. That truly pleases the Lord. When love is lacking in the church, the Lord is dishonored because he is misrepresented, and therefore he is displeased.

In the early church, there was a display of mutual affection among the believers. The Bible says, "And all who believed were together and had all things in common. And they were selling their possessions and belongings and distributing the proceeds to all, as any had need" (Acts 2:44–45). We also read,

> Now the full number of those who believed were of one heart and soul, and no one said that any of the things that belonged to him was his own, but they had everything in common. . . . There was not a needy person among them, for as many as were owners of lands or houses sold them and brought the proceeds of what was sold and laid it at the apostles' feet, and it was distributed to each as any had need. (Acts 4:32, 34–35)

This is how the church should be. This was truly pleasing to the Lord, and he blessed the early church tremendously.

Love is not an optional extra to a church. Where there is love, the Lord is pleased. Where there is no love, the Lord is offended. Can you describe your church as a place where love flows or as a place where people are leaving because of a lack of tender loving care? Do not treat this matter lightly. God wants his church to manifest his love for his children. The psalmist says,

> Behold, how good and pleasant it is
> > when brothers dwell in unity!
> It is like the precious oil on the head,
> > running down on the beard,
> on the beard of Aaron,
> > running down on the collar of his robes!
> It is like the dew of Hermon,
> > which falls on the mountains of Zion!
> For there the LORD has commanded the blessing,
> > life forevermore. (Psalm 133)

There are other areas in which the church offends or pleases God. I have pulled out the main areas. It is all about the honor of God. A good exercise would be to look at the letters of Christ to the seven churches of the book of Revelation. He is displeased with a number of them. You will soon find that the main issues he has against them are the ones we have covered above. On one hand, if you want your church to please God you should ensure that you do everything to his glory, you should jealously preserve and propagate his truth, you should be intentional about preserving godliness in your midst, and you should maintain an ambience of love among the brethren. On the other hand, you will surely incur God's displeasure if you turn the church into a playground, or if you no longer treasure God's truth as it is revealed in Scripture, or if you allow sin and hypocrisy to reign among your members, or if you relegate brotherly affection to the any-other-business category of the life of the church. You should want to please God because that is why your church is there in the first place. The church is not there primarily to keep everyone happy. That is the job of many social clubs but certainly not of the church. If there is anything that you know to be displeasing to God in your church, you should want to address it and rectify it so that, in the end, yours may be a church with which God is pleased. How to do that wisely and in a God-honoring way will be the subject of our final chapter.

STUDY GUIDE FOR CHAPTER 19
How Does the Church Offend or Please God?

Summary

The church pleases God when believers seek to glorify him in their worship and in all other areas of church life. When that glory is bestowed upon any creature, including ourselves, God is offended and is sinned against. The church especially glorifies God by being loyal to his word, by not treating sin lightly or hiding it, and by being characterized by sincere, active love for one another. A church without these things is displeasing to God, even if it is flourishing in other ways. Today's churches need to reflect the holiness and purity we observe in Scripture.

Study Questions

1. We are to "intentionally do everything with an eye on [God's] glory and pleasure" (p. 253). In what areas of your life have you made *your* glory and pleasure, instead of God's glory and pleasure, your motivation? (Consider specifics in the family, at work, and in your private life.)

Confess these things in light of the promises of Romans 8:1 and 1 John 1:9.

2. What African traditional practices have churches or denominations in your country mixed up with the biblical worship of God? Identify at least two.

3. When leaders show favoritism in how they deal with sinning members, what harm does this do to the congregation?

4. Is it possible to practice some of the biblical marks of a well-ordered church—e.g., how we process membership and church discipline—without the inner qualities of holiness or love?

   How can we go about implementing these external biblical marks without forgetting the very heart of the matter?

5. One of the reasons why some members don't love others is simply because they don't know them. What practices or tools could a church use to help members know one another?

20

How Can You Help in Reforming Your Church?

If you have read this book from the first chapter you probably have seen some areas of your church life that seriously need reforming. By the word "reforming" I mean the need to bring some aspects of the belief and practice of your church to conform with God's design for the church as taught in the Bible. There are two possible responses you can have toward that realization. The first response is to do nothing about it. This is often due to the benefits you are getting from an unbiblical practice in your church, or because you do not think that it is worth the trouble that attempting to change will bring upon you. In short, your conscience is not sufficiently captive to the word of God to make you lose your peace until you rectify what is a patently unbiblical practice in your church. Sadly, this attitude represents the majority of people. They see wrong and unbiblical practices in their church and they look the other way. They will not and cannot be bothered.

The second response is to do something about it. It matters how you then proceed to help make the change. Too many well-meaning individuals have destroyed the very church they have tried to reform because they have gone about the work of reforming in the wrong way. This chapter is meant to help the person who wants to help his church to conform to God's design for the church. It is meant to counsel such a person to do this in the most God-honoring way. I am working on the assumption that the person trying to make changes in the church is already a church leader, perhaps even the church pastor. Along the way I will also address the possibility of non–church leaders seeking to help in reforming their church. So, then, how can you help in reforming your church as a church leader?

Pray for God's Help

If you are in a position where you can see some area of glaring malpractice in your church and see the need to address that area, your first responsibility is to pray. Whether you are a leader in the church or not, this is one thing that you can certainly do—pray! In praying, you are talking to the owner of the church about his household. We have seen in this book that the church is "the household of God, which is the church of the living God" (1 Tim. 3:15). You are praying to the one who should be most interested in its well-being. You are also praying to him as Jesus taught us to pray. You are saying, "Our Father in heaven, hallowed be your name. Your kingdom come, your will be done, on earth as it is in heaven" (Matt. 6:9–10). You want God to be glorified in his church by a greater yielding of his people to his kingship, his rule, and his will. You want to see a greater readiness to obey God in his church on earth that is more and more like the readiness with which he is obeyed in heaven. So, pray!

Pray for wisdom and for favor. Wisdom is the ability to apply your knowledge in a way that is most helpful to yourself and to those around you. In reading this book you have acquired knowledge. You now need wisdom to know how best to apply that knowledge so that it helps those who should benefit from it. Ultimately, wisdom comes from God. The Bible says, "If any of you lacks wisdom, let him ask God, who gives generously to all without reproach, and it will be given him" (James 1:5). Pray that God will enable you to know how to talk to those who need to be talked to in a way that will not be offensive but winsome. Ask him to show you how what you now know can be applied in your church in the most suitable way. In a sense, you are also praying for favor, so that the people who have the power to make the necessary decisions and changes will have a favorable disposition toward you and your suggestions. Wisdom is what is coming from you to them, and favor is what is coming from them to you. Where these two come together, your recommendations for reform will most likely be accepted in the church.

With respect to wisdom, it is good to go beyond praying. While you are praying, you should also consult those whose many years of experience in church ministry and church leadership have taught them biblical wisdom. Theirs is not textbook knowledge. They have been in the trenches. They have made mistakes and learned from them. Do not be like Rehoboam, the son of King Solomon, who rejected the advice of the elderly men who had served with his father and opted for the advice of the young men he had grown up with. In the end, the people rejected his rule and Israel ended up splitting into two nations (see 1 Kings 12). They say experience is the best teacher. Seek wisdom from those who have a proven track record.

Pray for the grace and power of God to prevail. God-honoring changes in individuals and in churches can come about only by the direct working of the Holy Spirit in the human heart. No gimmicks or tricks can bring this about. You are not wrestling against flesh and blood, but against spiritual forces of evil in the heavenly places (Eph. 6:12). God must act by the power of his Spirit, or else you are totally toothless and will surely be vanquished. As we shall soon see, the chief instrument to bring about such changes is the teaching of the word of God. However, the Spirit of God must burn the word of God into the hearts of the people of God with convicting power in order for them to surrender to the will of God. Pray that this will happen, so that church members may see with renewed spiritual eyes what God's design for the church is and may want to see that realized in the life of their church. Often, it means that they will have to turn their backs on cherished practices. They will have to face friends who may mock them for the changes they are making in their church. Pray that they may so cherish the smile of God above all else that they will follow his leading with joy.

Teach the Word of God

The chief instrument of reform in our individual lives and in the life of the church is the word of God—the Bible. The apostle Paul says that it is the instrument that Jesus uses to clean up his church. As we have already seen in previous chapters, he says that Jesus loved the church and gave himself up for her, "that he might sanctify her, having cleansed her by the washing of water with the word, so that he might present the church to himself in splendor, without spot or wrinkle or any such thing, that she might be holy and without blemish" (Eph. 5:26–27). Your role is to be God's servant who faithfully teaches God's word so that Jesus can use that word in the lives of his people, to sanctify them and conform them more and more to his image individually and to his design corporately. As a pastor or a church leader, this is such a privilege. As you faithfully teach God's word week by week, you get to see the lives of God's people and the life of the church transformed.

Learn to apply God's word relevantly to the life of the church. Preaching is meant to inform the mind, warm the heart, and move the will of the listener to do what God wants him or her to do. That last part is often aided when the preaching itself clearly and relevantly applies the truth being taught to the lives of those who are listening. If the passage being taught is about Christ as the head of the church, challenge your listeners as to whether they are intentional about obeying the will of Jesus in the way they are involved in church life. If the passage is about the Great Commission, challenge them about whether they are being faithful senders or goers. Are they doing their part in the work of evangelism and missions? If the passage is about baptism or the Lord's Supper, again press the issue on the consciences of your listeners as to whether they have been baptized in obedience to Christ and whether they regularly participate in the Lord's Supper. If the passage is about financial stewardship, do not be hesitant to challenge your hearers to be faithful and generous when it comes to supporting the Lord's work. Ensure that the passage of Scripture being preached is properly explained before beginning to apply it. Do not rush to application. Let the minds of God's people first be filled with truth before you ask the people what they will do with the truth.

In order to see transformation taking place in your church, you must be a good example of someone who repents and obeys God's word when you learn about areas in your life in which you must change. Paul's challenge to the Jews of his day applies equally to church leaders today. He wrote,

> But if you call yourself a Jew and rely on the law and boast in God and know his will and approve what is excellent, because you are instructed from the law; and if you are sure that you yourself are a guide to the blind, a light to those who are in darkness, an instructor of the foolish, a teacher of children, having in the law the embodiment of knowledge and truth—you then who teach others, do you not teach yourself? While you preach against stealing, do you steal? You who say that one must not commit adultery, do you commit adultery? You who abhor idols, do you rob temples? You who boast in the law dishonor God by breaking the law. For, as it is written, "The name of God is blasphemed among the Gentiles because of you" (Rom. 2:17–24)

Those who teach God's word should be the first to conform to its teaching. If they do not, then the people who listen to them only get hardened in their disobedience. So, *be* the change that you want to see happen in the lives of the people of God and in the church.

Provide for opportunities for discussion and time for transition. The fact that the truth has become very well-defined to you does not mean that it has become equally clear to everyone. Some people are genuinely slow learners and will need more time for the truth to really sink in. Having the opportunity to ask questions and get clarifications helps them to think through matters and gain a firmer understanding of what is being taught. Others are strong traditionalists and take longer to let go of long-cherished practices even when they have finally seen that the practices are not in line with God's word. Someone once said that the last words of a dying church are, "But we have always done it this way." It is good to give them time to see how biblically untenable the practices are in the hope that they will finally see the need for change. A leader who thinks that, simply because he has taught about a needed change, everyone is ready to make the change, is probably a very young upstart and still has a lot to learn about fallen human nature. You need to learn to be very patient with people if you are going to finally see the desired change in the church. An impatient leader will break the people, or the people will break him.

Talk with Your Fellow Leaders

Reforming a church in its beliefs and practices must start from the top and go down to the grassroots. The church leaders must be convinced that this is God's will and must be favorably disposed to it. Where goodwill is missing from the leaders, you will have not a reformation but a rebellion. So, there is nothing more important than talking with your fellow church leaders about what you are seeing in the Bible about church life and how that seems to contradict the way in which you are currently doing church. Even if you are the church pastor, it is vital that you carry your church leaders with you as you seek to implement change. They must not be taken by surprise, because once they reject the proposed changes there is precious little that you can do to implement them. They are the undershepherds of the sheep; you can be sure that the majority of the sheep will follow them.

It is often in talking with church leaders that you especially need wisdom and favor. This is where your praying to God for such wisdom and favor comes in. You need wisdom in how best to present the issue about which you see the need for reform. You need goodwill from the other leaders as they consider the issue you are presenting, so that they can do so in a favorable light. If they are truly God's servants and they see you as a humble child of God who simply wants to see God glorified in his church, you are likely to win their favor. If they see you as a proud know-it-all and self-appointed little messiah, then you will have already shot yourself in the foot. You are not likely to get anywhere.

You also need a lot of patience as you deal with your church leaders. You did not learn the truths that make you uncomfortable with your church practice overnight. So, why should you expect your church leaders to see those truths after just a few words of explanation? Remember how difficult it was in the New Testament for the church in Jerusalem to accept Gentiles as "no longer strangers and aliens, but [as] fellow citizens with the saints and members of the household of God" (Eph. 2:19). God had to show Peter in a vision, while he was in the home of Simon the tanner, not to call unclean what God had now made clean. It was not until Peter arrived in Cornelius's house that he understood what the vision was all about. He said, "Truly I understand that God shows no partiality, but in every nation anyone who fears him and does what is right is acceptable to him" (Acts 10:34–35). What Peter now understood was not that easily understood by the brethren in Jerusalem. They were incensed when they heard that Peter had gone into the home of a Gentile and socialized with him (Acts 10:28; 11:3). Peter painstakingly and patiently explained to the church in Jerusalem how God had led him to understand this historic truth. That was how, in the end, the other leaders came to the same understanding. Later, in Acts 15, it is evident that some who "understood" this truth did not really understand it and wanted the Gentiles to be circumcised first before they could be full heirs of God's promises. This necessitated a meeting between these brothers, Paul and Barnabas, and the apostles and elders in Jerusalem. Only when the leaders were convinced did they proceed to call the rest of the church into the discussion and conclusion. That is how it should be. This process demands a lot of patience.

Sometimes the best way to handle this phase is not only to talk with the leaders but also to study the subject together in the leadership. Whether you are a leader yourself or not, at least one thing you can do is to give your leaders a book (or a CD or a link to a website) that teaches on that subject so that they can learn for themselves at their own pace. Then tell them that you would want to discuss this subject with them afterwards. In studying and discussing the subject with them, learn to listen to their doubts and fears. Gently and patiently show them from the Scriptures what the mind of Christ for his church seems to be and how "to obey is better than sacrifice" (1 Sam. 15:22). Undershepherds should lead the flock where the great shepherd of the sheep wants them to go. Hopefully, with time, the doubts and fears will be overcome and the leadership together will go forward to lead the church in reforming its beliefs and practices so that they better reflect God's design for the church.

Here is where I need to address those who are not yet leaders but who may read this book and find areas in which they would like to help bring about reform in their church. You should do everything stated above, though you may not have the opportunity to teach the congregation directly. You should avoid going from house to house talking to church members about what you see to be wrong in the church. Instead, talk to your church leaders. The greatest mistake that young "reformers" in the church make is that they discover truth in the Bible and they see how wrong their church is in belief or practice. Then they start attacking their church leaders for their erroneous ways and start demanding change. They foolishly think that in doing so they can shame their leaders into changing the beliefs and practices of the church. Publicly criticizing leaders never works. All that happens is that the critics lose the little goodwill that they once had with the leaders and they are labeled as troublemakers and rebels. If they continue to agitate for change, they soon are shown the exit door. Sometimes they even get excommunicated for causing disunity in the church. Their good ends up being spoken of as evil. They lose what they had been hoping to gain. You must never try to drive the car from the backseat. You will only agitate the driver, who may stop the car and ask you to jump out! Youthful passion needs to be regulated with spiritual wisdom and patience.

Sometimes Change Is Rejected

The most difficult situation to handle in the life of any true child of God is when you see from the teaching of Scripture what to believe or how to live and then, when you share this with those who mean so much to you, they totally reject it. For you, it is as clear as daylight, while for them it is like you want to go back to the dark ages. You are torn between staying with them and being miserable or leaving to look for happiness elsewhere. How should you handle this when it is in the context of reforming your church in its beliefs or practices? Consider how the prophets of the Old Testament suffered rejection from the people of Israel when they spoke the word of God to them. You will find great encouragement from their example.

1. **Consider how important the issue is that you are seeking to see changed.** Some issues are more important than others. This will determine whether you should press the panic button or not. On one hand, if the issue is something as serious as idolatrous worship, or if

it is something that undermines the gospel so that the souls of men and women are at stake, then you may need to seriously consider whether you need to leave your church and find a new one. On the other hand, if it is something that hinges on how well the finances are being accounted for or whether your church is contributing toward the training of future pastors, you may want to let the matter lie for now. You should not paint all attempts at reform with the same brush. Some are darker and deeper than others. Choose your battles wisely. Not every hill is worth dying on.

2. Consider also why your suggested changes have been rejected. Is it that your church is so traditional that what the Bible says is always secondary to their church constitution and practice? In that case, instead of concentrating on those changes, you may need to first help the church appreciate the authority and sufficiency of the Scriptures. Fix that issue first, and the rest will follow more easily. Is it that you have not yet earned the right to be listened to at such a level, and the person who is the real leader in the church is opposed to change? Perhaps you rushed and did not carry the consciences of God's people with you. Then postpone this matter and continue serving in the church until the center of gravity shifts. Paul counseled Timothy,

> The Lord's servant must not be quarrelsome but kind to everyone, able to teach, patiently enduring evil, correcting his opponents with gentleness. God may perhaps grant them repentance leading to a knowledge of the truth, and they may come to their senses and escape from the snare of the devil, after being captured by him to do his will. (2 Tim. 2:24–26)

Also, remember the issue of prayer. Pray for patience on your part as you live within a situation where your conscience troubles you in the light of what you have come to know from God's word. You can then reintroduce this subject and help the church to reform. Often the rejection of reform is a symptom of something else. Incisive diagnosis can be a great help for future plans.

3. Consider the spiritual state of the leadership of the church. In the worst-case scenario, you might find that you are dealing with an unconverted church leadership. Often, in Israel, that was where the problem lay. Before God's judgment fell upon the nation of Israel, they would have a series of wicked kings who sinned greatly against God and allowed the worst forms of idolatry. They would even persecute the prophets who were seeking to bring them back to God. This is what led to the lament of the Lord Jesus Christ when he said, "O Jerusalem, Jerusalem, the city that kills the prophets and stones those who are sent to it! How often would I have gathered your children together as a hen gathers her brood under her wings, and you were not willing!" (Matt. 23:37). That is how unregenerate people are. They do not care about the glory of God. They do not really care about what God's word says, especially if it goes against their personal or cultural inclinations. They will resist giving up their darling sins even if you preach your head off. They will live in a context of personal hatred, unforgiveness, gossip, and slander as long as they remain in leadership. In fact, they seem to thrive better in such a context. If you find yourself in such a situation, the best you can do for yourself is to preach the gospel before your time runs out. It is only a matter of time before those leaders will hound you out of the church the moment they realize you are trying to disturb their comfort zone—whether you are the church pastor or an ordinary member of the church. Seek to leave the church in the most God-glorifying and peaceable way. Remember, there are God's sincere children in the church, though they are in wrong hands. Do not destroy their faith by the way you leave. Clarify the issues where you have begged to differ and leave that in the records of the church. Then ask the Lord to lead you to a church whose leaders are more willing to listen to the voice of the great shepherd, the Lord Jesus Christ.

STUDY GUIDE FOR CHAPTER 20
How Can You Help in Reforming Your Church?

Summary

Once we see areas where God's will is not being done in the church, our consciences should be held captive to witness biblical change. Depending on our position in the church and the authority God has given us to be able to implement what is right, we should seek these reforms prayerfully, wisely, patiently, trusting the word of God, being examples of the things we want to see, and consulting with other leaders.

Study Questions

1. Make a list of the things you most urgently wish to see changed in your current local church.

2. Compare the list in (1) above with the list you made in response to question 5 on the Introduction to this book. What has been added or removed?

3. It is said that in Africa you cannot correct those who are above you in age or position. If you are a pastor, do you think you have the humility to hear the truth from someone under you?

What advice does the book give on how to go about pursuing the changes you wish to see, if you're not a leader in the church?

4. If you are a church leader and you have some changes you wish to introduce, what are the top three obstacles you anticipate? List them, and begin praying for success and wisdom to handle them.

5. If you are a pastor in your local church, or a regular preacher, consider three ways you could have applied God's word in your most recent sermon in a way that applies to the communal life of the local church.

Epilogue

The aim of writing this book was to show God's design for the church so that our generation can ensure that our churches across the African continent will indeed be what God meant them to be. This is because the glory of God shines brightest when the church fits his design as taught in the Bible.

As I wrote in the introduction, there is a lot to thank God for in what is happening in the church across Africa. The church is growing by leaps and bounds. It is bursting at the seams with young people, which speaks well for its future. There is a lot of zeal, and the communal culture on the continent is having an enriching effect on fellowship among believers. So, in writing a book on the church and sometimes sounding very negative, we must not lose sight of these blessings that God has bestowed on the church in Africa.

In the pages of this book, I have sought to answer the most basic questions related to God's design for the church. They are the kind of questions that, if answered faithfully from the Scriptures, will enable anyone who reads these pages to have a three-dimensional view of how God wants his church on earth to be run. I have tried to avoid being dogmatic on the finer details that the Bible is not very clear on and which we will probably understand only when we get to heaven. Where the Bible is definitive, I have also tried to be definitive.

I have written as a son of the African soil who has seen the many ways in which the church in Africa is caught in a rut that deprives it of the capacity to rise beyond its current levels. I have written in a way that foreign missionaries and visiting international preachers cannot speak or write without being grossly misunderstood. In applying the biblical teachings in each chapter, I have scratched where it itches the most. I have done so with the prayer that readers may see where changes need to be made so that their churches would begin to function in a more biblical and, thus, in a more God-glorifying way.

What remains now is for the readers of this book to apply its lessons. Change does not come easy. Yet, if we can pay the price and be deliberately intentional in addressing the areas of our shortcomings, there is no doubt that the church of Christ on the African continent will prove a great blessing to the rest of the global church as we actively await our Savior from heaven, Jesus Christ the righteous one. My prayer is that what God intended to achieve through designing his church as he did will be realized to some extent through the reading of this book. Part of that intention was "so that through the church the manifold wisdom of God might now be made known to the rulers and authorities in the heavenly places," and that, "to him [will] be glory in the church and in Christ Jesus throughout all generations, forever and ever. Amen" (Eph. 3:10, 21).

Index of Scripture References

THE GOSPEL **COALITION**

The Gospel Coalition is a fellowship of evangelical churches deeply committed to renewing our faith in the gospel of Christ and to reforming our ministry practices to conform fully to the Scriptures. We have committed ourselves to invigorating churches with new hope and compelling joy based on the promises received by grace alone through faith alone in Christ alone.

We desire to champion the gospel with clarity, compassion, courage, and joy—gladly linking hearts with fellow believers across denominational, ethnic, and class lines. We yearn to work with all who, in addition to embracing our confession and theological vision for ministry, seek the lordship of Christ over the whole of life with unabashed hope in the power of the Holy Spirit to transform individuals, communities, and cultures.

Through its pastoral resources, The Gospel Coalition aims to encourage and equip current and prospective pastors for faithful endurance over a lifetime of ministry in the church. By learning from experienced ministers of different ages, races, and nationalities, we hope to grow together in godly maturity as the Spirit leads us in the way of Jesus Christ.

Join the cause and visit TGC.org for fresh resources that will equip you to love God with all your heart, soul, mind, and strength, and to love your neighbor as yourself.

TGC.org

IX 9Marks

Building Healthy Churches

9Marks exists to equip church leaders with a biblical vision and practical resources for displaying God's glory to the nations through healthy churches.

To that end, we want to see churches characterized by these nine marks of health:

1. Expositional Preaching
2. Gospel Doctrine
3. A Biblical Understanding of Conversion and Evangelism
4. Biblical Church Membership
5. Biblical Church Discipline
6. A Biblical Concern for Discipleship and Growth
7. Biblical Church Leadership
8. A Biblical Understanding of the Practice of Prayer
9. A Biblical Understanding and Practice of Missions

Find all our Crossway titles and other resources at 9Marks.org.

Also Available from the Gospel Coalition

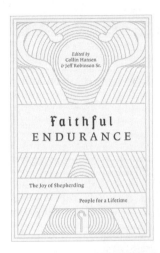

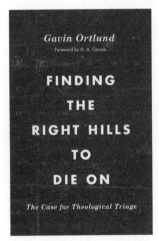

For more information, visit **crossway.org**.